WHAT THE BIBLE SAYS TO THE
MINISTER

The Minister's Personal Handbook

King James Version Edition

Leadership Ministries Worldwide
Chattanooga, TN

Third Edition
Copyright © 2017 by Alpha-Omega Ministries, Inc.

Second Edition
Copyright © 1996 by Alpha-Omega Ministries, Inc.

First Edition
Copyright © 1991 by Alpha-Omega Ministries, Inc.

All rights reserved throughout the world. No part of *The Minister's Personal Handbook* may be reproduced in any manner without written permission.

The Minister's Personal Handbook has been compiled for God's people to use both in their personal lives and in their teaching and preaching of God's Holy Word. The purpose of the copyright is to prevent the reproduction, misuse, and abuse of the material.

Please address all requests for information or permission to:
Leadership Ministries Worldwide
PO Box 21310
Chattanooga, TN 37424-0310
Ph.# (423) 855-2181   FAX (423) 855-8616
E-Mail info@outlinebible.org   http://www.outlinebible.org

Library of Congress Catalog Card Number: 96-077026

International Standard Book Number (Black cover) 978-1-57407-048-4
International Standard Book Number (Brown cover) 978-1-57407-233-4
International Standard Book Number (Paperback) 978-1-57407-055-2
International Standard Book Number (Hardback) 978-1-57407-138-2

PRINTED IN THE UNITED STATES OF AMERICA

PUBLISHED BY LEADERSHIP MINISTRIES WORLDWIDE

21 22 23 24 25   17 18 19 20 21

Dedicated

To all the men and women of the world who preach and teach the Gospel of our Lord Jesus Christ.

And to the mercy and grace of God Demonstrated to us through Christ.

"In whom we have redemption through His blood, the forgiveness of sins, according to the riches of His grace." (Eph. 1:7)

Out of the mercy and grace of God, His Word has flowed. Let every person know that God will have mercy upon him, forgiving and using him to fulfill His glorious plan of salvation.

"For God so loved the world, that he gave his only begotten Son, that whosoever believeth in him should not perish, but have everlasting life. For God sent not his Son into the world to condemn the world; but that the world through him might be saved." (Jn. 3:16-17)

May our Lord bless us all as we live, preach, teach, and write for Him, fulfilling His great commission to live righteous and godly lives and to make disciples of all nations.

"For this is good and acceptable in the sight of God our Saviour; who will have all men to be saved, and to come unto the knowledge of the truth." (1 Tim. 2:3-4)

Dear Friend,

Picture this: a business or professional person in the secular world has to speak at a conference before one or two hundred of his professional peers. How much time will he take out of his weekly work schedule to prepare for his speech? Two hours? Five hours? Ten hours? What if he had to speak to the same group two times—or three times—all in the same week? How much time would he then take out of his regular duties to prepare two or three different speeches?

But what if he had to do more than just prepare and deliver two or three speeches? What if he had to look after and minister to every one of the two hundred persons who attended the conference? What if he had to minister—to personally minister—to every one of them . . .

- when one of them got sick and went to the hospital
- when one of their family members was hospitalized
- when a serious problem arose
- when some counseling was needed
- when a family member died
- when a child got married
- when a major committee met

And on top of this . . .

- What if the professional had to *manage the conference*: its business, work, committees, schedules, finances, building program, whatever came up—with all the surrounding problems of management?
- What if the professional had to be constantly out *visiting and reaching new people* to attend and join the conference association?
- What if the professional had to constantly *face the scrutiny of his peers* and handle any and all criticisms, grumblings, and divisions that arose?

Many a professional person would throw up his hands, walk off the job, and quit.

But this is your task—the task of the minister—in today's industrialized world. And what a task it is, humanly impossible! But not with God. You are God's minister—His choice servant, His dear servant—whom He has called to minister to His precious people. God knows every throb of your heart . . .

- every joy, pleasure, ache, burden, cry, tear, and care
- every trial and temptation that often attacks you
- every person who criticizes, opposes, and persecutes you

- every duty and demand you face
- every sermon you must prepare and deliver and the pressure of it
- every burden for your dear people and for the lost of the world
- every care you have for the church and its believers
- every moment of disappointment and discouragement you face

God knows—He knows all about you. He knows when you have need and exactly what the need is. He knows your need even better than you know. More importantly, God wants to meet your need. He wants to give you the exact provision you need—perfectly and completely. He wants to fill you with the very best, with His very own fullness, the fullness of His presence and provision.

This is what this book is all about: this is . . .

- God's Word to the minister.
- What God has to say to the minister.

Most if not all of the verses in the Bible that *speak directly to the minister* are here in this book—all arranged under the subjects to which they speak.

This is what God has to say to you, His dear minister—His choice servant—whom He has called to minister to His precious people.

It is our prayer—daily prayer—that in the following pages you will find God's voice speaking through His Word, speaking the exact message you need when you need it:

- Brokenness before God—Comfort
- Rededication—Encouragement
- A renewed call—Peace
- A new challenge and vision—Strength
- Purpose and meaning—Power
- Love and understanding—Assurance
- Correction and instruction—Security
- Restoration: repentance—Victory and forgiveness

May our wonderful Lord bless you ever so richly as you use this, "*The Minister's Personal Handbook*," in your own life and ministry for Christ. May He use it to speak the exact message you need as you live day by day and go forth for Him. Refer to it often and do exactly what He says, and our Lord will meet your every need and use you beyond all imagination.

With the very warmest regards, we are,
LEADERSHIP MINISTRIES WORLDWIDE

CONTENTS
CHAPTER BY CHAPTER

Part One: Your Ministry

You have been given the greatest ministry in all the world, that of ministering to people and reconciling them to the Lord and Majesty of the universe, God Himself. For this reason, *you must understand and be fully committed* to the great ministry He has given you.

1.	What Your Call as a Minister Is	1
2.	What Your Aim as a Minister Must Be	11
3.	What Your Purpose as a Minister Is	25
4.	What Your Resources as a Minister Are	39
5.	What Your Commission and Work as a Minister Are	53
6.	What Your Message—Your Preaching and Teaching—Must Be	91
	A. You and Your Message	93
	B. You and Your Preaching and Teaching	116
7.	What Your Duty as a Minister Toward False Teaching Must Be	135
	A. You and False Teachers or Heretics	137
	B. You and Other Gospels	162
	C. You and False Doctrine and Teaching	175

Part Two: Your Personal Life and Day by Day Walk

God's Word tells you how to live and walk in Christ day by day. *Consistency, obedience, faithfulness*—this is what God is after. Following Him—doing exactly as He says—bears the most fulfilling and fruitful life and ministry imaginable. For this reason, you must be diligent in living and walking exactly as God says. Again, God's Word stresses that *consistency, obedience,* and *faithfulness* must be the hallmarks of your life.

8.	**What Your Daily Walk as a Minister Must Be**	**189**
	A. You and Christ	191
	B. You and Scripture	202
	C. You and Prayer	208
9.	**What Your Personal Life and Behavior as a Minister Must Be**	**221**
	A. You and Your Body and Mind	223
	B. You and Your Conduct	229
	C. You and Your Financial Support	242
10.	**What Your Relationship With Others Must Be**	**247**
	A. You and Your Family	249
	B. You and Other Ministries	258
	C. You and Those Who Oppose, Criticize, and Persecute You	268
	D. You and Other Believers	280
	E. You and Unbelievers	280
11.	**What Your Attitude Toward Suffering Must Be**	**281**
12.	**What Your Death and Reward as a Minister Will Be**	**299**

CONTENTS
POINT BY POINT

Part One: Your Ministry

1. What Your Call as a Minister Is — 1

As a minister, you have been given the greatest privilege and responsibility in all the world: called to be a minister of the living God, called by the Sovereign Lord and Majesty of the universe.

1. You are chosen by God Himself. — 3
2. You are chosen by Jesus Christ. — 3
3. You are chosen by the Holy Spirit of God. — 4
4. You are counted faithful—counted trustworthy—by Christ. — 5
5. You have been called to be a minister by the gift of God's grace. — 6
6. You have been called to be a steward—a servant—of God. — 7
7. You have been called to be an ambassador for Christ. — 8

2. What Your Aim as a Minister Must Be — 11

As a minister, the aim—the target and mark—of your life is clearly spelled out in Scripture. You are to set your life upon these goals. You are to adopt these goals and be utterly consumed with reaching them.

1. You must know, believe, and understand God. — 13
2. You must personally know Christ and the power of His resurrection. — 14
3. You must forget the past and press on for the prize. — 15
4. You must set this as your great aim and eagerly expect and hope to reach it. — 16

	5. You must have one great concern: consistency, not to offend in anything. You must prove that you are a true minister of God—that you are faithful through all the experiences of life, through all trials and temptations.	17
	6. You must fulfill the supreme requirement of God: that you be faithful.	18
	7. You must be faithful, so faithful that you are totally abandoned and surrendered to Christ.	19
	8. You must be faithful to the end of life.	21

3. What Your Purpose as a Minister Is — 25

Why has God called you to be a minister? What are His purposes for calling you? God has several very specific purposes He wants to accomplish through you. Scripture is clear in describing just what these purposes are.

1. You are to be a pattern of the glorious truth that God saves sinners—a living example of God's mercy. — 27
2. You are to go and make disciples of all nations. — 28
3. You are to present every man perfect in Christ Jesus. — 30
4. You are to be a witness for the Lord Jesus Christ. — 30

4. What Your Resources as a Minister Are — 39

How can you fulfill the purposes of God for your life and ministry? God has not left you alone, He has not left you with only human wisdom and strength to accomplish your task. God has provided great help—unbelievable resources—to equip you to live for Him and to carry out His great purposes for you.

1. You are given the grace and power of Christ. — 41
2. You are given the presence and power of the Holy Spirit. — 42
3. You are given the presence and power of God. — 43
4. You are given the assurance—absolute assurance—of victory by God Himself. — 45
5. You are given a spiritual gift by God. — 47
6. You are given faith to sustain you in the ministry. — 48
7. You are given the love of Christ to compel you in the ministry. — 49
8. You are given the hope of the resurrection to sustain you in the ministry. — 51

5. **What Your Commission and Work as a Minister Are** — 53

As a minister, God has given you the greatest commission and work imaginable. Scripture spells out in great detail just what your duties are.

1. You must challenge and lead people to worship the Lord, the only living and true God, in spirit and in truth. — 55
2. You must minister and serve even as Christ ministered and served. — 57
3. You must seek and save the lost even as Christ sought and saved the lost. — 58
4. You must work and labor for God right now: the harvest is ripe and the task is urgent. — 59
5. You must preach the Word of God: correcting, rebuking, and exhorting people. — 61
6. You must teach. You must instruct—root and ground—people in Jesus Christ and in the Word of God. — 67
7. You must edify and build up believers and equip them to do the work of the ministry. — 69
8. You must feed believers. — 72
9. You must watch over and warn believers. — 76
10. You must lead believers into a pure and faultless religion. — 78
11. You must do the work of an evangelist. — 80
12. You must oversee the administration of the church, set in order the affairs and organization of the church. — 81
13. You must build the church first and foremost in the homes, as instructed by Christ. — 83
14. You must build up the church as a wise masterbuilder. — 87

6. **What Your Message—Your Preaching and Teaching—Must Be** — 91

God wants to reveal Himself to the world; He longs for all men to know Him, to know Him personally. This was the very reason God created man, that man might know Him personally. Consequently, your first duty is to share the Word of God—His message, His revelation—with the world. What you preach and teach is, therefore, of critical importance to God. As a minister of Christ, Scripture has far more to say to you about your preaching and teaching than it does about any other subject. (See both Chapters VI and VII.)

A. You and Your Message		93
1. You must hold fast to sound doctrine and you must preach and teach sound doctrine.		93
2. You must preach and teach the Word of God, the Holy Scripture.		95
3. You must proclaim Jesus Christ and Him crucified.		99
4. You must proclaim that Jesus Christ was buried and raised from the dead.		106
5. You must preach and teach the kingdom of God and of heaven.		110
6. You must not mishandle the Word of God.		114
B. You and Your Preaching and Teaching		116
1. You must make absolutely sure that you live what you preach and teach.		116
2. You must preach the gospel with a sense of urgency.		120
3. You must preach in the power of God's Spirit, not with the persuasive thoughts and ideas of men.		122
4. You must preach and teach to please God, not men. You must not tone down the gospel and use flattering words in order to secure support.		124
5. You must not glory in yourself; you must glory only in the cross. You must not seek worldly popularity and recognition, nor seek to make a good impression and attract attention to yourself.		127
6. You must not preach yourself—lift yourself up—but preach Christ Jesus the Lord.		131
7. You must be consistent and teach over a long period of time.		133

7. What Your Duty as a Minister Toward False Teaching Must Be — 135

As a minister of Christ, you face false teaching at every turn of life. The world—both the secular and the religious world—is bombarded with false teaching. What does Scripture say about false teaching? What is your duty as a minister toward false teaching? Scripture is very clear in its instructions to you as you deal with false teaching.

A. You and False Teachers or Heretics		137
1. You must make sure you are genuine, that you yourself are not a false teacher—not a ravenous wolf in sheep's clothing.		137

2. You must test yourself: Do you believe—really confess and preach—that Jesus Christ has come in the flesh: that God actually sent His Son to earth to save the world?	140
3. You must ask yourself: Am I really truthful? Do I honestly believe and confess that Jesus is the Christ, the Messiah, the Son of God?	145
4. You must not depart from the faith.	147
5. You must guard against those who resist the truth.	151
6. You must guard against those who deny the only Lord God and our Lord Jesus Christ.	152
7. You must reject heretics, false teachers.	154
8. You must reject those who do not teach the words of Christ and the doctrine of godliness.	156
B. YOU AND OTHER GOSPELS	**162**
1. You must not pervert the gospel of Christ nor preach any other gospel.	162
2. You must not bring destructive heresies into the church, heresies that deny the Lord and His death for man.	167
3. You must not preach another Jesus, a Jesus other than the Jesus proclaimed by Scripture and true ministers.	171
C. YOU AND FALSE DOCTRINE AND TEACHING	**175**
1. You must not teach the traditions, ideas, and commandments of men as doctrine.	175
2. You must not be carried away with different kinds of teachings. You must not preach or teach the fables, myths, speculations, ideas, and false doctrines of men.	177
3. You must turn away from empty talk and the opposition of false science and false knowledge.	180
4. You must guard against the false teaching of religion and of the state.	183
5. You must not preach man's empty ideas and discussions—questionable things—but love and faith and the need for a pure conscience.	185

Part Two: Your Personal Life and Day by Day Walk

8. What Your Daily Walk as a Minister Must Be — **189**

As a minister of Christ, you must walk in three things every day of your life: in Christ, in the Scriptures, and in prayer. These three things are absolute essentials as you live and minister for Christ in the midst of a broken and hurting world.

   A. YOU AND CHRIST — **191**

      1. You must make sure—absolutely sure—that your belief in Christ is the right kind of belief. — 191

      2. You must make sure—absolutely sure—that you are a new creation in Christ Jesus. — 192

      3. You must constantly examine yourself—make sure you continue in the faith of Christ—lest you become disqualified, unfit, and rejected. — 194

      4. You must always walk in Christ: you must always seek first the kingdom of God and His righteousness. — 194

      5. You must live a crucified life in Christ, a life of self-denial and sacrifice. — 195

      6. You must be inwardly renewed day by day, changed into the image of Christ. — 197

      7. You must put on the whole armour of God and be strong in Christ. — 200

   B. YOU AND SCRIPTURE — **202**

      1. You must study and obey the Scriptures daily: you must live by the Word of God and proclaim it. — 202

      2. You must memorize the Word of God; let it dwell in your heart and life all day every day — 205

      3. You must be consistent in the Scriptures—studying and living as Scripture dictates. — 207

   C. YOU AND PRAYER — **208**

      1. You must pray daily, pray as Christ taught you to pray in the Lord's prayer. — 208

	2. You must pray daily for the church and for believers. Paul's prayer for the church and for believers is a good pattern to use and to pray through.	210
	3. You must pray daily for the whole world—for all people everywhere.	211
	4. You must pray daily for more laborers.	213
	5. You must pray always—moment by moment—striving to gain an unbroken consciousness of the Lord.	214
	6. You must take some extended time for fervent prayer when very special needs exist.	218

9. What Your Personal Life and Behavior as a Minister Must Be   221

How you take care of you body and mind, how you behave and conduct yourself, and how you handle financial matters are of critical importance to God. He cares deeply about how you live and behave among both the godly and ungodly of the world.

A. YOU AND YOUR BODY AND MIND	**223**
1. You must present your body as a living sacrifice to God.	223
2. You must know that your body is the temple of the Holy Spirit.	224
3. You must struggle to control your mind—even every thought—and think only positive thoughts.	225
4. You must discipline and subject your body to Christ lest you become a castaway.	227
5. You must exercise your body both spiritually and physically.	228
B. YOU AND YOUR CONDUCT	**229**
1. You must live a life of godly character.	229
2. You must live a life of separation, a life separate from the world.	231
3. You must be a man of God.	233
4. You must be faithful through temptations and trials, faithful no matter how severe the temptations and trials may be.	235
5. You must flee youthful lusts.	236
6. You must shun godless and empty talk and avoid questionable teachings and arguments.	237
7. You must know that perilous times are coming and turn away from selfish and ungodly men.	240

    C. You and Your Financial Support **242**
        1. You must receive financial support without being embarrassed or feeling guilty, but you must not seek luxury. 242
        2. You must not covet worldly wealth. 243
        3. You must work at secular employment if needed in order to preach the gospel. 244
        4. You must trust God to meet your financial needs. 245

10. What Your Relationship With Others as a Minister Must Be 247

Relationships are very sensitive within any society or body of people, no matter how small or large. The relationship you are to have with your family and with other ministers, and even with those who oppose and criticize you, is clearly spelled out by Scripture.

    A. You and Your Family **249**
        1. You must walk in a spirit of submission and love with your wife. 249
        2. You must be the husband of one wife. 254
        3. You must manage your own family well. 256

    B. You and Other Ministers **258**
        1. You must understand that you are one with all other ministers and that you are equal in God's eyes, that all ministers are coworkers together with God. 258
        2. You must leave judging other ministers up to God. 260
        3. You must receive and support travelling ministers: evangelists, Bible teachers, missionaries, and other preachers. 262
        4. You must not ordain other ministers too quickly, and you must restore fallen ministers. 264
        5. You must make sure—absolutely sure—that accusations against another minister are true before correcting the other minister. 266

    C. You and Those Who Oppose, Criticize, and Persecute You **268**
        1. You must go forth and preach the gospel, but know that you go into an antagonistic world. 268
        2. You must know that the world will persecute you. 269
        3. You must trust God when you are criticized, judged, slandered, censored, and attacked. 272

	4. You must love your enemies, love all who curse, hate, persecute, and despitefully use you.	276
	D. **YOU AND OTHER BELIEVERS**	**280**
	E. **YOU AND UNBELIEVERS**	**280**

11. What Your Attitude Toward Suffering Must Be — 281

Suffering is a universal experience: we all suffer and suffer much throughout life. As a minister of God—as a leader within society—you must help to ease the suffering of everyone. To do this, you must have both a healthy and a Biblical attitude toward suffering.

1. You must trust God to deliver you through whatever suffering afflicts you, no matter its severity. — 283
2. You must conquer your sufferings—your thorn in the flesh—for Christ's sake. — 293
3. You must triumph over all sufferings—all the trials and temptations—that attack you. — 297

12. What Your Death and Reward as a Minister Will Be — 299

1. You will be carried immediately into heaven, transferred quicker than the blink of an eye into God's heavenly kingdom. — 301
2. You will receive eternal life. — 301
3. You will receive a new body, a transformed body, a glorious incorruptible body. — 304
4. You will receive the crown of righteousness. — 306
5. You will receive the crown of life. — 308
6. You will receive the crown of incorruption. — 309
7. You will receive the crown of rejoicing or soul-winning. — 309
8. You will receive the crown of glory. — 311
9. You will receive the perfection of all things. — 311
10. You will receive an eternal inheritance, be made an heir of God and a joint-heir with Christ. — 314

CHAPTER 1
What Your Call as a Minister Is

As a minister, you have been given the greatest privilege and responsibility in all the world: called to be a minister of the living God, called by the Sovereign Lord and Majesty of the universe.

Contents

1. You are chosen by God Himself.	3
2. You are chosen by Jesus Christ.	3
3. You are chosen by the Holy Spirit of God.	4
4. You are counted faithful—counted trustworthy—by Christ.	5
5. You have been called to be a minister by the gift of God's grace.	6
6. You have been called to be a steward—a servant—of God.	7
7. You have been called to be an ambassador for Christ.	8

Chapter 1
What Your Call as a Minister Is

1. *You are chosen by God Himself.*

    "Ye are my witnesses, saith the Lord, and my servant whom I have chosen: that ye may know and believe me, and understand that I am he: before me there was no God formed, neither shall there be after me" (Is.43:10).

    "Then answered Amos, and said to Amaziah, I was no prophet, neither was I a prophet's son; but I was an herdman, and a gatherer of sycamore fruit: and the Lord took me as I followed the flock, and the Lord said unto me, Go, prophesy unto my people Israel" (Amos 7:14-15).

    "There was a man <u>sent from God</u>, whose name was John" (Jn.1:6).

Thought

It is God the Father—the only living and true God, the Sovereign Lord and Majesty of the universe—who has called and chosen you to be a minister. You have been given the highest privilege in all the world: you have been called and chosen to be a minister by the Lord God Himself.

   "Before I formed thee in the belly I knew thee; and before thou camest forth out of the womb I sanctified thee, and I ordained thee a prophet unto the nations. Then said I, Ah, Lord God! behold, I cannot speak: for I am a child. But the Lord said unto me, Say not, I am a child: for thou shalt go to all that I shall send thee, and whatsoever I command thee thou shalt speak" (Jer.1:5-7).

2. *You are chosen by Jesus Christ.*

    "Ye have not chosen me, but I have chosen you, and ordained you, that ye should go and bring forth fruit, and that your fruit should remain: that whatsoever ye shall ask of the Father in my name, he may give it you" (Jn.15:16).

> "Then said Jesus to them again, Peace be unto you: as my father hath sent me, even <u>so send I you</u>" (Jn.20:21).
>
> "And I thank Christ Jesus our Lord, who hath enabled me, for that he counted me faithful, <u>putting me</u> into the ministry" (1 Tim.1:12).

Thought

It is the Son of the living God, Christ Jesus, who has called and chosen you to be a minister. He has chosen you to go and bear fruit among men. You are the most privileged person in all the world: you have been chosen to be a minister—chosen by the Son of God Himself.

3. *You are chosen by the Holy Spirit of God.*

> "Take heed therefore unto yourselves, and to all the flock, over the which the <u>Holy Ghost hath made you overseers</u>, to feed the church of God, which he hath purchased with his own blood" (Acts 20:28).
>
> "What? know ye not that your body is the temple of the Holy Ghost which is in you, which ye have of God, and ye are not your own? For ye are bought with a price: therefore glorify God in your body, and in your spirit, which are God's" (1 Cor.6:19-20).

Thought

It is the Holy Spirit of God who has called you to be a minister. He has chosen you so that He can live within you—chosen you to be His instrument, His channel, His person through whom He can live and work upon earth.

- The Holy Spirit wants to use your body and your life to show how a person is to live upon earth.

- The Holy Spirit wants to conform you to the image of Christ—to make you an example for the world, an example of how God wants people to live: in all godliness and righteousness.

- The Holy Spirit wants to use you to preach and teach the glorious gospel of Jesus Christ.

You have been given the most glorious privilege in all the world. You have been called and chosen by the Holy Spirit of

God: you have been called to live just like Christ lived—a holy and righteous life—and you have been called to proclaim the gospel of Christ to a world lost and reeling under the weight of enormous need.

4. *You are counted faithful—counted trustworthy—by Christ.*

> "And I thank Christ Jesus our Lord, who hath enabled me, for that he <u>counted me faithful</u>, putting me into the ministry" (1 Tim.1:12).
>
> "Moreover it is required in stewards, that a man be found faithful" (1 Cor.4:2).
>
> "I am made a minister, according to the dispensation [stewardship, trust] of God which is given to me for you, to <u>fulfil</u> the word of God" (Col.1:25).
>
> "Also I heard the voice of the Lord, saying, Whom shall I send, and who will go for us? Then said I, here am I; send me" (Is.6:8).

Thought

This is a most wonderful thought, that Christ Jesus counts you trustworthy (1 Tim.1:12). He trusts you to be faithful, and in the final analysis, He knows that you will be faithful to Him. This is one of the reasons He has chosen you and put you into the ministry.

Note the word "enabled." It means strength and power. The power of your ministry comes from Christ. Christ gives you the power to minister and to conquer all. You must always remember this:

- No matter what may confront you or how far down you may fall, Christ counts you faithful and Christ will give you the power to be faithful. Christ knows that you will arise and begin to serve with renewed fervor.

This is the reason Christ called you: because in the final analysis you will be faithful. How can you know and be assured of this? Because of the forgiveness and the power and faithfulness of Christ. Christ will lift you up. Therefore when you fall, you must arise and seek the forgiveness of Christ and begin to walk anew in the strength and power of Christ.

5. *You have been called to be a minister by the gift of God's grace.*

> "I was made a minister, <u>according to the gift of the grace of God</u> given unto me by the effectual working of his power. Unto me, who am less than the least of all saints, is this grace given, that I should preach among the Gentiles [unbelievers] the unsearchable riches of Christ" (Eph.3:7-8).
>
> "Let a man so account of us, as of the <u>ministers of Christ</u>, and stewards of the mysteries of God" (1 Cor.4:1).

Thought

You have been called to be a minister of Christ (1 Cor.4:1). Note four significant facts.

a) The word "minister" means an *under-rower*. It refers to the slaves who sat in the belly of the large ships and pulled at the great oars to carry the boat through the sea. Christ is the Master of the ship and the minister is *one of the slaves of Christ*. Note: you are only one of many under-rowing servants. Remember also that slaves in the belly of the ship were bound by chains. They were allowed to do nothing but serve the master of the ship. You are a bound slave of Christ: you exist only to row for the Master. You do not and cannot serve anyone else.

b) God has showered His grace upon you and made you a minister (Eph.3:7-8). God has been merciful to you, forgiven you so much. You owe God your life, to preach the unsearchable riches of Christ. No greater call and privilege could ever be given a person.

c) Your greatest glory is God's call and God's work. This was certainly true of Paul (Eph.3:7-8). Paul saw the dignity of the ministry, the dignity of being especially chosen by God. William Barclay points out that the ministry was a radiant privilege for Paul. God did not have to persuade Paul to be a minister. No one had to persuade Paul to teach (Eph.4:1); to sing (Eph.5:19); to speak for God (Eph.4:17); to visit (2 Cor.13:1f); to administer the affairs of the church (1 Cor.7:1f); to give his money (2 Cor.8:1f; 9:1f). Paul did not have to be coerced. He saw his call to be a minister as the greatest of all privileges. As a minister of God, you must see the glorious privilege you have in serving Christ (*The Letters to the Galatians and Ephesians*, p.145).

d) Your call to be a minister and a preacher is a gift, a free gift of God's grace. This is exactly what Paul says (Eph.3:7-8). God had the right to call Paul simply because God has all rights. God is God. There was no merit, no worth, no value within Paul that caused God to choose him as a minister and as a preacher. Paul simply exclaims, "What a privilege! What a responsibility! The less of the least called by God to minister and to preach!"

- The salvation in Christ caused Paul to become a minister (Eph.3:7).
- The salvation in Christ caused Paul to become a preacher. Note Paul's utter humility. He had what we all need: a deep, intense sense of unworthiness before God.

As a minister of God, you have the greatest of all calls. You have been privileged with the highest of privileges. God has *showered His grace* upon you and called you to be His minister to a world that reels under the weight of suffering and death.

6. *You have been called to be a steward—a servant—of God.*

> "**Let a man so account of us, as of the ministers of Christ, and <u>stewards</u> of the mysteries of God**" (**1 Cor.4:1**).
> "**For a bishop [minister] must be blameless, as the <u>steward</u> of God**" (**Tit.1:7**).
> "**As every man hath received the gift, even so minister the same one to another, as <u>good stewards</u> of the manifold grace of God**" (**1 Pt.4:10**).

Thought

You are the steward of God. The word "steward" (oikonomos) means the overseer of an estate. The steward was always a slave, subject to a master, but he was *placed in charge* of the other slaves throughout the master's house or estate. He controlled the staff and ran the whole operation for the master. He was set over others, yet he himself was still a slave of the master. His work was not closely supervised; therefore, he had to be trustworthy and responsible.

Note what the minister is made a steward over: the mysteries of God. A mystery is not something hard to understand. Rather, it is something that has been hidden and kept secret. It is something that was undiscoverable by human reason, but now is revealed by God. It is crystal clear to those to whom it is revealed, but it is completely alien to those who do not receive it. What are the mysteries of God? They are the truths—the glorious truths—of God's Word. Who are the ones to whom the mysteries are revealed? The stewards, the ministers, the believing servants of Christ.

As a minister of God, you are to be esteemed highly for your work's sake. You are *only* a servant of God's, but you are the servant whom God has made steward over His household, over His church and His people. You have been honored by God: you have been made responsible for the imperishable mysteries of God, the great truths of God's Holy Word. You do not deal with perishable things such as money and possessions, but with the eternal things of God Himself, the eternal truths that God wants proclaimed to the world.

7. *You have been called to be an ambassador for Christ.*

> "And all things are of God, who hath reconciled us to himself by Jesus Christ, and hath given to us the ministry of reconciliation; to wit [oh! to know], that God was in Christ, reconciling the world unto himself, not imputing their trespasses unto them; and hath committed unto us the word of reconciliation. Now then we are <u>ambassadors for Christ</u>, as though God did beseech you by us: we pray you in Christ's stead, be ye reconciled to God" (2 Cor.5:18-21).

Thought

God has called you to be His ambassador to the world. He has given you the ministry of delivering the message of God to the whole world, the message of reconciliation. No greater call could ever be issued; no higher position could ever be held. Note two significant points.

a) You are given the highest of titles: you are an "ambassador for Christ." The "ambassador" (presbeuomen) is a person who is sent forth as an official envoy to represent the Sender and to announce the message of the Sender. Four things are always true about the ambassador.

- You belong to the One who sent you out.
- You are commissioned to be sent out. You exist only for the purpose for which you were sent.
- You possess all the authority and power of the One who sent you out.
- You are sent forth with the message of the Sender. The message is not your own.

b) You are given the greatest of messages: "Be reconciled to God." The message is so critical that you are to "beseech" (deometha) men: beg, intreat, cry, and plead with them to be reconciled to God.

Note that it is "for Christ's sake" that you are to plead with men. Christ has paid the ultimate price to make reconciliation available to men: He has taken the sins of men upon Himself and borne the condemnation for them. Because He has done so much, every person owes his life to Christ—every person should be reconciled to God. For Christ's sake, a person should give himself to God.

Chapter 2

What Your Aim as a Minister Must Be

As a minister, the aim—the target and mark—of your life is clearly spelled out in Scripture. You are to set your life upon these goals. You are to adopt these goals and be utterly consumed with reaching them.

Contents

1. You must know, believe, and understand God.	13
2. You must personally know Christ and the power of His resurrection.	14
3. You must forget the past and press on for the prize.	15
4. You must set this as your great aim: not to be ashamed in anything, but to exalt Christ.	16
5. You must have one great concern: consistency, not to offend in anything. You must prove that you are a true minister of God—that you are faithful through all the experiences of life, through all trials and temptations.	17
6. You must fulfill the supreme requirement of God: that you be faithful.	18
7. You must be faithful, so faithful that you are totally abandoned and surrendered to Christ.	19
8. You must be faithful to the end of life.	21

Chapter 2
What Your Aim as a Minister Must Be

1. *You must know, believe, and understand God.*

    "Ye are my witnesses, saith the LORD, and my servant whom I have chosen: <u>that ye may</u> know and believe me, and understand that I am he: before me there was no God formed, neither shall there be after me" (Is.43:10).

    Thought
    This is the reason God created you, saved you, and called you into the ministry: that you may know, believe, and understand Him.

    a) Your aim must be to know God: know Him personally and intimately—grow to know Him more and more as you walk day by day.

    b) Your aim must be to believe God.
    - Believe His love for the world.
    - Believe His salvation and call.
    - Believe His promise of eternal life.
    - Believe His Word, the Holy Scriptures.
    - Believe He is with you no matter the trial or temptation: that He will never forsake you, that He cares for you and is looking after you.
    - Believe He has called and commissioned you to proclaim His Word to a lost and dying world, a world reeling in desperate need.

    c) Your aim must be to understand God.
    - Understand that He alone is God, the only living and true God, the Sovereign LORD and Majesty of the universe.
    - Understand that God is loving as well as holy and righteous—that God is merciful and gracious as well as just—that God will forgive sin as well as judge sin.

- Understand that God loves and cares for man, that He has demonstrated His love in the most supreme way possible: He has given His Son to die for sin so that whoever believes in Him might not perish but have everlasting life.
- Understand that God alone saves man; therefore, He alone is to be worshiped and served by man.

You have been called to be God's witness and servant upon earth for this one great aim: that you may *know*, *believe*, and *understand* God.

2. *You must personally know Christ and the power of His resurrection.*

> "That I may know him, and the power of his resurrection, and the fellowship of his sufferings, being made conformable unto his death; if by any means I might attain unto the resurrection of the dead" (Ph.3:10-11).

Thought

As a minister, you must seek a victorious experience with Christ. You must seek to know Christ—to know Him personally and to know Him intimately—to know His glorious power over the world and all that is in the world. Your great pursuit in life must be to seek Christ.

a) Your aim must be to know Christ: know Him personally and intimately—grow to know Him more and more as you walk day by day.

b) Your aim must be to know the power of Christ's resurrection: to call upon the power of Christ in conquering this world with all its trials and temptations, sin and death.

c) Your aim must be to know the fellowship of Christ's sufferings: to suffer for the same reasons that Christ suffered—to save and minister to people.

d) Your aim must be to be conformed to Christ's death: to subject yourself totally to God—to deny yourself and put your desires and flesh to death and to do only the will of God.

"If any man will come after me, let him deny himself, and take up his cross daily, and follow me" (Lk.9:23).

"I beseech you therefore, brethren, by the mercies of God, that ye present your bodies a living sacrifice, holy, acceptable unto God, which is your reasonable service" (Ro.12:1).

3. *You must forget the past and press on for the prize.*

"Brethren, I count not myself to have apprehended: but this one thing I do, forgetting those things which are behind, and reaching forth unto those things which are before, I press toward the mark for the prize of the high calling of God in Christ Jesus" (Ph.3:13-14).

Thought

Forgetting the past and pressing on is a difficult thing to do. But as a minister you must do it. How? By concentrating and controlling your mind and by reaching forth to those things which are before you. Note the concentration and focus:

- BUT THIS ONE THING I DO.

In one focused act, you must forget the past and reach forth to those things that are before you. This act involves two steps: both forgetting and reaching forth. The past cannot be forgotten without reaching forth to what lies ahead. You must not sit around moaning and regretting the past. You must not wallow around in self-pity when you come short or fail. You must not allow the feelings of being unworthy to grip you. We are all unworthy, *totally unworthy*, and we cannot be more unworthy than to be *totally unworthy*. This is not to excuse our failure and shortcoming. God holds us accountable. But we are to confess and forsake sin and failure. This is what you—all ministers of God—must always do. Confess and repent and get up and begin to serve Christ with a renewed commitment. You must not concentrate upon the past. The things of the past are to be forgotten. The things of the future are to be the focus of your mind. You are to zero in on the things at hand and on the things that lie ahead. If you do this, you will conquer and overcome in life, and you will complete and fulfill your ministry for the Lord Jesus Christ.

4. *You must set this as your <u>great aim</u> and eagerly expect and hope to reach it:*
   - *not to be ashamed in anything*
   - *to exalt Christ whether it be by life or by death*

> "According to my <u>earnest expectation and my hope</u>, that in nothing I shall be ashamed, but that with all boldness, as always, so now also Christ shall be <u>magnified in my body</u>, whether it be by life, or by death" (Ph.1:20).
>
> "I beseech you therefore, brethren, by the mercies of God, that ye <u>present your bodies a living sacrifice</u>, holy, acceptable unto God, which is your reasonable service. And be not conformed to this world: but be ye transformed by the renewing of your mind, that ye may prove what is that good, and acceptable, and perfect, will of God" (Ro.12:1-2).
>
> "I thank God, whom I serve from my forefathers with <u>pure conscience</u>" (2 Tim.1:3).

Thought
The only place people can see Jesus Christ living is in the body and life of a believer. Consequently, there is only one place where you can magnify and glorify Jesus Christ: that place is in your body. You must, therefore, commit your body totally to Jesus Christ.

a) You must guard and keep your body from . . .
   - wondering and questioning God and His Word
   - becoming discouraged and depressed
   - becoming complacent and slothful
   - becoming lazy and undisciplined
   - sinning and failing
   - denying and turning away from Christ
   - overeating and drunkenness
   - immorality and drugs

b) You must commit your body totally to Jesus Christ . . .
- so that you will not be ashamed of anything
- so that you will exalt Christ, whether it be by life or by death

5. *You must have one great concern: consistency, not to offend in anything. You must prove that you are a true minister of God—that you are faithful through all the experiences of life, through all trials and temptations.*

   "**Giving no offence in any thing, that the ministry be not blamed: but in all things <u>approving ourselves</u> as the ministers of God,**
   - **in much patience**
   - **in afflictions**
   - **in necessities**
   - **in distresses**
   - **in stripes**
   - **in imprisonments**
   - **in tumults**
   - **in labours**
   - **in watchings**
   - **in fastings**
   - **by pureness**
   - **by knowledge**
   - **by longsuffering**
   - **by kindness**
   - **by the Holy Ghost**
   - **by love unfeigned**
   - **by the word of truth**
   - **by the power of God**
   - **by the armour of righteousness on the right hand and on the left**
   - **by honour and dishonour**
   - **by evil report and good report**
   - **as deceivers, and yet true**
   - **as unknown, and yet well known**
   - **as dying, and, behold, we live**
   - **as chastened, and not killed**
   - **as sorrowful, yet always rejoicing**
   - **as poor, yet making many rich**
   - **as having nothing, and yet possessing all things**"
   (2 Cor.6:3-10; cp. 2 Cor.4:8-10).

> "There hath no temptation taken you but such as is common to man: but God is faithful, who will not suffer you to be tempted above that ye are able; but will with the temptation also make a way to escape, that ye may be able to bear it" (1 Cor.10:13).

Thought
As a minister, you must have one great concern: consistency, to offend in nothing. You must aim to be so consistent . . .

- that you will never cause anyone to reject or turn sour on the Lord Jesus Christ.
- that you will never cause a person to stumble or fall.
- that you will never be a poor reflection upon the ministry.

You must aim and seek diligently to bring only honor to the ministry and the name of the Lord Jesus Christ. You must prove that you are a true minister of God, no matter the severity of the trial or temptation. You must be strong against all trials and temptations, struggling to conquer them all. You must not offend anyone in anything. This must be your great concern, your great aim in the ministry.

6. *You must fulfill the supreme requirement of God: that you be faithful.*

> "Let a man so account of us, as of the ministers of Christ, and stewards of the mysteries of God. Moreover it is required in stewards, that a man be found **faithful**" (1 Cor.4:1-2).

Thought
As a minister of Christ, God requires one thing of you: faithfulness. Faithfulness is the one essential demanded of you.

- You are not required to be eloquent, brilliant, intelligent, loaded with ability, or successful. You are required to be *faithful*.
- You are not required by God to be an administrator, counsellor, visitor, door-greeter, or socializer—as important as these ministries are. You are required to be *faithful*.

You are required to be faithful in ministering the mysteries of God. By mysteries is meant the *truths of God's Word*. You are held accountable and shall be judged for how well you minister the truths of God's Word.

- You must not hold back or fail to share the truths of God.
- You must not substitute some other message for the truths of God.
- You must not mix some other message with the truths of God.

You must be faithful to your call. You are the minister of Christ and the steward of God's mysteries, of the truths of His Word. You must—absolutely must—proclaim the mysteries of God, His Holy Word.

> "According to the <u>glorious gospel</u> of the blessed God, which was committed to my trust. And I thank Christ Jesus our Lord, who hath enabled me, for that he counted me faithful, putting me into the ministry" (1 Tim.1:11-12).
>
> "Now the word of the LORD came unto Jonah the son of Amittai, saying, Arise, go to Nineveh, that great city, and cry against it; for their wickedness is come up before me. But Jonah <u>rose up to flee</u> unto Tarshish from the presence of the LORD, and went down to Joppa; and he found a ship going to Tarshish: so he paid the fare thereof, and went down into it, to go with them unto Tarshish <u>from the presence of the</u> LORD" (Jonah 1:1-3).
>
> "And the word of the LORD came unto Jonah the second time, saying, Arise, go unto Nineveh, that great city, and preach unto it the preaching that I bid thee. So <u>Jonah arose, and went</u> unto Nineveh, according to the word of the LORD" (Jonah 3:1-3).

7. *You must be faithful, so faithful that you are totally abandoned and surrendered to Christ.*

    > "But none of these things move me, <u>neither count I my life dear unto myself,</u> so that I might finish my course with joy, and the ministry, which I have

received of the Lord Jesus, to testify the gospel of the grace of God" (Acts 20:24).

Thought
This is a striking verse, but it is also a precious verse, and should be read many times to get the full impact of its message.

Paul did not count his life "dear" unto himself. His life was not for him to use as he pleased, not for earthly comfort or pleasure. His life was not for himself; it was for Christ. His life was "dear" (timian), that is, *precious* and *valuable*; but it was not for himself, not for his own use. His life was the *precious* and *valuable* possession of the Lord. The Lord possessed his life, for he had given it to the Lord, and the Lord was using it to the maximum. Paul had given his life to the Lord for two reasons.

First, Paul wished to finish the course of his life with joy. He wished to be faithful and diligent, running the Christian race to the end (1 Cor.9:24-27; Ph.3:13-14). Note: he did complete his course, proclaiming its fulfillment to all believers.

> **"For I am now ready to be offered, and the time of my departure is at hand. I have fought a good fight, I have finished my course, I have kept the faith: henceforth there is laid up for me a crown of righteousness, which the Lord, the righteous judge, shall give me at that day: and not to me only, but unto all them also that love his appearing" (2 Tim.4:6-8).**

What a glorious *testimony and challenge* to you and to all others who preach the gospel of Christ. May God grant that you—that every true minister of God—finish your course with joy, faithfully and diligently running the race to the end.

> **"Know ye not that they which run in a race run all, but one receiveth the prize? So run, that ye may obtain. And every man that striveth for the mastery is temperate in all things. Now they do it to obtain a corruptible crown; but we an incorruptible. I therefore so run, not as uncertainly; so**

> fight I, not as one that beateth the air: but I keep under my body, and bring it into subjection: lest that by any means, when I have preached to others, I myself should be a castaway" (1 Cor.9:24-27).

Second, Paul wished to finish the ministry which the Lord Jesus Christ had given him. Note what his ministry was—to proclaim the gospel of the grace of God.

As the minister of Christ, you must do just what Paul did; you must have the same testimony that Paul had: you must abandon and surrender yourself totally to Christ.

> "Also I heard the voice of the Lord, saying, Whom shall I send, and who will go for us? Then said I, Here am I; send me" (Is.6:8).
>
> "And thou [Ezekiel] shalt speak my words unto them, whether they will hear, or whether they will forbear: for they are most rebellious" (Ezk.2:7).

8. *You must be faithful to the end of life.*

Thought
As a minister, when you come to the end of life, you must have the most glorious of testimonies. You must be able to say with Paul:

> "I have fought a good fight, I have finished my course, I have kept the faith: henceforth there is laid up for me a crown of righteousness, which the Lord, the righteous judge, shall give me at that day" (2 Tim.4:7-8a).

The way Paul describes his life is full of meaning. He quickly glances back over his life and uses three pictures to describe it, the pictures of a soldier, an athlete, and a steward. As a minister, you must be able to say the same things about your life.

a) You must live life just like a faithful soldier: "I have fought a good fight." Paul had responded to the call of the Lord Jesus Christ...

- He had volunteered to serve Christ.
- He had separated himself from this world, sacrificing *all that he was and had* to be a soldier for Christ—a soldier totally committed to the mission of Christ.

- He had suffered through the trials, temptations, criticisms, and attacks launched by the enemies of Christ, both the human and spiritual enemies.
- He had fought a "good" (kalos) fight: a fight that was worthy, honorable, noble, and commendable.
- He had done his time, stuck to the mission of Christ to the very end.

Therefore, Paul could victoriously declare, "I have fought a good fight." He was being released from his service as a soldier for the King, released to go home to live at peace in the kingdom of his dear Lord forever and ever. This, too, must be your testimony: as a good soldier of Jesus Christ, you must be able to declare, "I have fought a good fight."

> **"Fight the good fight of faith, lay hold on eternal life, whereunto thou art also called, and hast professed a good profession before many witnesses" (1 Tim.6:12).**
>
> **"But call to remembrance the former days, in which, after ye were illuminated, ye endured a great fight of afflictions" (Heb.10:32).**

b) You must run and finish the course of your life; you must complete the race of life just like the athlete runs and finishes the course of his race. This is powerful, for it means that Paul disciplined and controlled his life to the utmost—just like the Olympian athlete.

- He controlled what he ate and drank and what he did with his body and mind.
- He focused upon the course of life, how he ran it. He could not risk being distracted by the things of the world nor of the flesh lest he become a castaway and be disqualified from running the race.

> **"Know ye not that they which run in a race run all, but one receiveth the prize? So run, that ye may obtain. And every man that striveth for the mastery is temperate in all things. Now they do it to obtain a corruptible crown; but we an**

incorruptible. I therefore so run, not as uncertainly; so fight I, not as one that beateth the air: but I keep under my body, and bring it into subjection: lest that by any means, when I have preached to others, I myself should be a castaway" (1 Cor.9:23-27).

c) You must keep the faith. You must look after the faith just like a good steward looks after the estate of his master. The Lord had *entrusted* the faith to Paul, and Paul had kept the faith. He had proven faithful; he had faithfully managed the faith for his Master, the Lord Jesus Christ. The idea is that of a trust, of a management contract between Christ and Paul. Paul is saying that he had kept the terms of the contract; he had managed and looked after the trust faithfully and well. Think about this for a moment—all the sufferings that Paul went through—the terrible trials—the times that he could have . . .

- dumped the trust of the faith or laid it aside and ignored it. But he never did. He had been chosen by the Lord and Master of life to manage the trust of God, even the faith of our Lord Jesus Christ. Therefore, Paul took the trust and managed it through all—both good and bad times. He never forsook the faith. And because he had been faithful, it was time for him to bear the fruit of his labor. He was now to reap the benefits of the faith; he was to be given all the rights and privileges of the Lord's estate—to live and enjoy its pleasures forevermore.

CHAPTER 3
What Your Purpose as a Minister Is

Why has God called you to be a minister? What are His purposes for calling you? God has several very specific purposes He wants to accomplish through you. Scripture is clear in describing just what these purposes are.

Contents

1. You are to be a pattern of the glorious truth that God saves sinners—a living example of God's mercy.   27
2. You are to go and make disciples of all nations.   28
3. You are to present every man perfect in Christ Jesus.   30
4. You are to be a witness for the Lord Jesus Christ.   30

CHAPTER 3
What Your Purpose as a Minister Is

1. *You are to be a pattern of the glorious truth that God saves sinners—a living example of God's mercy.*

    "Howbeit for this cause I obtained mercy, that <u>in me first</u> Jesus Christ might show forth all longsuffering, for a <u>pattern</u> to them which should hereafter believe on him to life everlasting" (1 Tim.1:16).

    "Let no man despise thy youth; but be thou an <u>example</u> of the believers, in word, in conversation, in charity, in spirit, in faith, in purity" (1 Tim.4:12).

    "In all things showing thyself a <u>pattern</u> of good works: in doctrine showing . . .
    - uncorruptness
    - gravity
    - sincerity
    - sound speech

    . . . that cannot be condemned; that he that is of the contrary part may be ashamed, having no evil thing to say of you" (Tit.2:6-8).

Thought

God has been longsuffering toward you—very longsuffering. He has had mercy upon you, saved you, and called you to be His minister to the world. But there is a reason God has done so much for you: that you might be a living example of His longsuffering and mercy.

a) You are to be a pattern—a demonstration, an example—that God is longsuffering and not willing that any should perish or die. You are to be a pattern of God's mercy, that He will have mercy upon anyone who comes to Him for mercy. And note: you are God's minister to the world; therefore, you are to be *the first—the foremost—example* of God's longsuffering and mercy. You are to be the first to live and proclaim the longsuffering and mercy of God.

b) You are to be an example to all believers . . .
- in word
- in purity
- in love
- in the Holy Spirit
- in behavior
- in faith

c) You are to be a pattern—an example—of good works in doctrine and teaching:
- in proclaiming a pure doctrine
- in proclaiming the message sincerely and with dignity
- in proclaiming the message with sound words

As stated, you are to be the first—the foremost—example of God's longsuffering and mercy to the human race. You are to set a blazing example in all good works and in keeping the message of God uncorrupted.

2. *You are to go and make disciples of all nations.*

> "Go ye therefore, and teach all nations, baptizing them in the name of the Father, and of the Son, and of the Holy Ghost: teaching [making disciples of] them to observe all things whatsoever I have commanded you: and, lo, I am with you alway, even unto the end of the world" (Mt.28:19-20).
>
> "And the things that thou hast heard of me among many witnesses, the same commit thou to faithful men, who shall be able to teach others also" (2 Tim.2:2).

Thought

This is the great commission of Jesus Christ to His followers (Mt.28:19-20). This is one of the most important verses in all the Bible, for it tells you as a minister of the gospel exactly what your purpose and task are: you are to go and make disciples of all nations. The word "teach" in some translations is the Greek word *make disciples*. What does it mean to *make disciples*? It means to do exactly what Christ did. When Christ found a person who was willing to commit his life to God—totally commit his life—Christ attached Himself to that person. Christ began to mold and make that person into His image. The word *attach* is the key word. It is probably the word that best describes discipleship. Christ made disciples of men by attaching Himself to them, and through that personal attachment, they were able to observe His life and conversation. In seeing and hearing Him, they began to absorb and assimilate His very character and behavior. They began to follow Him and to serve Him more closely. In simple terms this is what our Lord did. This is the way He made disciples. This was His mission and His method, His obsession: to attach Himself to willing believers.

There is another way to describe what Christ did. Christ envisioned something beyond Himself and beyond His day and time. He envisioned an *extension* of Himself, an *extension* of His very being, and an *extension* of His mission and method. The way He chose to extend Himself was discipleship, attaching Himself to committed persons, and through attachment, the persons absorbed and assimilated the Lord's very character and mission. They in turn attached themselves to others and discipled them. They, too, expected their disciples to make disciples of others who were willing to commit their lives to Christ. This was the way the glorious message of Christ was to march down through the centuries (2 Tim.2:2).

There is no question what our Lord's commission is: we are to go. But more than that, we are to make disciples, to *attach* ourselves to those persons who will follow our Lord until they in turn can make disciples (2 Tim.2:2).

Your purpose as a minister of God is . . .

- to disciple others: pick out several believers who are willing to commit all they are and have to Jesus Christ and *attach* yourself to them. (Pick out as many as you can handle.)
- to teach the willing believer all you know: let him walk and talk with you and see you live, pray, teach, minister, eat, and relax. Let him observe you day by day as much as possible and absorb *Christ in you*.
- to always be discipling some believers, and then turning them loose to disciple others. (Set a goal as to how long you think it will take to train each disciple, and then turn each one loose to disciple others. As you turn each one loose, then

pick out another committed believer to replace him in your group of disciples.)

Do this—disciple others—for it is the great commission of Christ, the very method He used. We can soon reach the world if you and all other ministers will follow this simple instruction of Christ: disciple—pick out and attach yourself to all who are willing to commit their lives to the ministry.

3. *You are to present every man perfect in Christ Jesus.*

> "[Christ] whom we preach, warning every man, and teaching every man in all wisdom; that we may present every man perfect in Christ Jesus" (Col.1:28).

Thought
God wants every person to be reached and presented perfect before Him. "Perfect" means mature and complete. This is your overriding purpose, your supreme objective: to go after every person—try to reach every single soul—and present every person to God as a mature and complete believer in Christ Jesus. How can you accomplish this task? Note the verse:

- Preach Christ.
- Warn every man.
- Teach every man in all wisdom.

4. *You are to be a witness for the Lord Jesus Christ. Jesus Christ came to earth that you might have life, both abundant and eternal life. He came to save you from the enslavement of sin, death, and judgment to come. You have been called by Christ to be a witness of His salvation. Your very purpose for existing—for being a minister—is to be a witness for Christ.*

FIRST, YOU ARE TO BE AN UNASHAMED WITNESS.

> "<u>Be not</u> thou therefore <u>ashamed</u> of the testimony of our Lord, nor of me his prisoner; but be thou partaker of the afflictions of the gospel according to the power of God" (2 Tim.1:8).

> "I will speak of thy testimonies also before kings, and will not be ashamed" (Ps.119:46).
>
> "And spared not the old world, but saved Noah the eighth person, a <u>preacher of righteousness</u>, bringing in the flood upon the world of the ungodly" (2 Pt.2:5).

Thought

You are not to be ashamed of the gospel nor of strong believers who are living and witnessing for Christ. The point and verse are clear enough. You are not to shrink . . .

- from identifying with the gospel and the Lord of the gospel.
- from identifying with strong believers who are sharing and living for Christ.

You are to share the gospel—share by living for Christ and by speaking up for Him, bearing testimony of His saving grace. You are to stand up for those who share Christ when they are being ridiculed and persecuted. In fact, note the verse: you are to share in the sufferings of the gospel. You will be opposed and misunderstood by the world. Why? Because you do not live like the world; you do not live a sensual, immoral, ungodly, and worldly life. You do not follow after the things of the world. Therefore, your righteous and godly life convicts the world of its ungodly deeds. Hence, the world will ridicule and persecute you. But you are not to let this stop you: you are not to shrink from living for and sharing the gospel. You are to jump right in with other strong believers and share the gospel with a starving and lost world that reels under the weight of evil, corruption, and death.

SECOND, YOU ARE TO BE A STRONG, BOLD WITNESS.

> "Who gave himself for us, that he might redeem us from all iniquity, and purify unto himself a peculiar people, zealous of good works. These things <u>speak</u>, and <u>exhort</u>, and <u>rebuke</u> with all authority. Let no man despise thee" (Tit.2:14-15, cp. v.11-13).
>
> "Then spake the Lord to Paul in the night by a vision, <u>Be not afraid, but speak</u>, and hold not thy

peace: for I am with thee, and no man shall set on thee to hurt thee: for I have much people in this city" (Acts 18:9-10).

Thought

The death of Jesus Christ is to be proclaimed with all authority—strongly and boldly (Tit.2:14-15).

- You are to speak about the death of Christ, that His death redeems man. There is no argument about the grace of God, no argument about the Lord Jesus Christ and His death. Unquestionably, God loves the world. He has demonstrated His love by sending His Son into the world to redeem man. You are, therefore, to proclaim the death of Christ for the sins of the world.

- You are to use every method of speech and communication there is. You are to declare the grace of God and the death of His Son for the sins of the world.

- You are to exhort people in the death of Christ, how His death redeems man. The word *exhort* means to encourage. People are lonely, empty, without purpose, discouraged, distressed, and without hope. They need to hear the glorious message of God's grace, of the Lord Jesus Christ. They need to hear about the wonderful life God gives us now and eternally—all through the Lord Jesus Christ and His death.

- You are to rebuke people in the death of Christ. There is no excuse for men living in sin and rejecting the grace of God. God has done too much for us in Christ Jesus, His Son. A man is a fool to reject eternal life, the glorious redemption and hope which Christ gives. Men need to be told the truth, rebuked, and put under conviction by your proclaiming the grace of God and the death of Jesus Christ.

THIRD, YOU ARE TO BE CHRIST'S WITNESS.

"Now then we are ambassadors for Christ, as though God did beseech you by us: we pray you in Christ's stead, be ye reconciled to God" (2 Cor.5:20).

Thought
You are an ambassador for Christ. In God's eyes, you have the highest of titles, that of being an *ambassador* for your Lord and Master. As the ambassador of Christ, four things are true of you (the same four things are always true of the ambassador of a nation):

- You—the Lord's ambassador—belong to Christ, the One who has sent you out to the world.
- You—the Lord's ambassador—are commissioned to be sent out. You now exist only for the purpose for which you were sent out.
- You—the Lord's ambassador—possess all the authority and power of Christ, of the One who has sent you out into the world.
- You—the Lord's ambassador—are sent forth with the message of Christ, the Lord of the universe. You are not free to deliver your own message nor the message of anyone else. You have been appointed by Christ as His ambassador to deliver His message and His message alone.

Note a most significant fact: you have been given the greatest of messages to deliver—"Be reconciled to God."

FOURTH, YOU ARE TO BE A FAMILY AND COMMUNITY WITNESS.

> **"Go home to thy friends, and tell them how great things the Lord hath done for thee, and hath had compassion on thee" (Mk.5:19).**

Thought
You are to witness first to your own family and home. Too often, the very opposite is true: our homes—both spouse and children—are often neglected and overlooked. We just fail to make a clearcut presentation of the gospel to our loved ones. But this is not to be, not if you are a minister of Christ. Your first duty is to witness to your family.

FIFTH, YOU ARE TO BE A WORLDWIDE WITNESS.

> **"Go ye therefore, and teach <u>all nations</u>, baptizing them in the name of the Father, and of the Son,**

and of the Holy Ghost: teaching them to observe all things whatsoever I have commanded you: and, lo, I am with you alway, even unto the end of the world" (Mt.28:19-20).

"And he said unto them, Go ye into <u>all the world</u>, and preach the gospel to every creature" (Mk.16:15).

"For thou shalt be his witness unto <u>all men</u> of what thou hast seen and heard" (Acts 22:15).

Thought
Christ has given you the method to follow as you bear witness for Him (Acts 1:8).

a) You are to witness where you are (Jerusalem) and move progressively outward (Judea and Samaria) until you have a part in reaching the uttermost part of the earth.

- You are to go—personally go—as far as you can.
- You are to give as sacrificially as you can so that others can go.
- You are to use every method and ministry you can to reach the world.

b) You are to witness where you are first. See to it that Christ is well known throughout your home and community before moving on. But once Christ is well known, you are to move out, ever pressing outward from where you are. Your first witness is to be . . .

- in Jerusalem: where you are, your home and local community. (See *The Preacher's Outline & Sermon Bible,*® note—Lk.9:4 for more discussion.)
- in all Judea: other communities and areas and cities and states. Note the word "*all* Judea."
- in Samaria: other nations and countries, perhaps even where people are antagonistic. There was bitter hatred between the Jews and Samaritans. Yet Christ tells His witnesses to carry the message of salvation even to their enemies.

- to the uttermost part of the earth: to the unknown countries and regions of the world.

A critical point is this: you are to see that each area receives the message of Christ. You are to stay where you are before reaching out. But once the area knows the message—has received your ministry and gift—the message is to be carried out into another area.

SIXTH, YOU ARE TO BE AN OBEDIENT WITNESS.

> **"Go, stand and speak in the temple to the people all the words of this life. And when they heard that, they entered into the temple early in the morning, and taught" (Acts 5:20-21a).**
>
> **"Then I said, I will not make mention of him, nor speak any more in his name. But his word was in mine heart as a burning fire shut up in my bones, and I was weary with forbearing, and I could not stay [refuse to witness any longer]" (Jer.20:9).**

Thought
Witnessing is often difficult. There are many reasons why:
- You may be busy or rushed.
- You may be tired and exhausted; you may need rest.
- You may face opposition, ridicule, imprisonment, or outright persecution.
- You may have other pressing duties demanding your immediate attention.
- You may have to go out and visit and witness alone. There may be no one available or willing to go with you.

But God's commission to you, His minister, is clear: "Go, stand and speak . . . to the people" (Acts 5:20-21a). The Greek is strong, demanding boldness and courage.
- "Go": go now, immediately.
- "Stand": take your stand; stand forth without reservation or hesitation.
- "Speak": proclaim, preach, teach—courageously, boldly, without fear.

- "All the words of this life": the whole gospel of salvation; the glorious message of the death and resurrection of Christ; not watering down or changing anything; not holding back; not trying to soften the message to make it more acceptable.

God has no one to go but His followers, and the leaders of His followers are His ministers. If you are not obedient in witnessing, then others—your people, your church, your class, your fellow ministers, your friends, your dynamic laymen—will not witness. You, as God's minister, must take the lead in witnessing. The highest authority in the universe—God Himself—has commissioned you to be His witness. You must, therefore, be obedient and bear witness to the glorious gospel of His Son, the Lord Jesus Christ.

SEVENTH, YOU ARE TO BE A CONSTANT WITNESS.

> "For we **cannot but speak** the things which we have seen and heard" (Acts 4:20).
>
> "But sanctify the Lord God in your hearts: and be ready **always** to give an answer to every man that asketh you a reason of the hope that is in you with meekness and fear" (1 Pt.3:15).
>
> "Then they that feared the LORD **spake often** one to another: and the LORD hearkened, and heard it, and a book of remembrance was written before him for them that feared the LORD, and that thought upon his name" (Mal.3:16).
>
> "My mouth shall show forth thy righteousness and thy salvation **all the day**; for I know not the numbers [of my days] thereof" (Ps.71:15).
>
> "I have set watchmen upon thy walls, O Jerusalem, which shall **never hold their peace** day nor night: ye that make mention of the LORD, keep not silence" (Is.62:6).

Thought

You have the most glorious message in all the world: man can now live abundantly and live forever. Man never has to die; he never has to suffer emptiness, loneliness, or anxiety; he never has to lack purpose, love, joy, or peace. The world is crying for this news, the news that they can have life—real life—both now and forever.

You must, therefore, proclaim the gospel and proclaim it *constantly*. You must grasp every opportunity, and even make opportunity, to share the gospel. You must never shirk your duty, never neglect or ignore anyone. Day by day as you cross the paths of others, you must constantly share the gospel, share the glorious news that the world so desperately needs, the news that man can now live both abundantly and eternally.

EIGHTH, YOU ARE TO BE A SPIRIT-FILLED WITNESS.

> "But when the Comforter is come, whom I will send unto you from the Father, even the Spirit of truth, which proceedeth from the Father, he shall testify of me: and <u>ye also shall bear witness</u>, because ye have been with me from the beginning" (Jn.15:26-27, cp. Acts 1:8).
>
> "And we are his witnesses of these things; and so is also the Holy Ghost, whom God hath given to them that obey him" (Acts 5:32).

Thought
You cannot witness on your own, in your own physical and mental strength, and win people to Jesus Christ. Neither you nor any other person can enter the heart of a person and place the divine nature—the incorruptible seed of God—into that person. Only the Holy Spirit can do this. You must, therefore, trust God's Spirit to convict and convert the souls of people when you share the gospel. Your task is twofold:

- to speak and share the gospel.
- to pray and trust the Holy Spirit to convict and convert the person.

When you pray and trust God's Spirit to work through you, then God's Spirit does just that. God's Word—His witness—never returns to Him void.

> "So shall my word be that goeth forth out of my mouth: it shall not return unto me void, but it shall accomplish that which I please, and it shall prosper in the thing whereto I sent it" (Is.55:11).

God's Spirit takes your witness, prayer, and trust, and He convicts the souls of people. He convicts and saves all who willingly receive Christ as their Savior.

NINTH, YOU ARE TO BE A BELIEVING WITNESS, A WITNESS WHO IS A TRUE BELIEVER.

> "And ye also shall bear witness, because ye have been with me from the beginning" (Jn.15:27).
>
> "We having the same spirit of faith, according as it is written, <u>I believed</u>, and therefore have I spoken; we also believe, and therefore speak" (2 Cor.4:13).
>
> "Come and hear, all ye that fear God, and I will declare what he hath done for my soul" (Ps.66:16).

Thought

The Son of God came to earth; He partook of flesh and blood and became a Man just like all other men. He is called Jesus Christ or Jesus the Messiah, the Savior of the world. He was heard, seen, intensely looked upon and handled by John and the other apostles and by many others who believed and followed Him (1 Jn.1:3). Jesus Christ did everything He could to show man that the Son of God had come to earth—that He had come to save and to deliver man from this corruptible world of sin and death and to give man life eternal. Jesus Christ did everything He could to show man that man can live with God forever and ever.

As a minister, you yourself believe the gospel. Now, it is your duty to declare to the world the very message proclaimed by John: "That which we have seen and heard declare we unto you, that ye also may have fellowship with us: and truly our fellowship is with the Father, and with his Son Jesus Christ" (1 Jn.1:3).

CHAPTER 4
What Your Resources as a Minister Are

How can you fulfill the purposes of God for your life and ministry? God has not left you alone; He has not left you with only human wisdom and strength to accomplish your task. God has provided great help—unbelievable resources—to equip you to live for Him and to carry out His great purposes for you.

Contents

1. You are given the grace and power of Christ. — 41
2. You are given the presence and power of the Holy Spirit. — 42
3. You are given the presence and power of God. — 43
4. You are given the assurance—absolute assurance—of victory by God Himself. — 45
5. You are given a spiritual gift by God. — 47
6. You are given faith to sustain you in the ministry. — 48
7. You are given the love of Christ to compel you in the ministry. — 49
8. You are given the hope of the resurrection to sustain you in the ministry. — 51

Chapter 4
What Your Resources as a Minister Are

1. *You are given the grace and power of Christ.*

   "And he said unto me, My grace is sufficient for thee: for my strength is made perfect in weakness. Most gladly therefore will I rather glory in my infirmities, that the power of Christ may rest upon me. Therefore I take pleasure in infirmities, in reproaches, in necessities, in persecutions, in distresses for Christ's sake: for when I am weak, then am I strong" (2 Cor.12:9-10; cp. 1 Cor.1:3-4; 2 Cor. 9:8).

   Thought
   Christ wants to reveal His grace and power in you. But note a most significant fact: the weaker the vessel, the more Christ is glorified. This is seen in four striking points.

   a) The grace of Christ is sufficient for you. The presence of God and His grace are sufficient to help you walk through any suffering. The word "sufficient" (arkei) means the power or strength to withstand any danger. Christ's grace within you can carry you through anything. In Paul's case, it was physical suffering. In your case it may be either physical or spiritual attacks, but no matter: Christ's grace is sufficient to see you through whatever you suffer.

   b) The strength of Christ is made perfect in your weakness. The weaker the minister, the more Christ can demonstrate His strength in the minister. If you are self-sufficient, you do not need Christ; but if you are weak, you need Christ: the help, provision, and sufficiency of Christ. You must, therefore, walk humbly before Christ, depending upon His grace and sufficiency.

   c) The power of Christ will rest upon you through all your infirmities and trials. Note the point of this statement: infirmities or weaknesses are purposeful. You suffer for a reason: that the power of Christ may be demonstrated and clearly seen in your life. The word "rest" (episkenosei) means to fix a tent upon. The idea is that the power of Christ rests upon the suffering minister just as the Shekinah glory dwelt in the holy place of the tabernacle. What a glorious thought! The strength of Christ fixes itself upon and dwells within you—filling you with the Shekinah glory of God—when you suffer trials and temptations.

d) When you suffer some infirmity or weakness, it gives Christ the chance to infuse power into you and to overcome the weakness for you. Your infirmity gives Christ an opportunity to prove Himself. Therefore, you are to take pleasure . . .

- "in infirmities": a general term meaning all kinds of sufferings and weaknesses, whether moral or physical. The power of Christ can overcome any weakness or temptation for the believer.
- "in reproaches": whether ridicule, insult, slander, rumor, or whatever.
- "in necessities": hardships, needs, deprivations, hunger, thirst, lack of shelter or clothing, or any other necessity.
- "in persecutions": verbal or physical attack, abuse, or injury.
- "in distresses": tight situations, perplexities, disturbances, anxious moments, inescapable problems and difficulties.

When you are weak, you are strongest. How? By the power of Christ. And the power of Christ is much stronger than all the combined forces of mankind.

Your great need is to acknowledge your weakness before the Lord. When you do, the Lord pours His strength into your mind and heart. The Lord empowers you to overcome and conquer all infirmities and weaknesses, and all trials and temptations.

2. *You are given the presence and power of the Holy Spirit.*

> **"But ye shall receive power, after that the Holy Ghost is come upon you: and ye shall be witnesses unto me both in Jerusalem, and in all Judaea, and in Samaria, and unto the uttermost part of the earth" (Acts 1:8).**

> "Now we have received, not the spirit of the world, but the spirit which is of God; that we might know the things that are freely given to us of God" (1 Cor.2:12).

Thought
As a minister, you are equipped with God's very own Spirit. No greater power could ever be possessed by anyone. This is clearly seen: once the early disciples experienced the coming of God's Spirit into their lives, they *never again asked* about earthly power. Experiencing the presence and power of God's Spirit within their lives was the summit, the supreme experience of their lives. Nothing else was ever needed. It is this for which the human heart craves, and once God's Spirit truly dwells within the minister, that minister is supremely fulfilled and satisfied. Nothing else can ever satisfy—not position or authority, recognition or fame—not if the minister has truly received the Spirit of God into his heart and life.

The point is this: you have been given a task by God, a mission to carry out on earth. You do not have the power to carry out that task, not within yourself. The power of God Himself, of His Spirit, is needed. Therefore, Christ promises: "Ye shall receive power after the Holy Spirit is come upon you" (Acts 1:8). Both the Spirit of God and His power are promised. But note a critical point: the Holy Spirit comes upon you as an *equipping power*. The major purpose for His coming is to *equip* you to carry out your task for God.

3. *You are given the presence and power of God.*

> "But we have this treasure in earthen vessels, that the excellency of the power may be of God, and not of us" (2 Cor.4:7).
>
> "For David speaketh concerning him, I foresaw the Lord always before my face, for he is on my right hand, that I should not be moved" (Acts 2:25).
>
> "But truly I am full of power by the spirit of the LORD, and of judgment, and of might, to declare unto Jacob his transgression, and to Israel his sin" (Micah 3:8).

Thought

This is a precious, yet very striking, verse (2 Cor.4:7). "This treasure" refers back to the former verse (v.6). The *treasure* is the presence of God Himself shining in the believer's earthly vessel, in his heart, in his earthly body. Note three significant points.

a) God's presence is a treasure, a precious and priceless treasure.

b) God's presence is placed into earthly vessels. God enters your body, a body that is like an earthly vessel made of pottery or glass. Your body is ever so weak and worthless, corruptible and perishable. Yet imagine—God's presence is placed into such an earthly body!

c) God's purpose for entering your body is to show His power by overcoming all weaknesses—all trials and temptations, all handicaps and infirmities—even death itself.

- "The excellency of the power" is a picture of the grandeur, glory, and preeminence of His power. It is the excellency, the great and overcoming power of God.

The presence of God in your heart and body is power.

- It is the power to convert and transform you into a new creature.

  "Therefore if any man be in Christ, he is a new creature: old things are passed away; behold, all things are become new" (2 Cor. 5:17).

- It is the power to convert and transform you into a new man.

  "And that ye put on the new man, which after God is created in righteousness and true holiness" (Eph.4:24).
  "And have put on the new man, which is renewed in knowledge after the image of him that created him" (Col.3:10).

- It is the power to deliver you from all temptations and trials.

  "There hath no temptation taken you but such as is common to man: but God is faithful, who will not suffer you to be tempted above that ye are able; but

will with the temptation also make a way to escape, that ye may be able to bear it" (1 Cor.10:13).

"Now thanks be unto God, which always causeth us to triumph in Christ, and maketh manifest the savour of his knowledge by us in every place" (2 Cor.2:14).

- It is the power to put His divine nature into you.

   "Whereby are given unto us exceeding great and precious promises: that by these ye might be partakers of the divine nature, having escaped the corruption that is in the world through lust" (2 Pt.1:4).

- It is the power to give you life, both abundant and eternal life.

   "I am come that they might have life, and that they might have it more abundantly" (Jn.10:10).
   "For God so loved the world, that he gave his only begotten Son, that whosoever believeth in him should not perish, but have everlasting life" (Jn.3:16).

The point is this: the treasure of God's presence is in your earthly vessel, your earthly body that is ever so weak and frail. God does so much for you, and it is all wrought by Him. Therefore, God and God alone gets all the credit, and He is thereby praised. As the verse says, the power is of God, not of us.

4. *You are given the assurance—absolute assurance—of victory by God Himself.*

   "Now thanks be unto God, which always causeth us to triumph in Christ, and maketh manifest the savour of his knowledge by us in every place" (2 Cor.2:14).

Thought
As a minister, you always triumph in Christ. God gives you absolute assurance of victory. God never fails His dear minister.

The picture of triumph is descriptive. It is the picture of a military commander returning to Rome after some great victory. The commander was always welcomed into the city in a great march of triumph. Most people have seen such scenes in films either on television or in movies.

What Paul pictures is the triumph of Christ. He sees God giving Christ the glorious and triumphant victory: the victory is gained as the Word of God is proclaimed throughout the world. And Paul sees himself, as a minister of God, being a part of that glorious and triumphant victory. Note several points.

a) It is God who causes you to triumph. God Himself is looking after you, never taking His eyes off you as His dear servant. The journey may sometimes get rough, and you may be attacked and abused, but God never forsakes you.

b) God always causes you to triumph. As a true minister of God, you will never know defeat—not permanently. Even if you fall and fail for a period of time, God will eventually reach you and restore you, and He will continue to use you. God will *always* cause His dear minister to triumph over all. There is nothing, absolutely nothing, that can conquer and gain the final victory and triumph over you—not if you are truly called of God—not if you truly serve Him. The glorious triumph over all is assured.

c) The triumph is *"in Christ"* and in Christ alone. You must . . .

- believe in Christ
- minister in Christ
- trust in Christ
- live in Christ
- be called in Christ
- move in Christ
- serve in Christ
- be in Christ

You are no different from anyone else: your only victory is in Christ. You must trust and live in Christ just like everyone else. You are not acceptable to God apart from Christ. Your acceptance before God is based upon the same thing as everyone else's: faith in Christ. Therefore, to triumph *"in Christ"* you must be "in Christ"; that is, you must *believe in* and *live in* Christ. Your triumph is in Christ and in Christ alone.

d) God uses you, the minister, to spread the knowledge of Christ everywhere. This is the reason God causes you to triumph: to spread the glorious message of Christ all over the world. God is out to reach every person He can: to see to it that every person knows about the love of Christ. The word "savour" simply means fragrance or aroma, like the fragrance of a flower. God spreads the fragrance of His Word through you, His minister.

5. *You are given a spiritual gift by God.*

> **"And he gave some, apostles; and some, prophets; and some, evangelists; and some, pastors and teachers" (Eph.4:11).**
>
> **"And God hath set some in the church, first apostles, secondarily prophets, thirdly teachers, after that miracles, then gifts of healings, helps, governments, diversities of tongues" (1 Cor.12:28; cp. Ro.12:6-8).**

Thought

God has equipped you for the ministry. Whatever He has called you to do, He has gifted you for that particular ministry. God has given you everything needed to complete your call and ministry:

- the spiritual office
- the spiritual gift and ability
- the authority and power
- the grace to bear all trials and temptations in order to complete your ministry.

It is important to note what is meant by spiritual gifts. A spiritual gift does not mean the natural ability or talent of a person. God, of course, keeps natural abilities and talents in mind when He gifts a person, but spiritual gifts are special gifts given to believers. They are highly specialized gifts—gifts that are given to build up believers in the church and in witnessing and ministering to the world. The point to note is this: you have received a spiritual gift, a highly specialized gift. You have received your gift to carry out the ministry of the Lord upon the earth.

Note another significant point: Jesus Christ gives you the grace to use your gift. Grace means the strength, wisdom, courage, motivation, love, concern, care, power—all the favor and blessings—of Christ. Whatever is needed to use the gift, Christ gives you. He measures out the exact amount of grace needed for the maximum use of a gift.

What a glorious truth! What a spark of encouragement! You are gifted by Christ—gifted with a highly specialized gift. And you have the measure of grace—whatever measure is needed—to use your gift. Christ pours out His grace upon you, equipping you to carry out your task upon earth. This is significant, for it means that your gift is the gift of Christ. It is the very best gift for you. You should not be displeased with your gift, nor covet someone else's gift. Christ has placed you into your ministry and given you the very best gift—if you are truly His, yielded and committed to serve Him.

6. *You are given faith to sustain you in the ministry.*

> **"We having the same spirit of faith, according as it is written, I believed, and therefore have I spoken; we also believe, and therefore speak" (2 Cor.4:13; cp. Acts 27:25; Ro.4:20-21; Heb.11:6).**

Thought
When nothing else sustains you as a minister, your faith will sustain you. You may be tempted to give up: the trouble and pressure against you may be so great that you are tempted to leave the ministry, to never again share the gospel. However as stated, when nothing else sustains you, your faith will sustain you.

> **"Above all, taking the shield of faith, wherewith ye shall be able to quench <u>all</u> the fiery darts of the wicked" (Eph.6:16).**

If you will hold on to your faith in Christ—pray and seek the face of God, believe and never give up no matter what attacks you—you will never fall, not for long.

Your faith will not allow you to become discouraged, not to the point that you would leave the ministry and fall into the depths of despair. By faith you must believe the promises of God. By faith you must stay in the ministry and continue to speak just as the Word of God exhorts you to do.

> "For whatsoever is born of God overcometh the world: and this is the victory that overcometh the world, even our faith. Who is he that overcometh the world, but he that believeth that Jesus is the Son of God?" (1 Jn.5:4-5).

7. *You are given the love of Christ to compel you in the ministry.*

> "For the love of Christ constraineth us; because we thus judge, that if one died for all, then were all dead" (2 Cor.5:14).

Thought
As a minister, the love of Christ constrains you to hold fast to the ministry. Note: Paul does not say that he is driven to minister because of . . .

- the great teaching of Christ
- the great example of Christ
- the great ministry of Christ
- the great life of Christ

All of these areas of the Lord's life are important, critically so, but they are not the foundation of our salvation and ministry. The foundation of the believer's life is the *love of Christ*. As the above verse says, the love of Christ is seen in His death upon the cross.

Christ died that all persons might die *in Him*. In the Greek this verse says:

- "One died for all" (heis huper panton apethanen).
- "Therefore, all died" (ara hoi pantes apethanon).

Note the exact words: "One died for all; therefore, all died." Paul is saying . . .

- that Jesus Christ died for all men; therefore all men died when He died.
- that since Christ died for all, then it follows that all men died in Him.
- that all men were represented in Christ when He died.
- that all men are counted as having died when Christ died.
- that Jesus Christ died the *ideal death*, the death that stands for all men.

Of course, this is simply saying the same thing in different ways so that we can more easily grasp exactly what Paul is saying. But note: the word "all" is not teaching universal salvation, that is, that every human being is saved by the death of Christ. This passage has to be kept in context with the rest of Scripture. The word *"all"* means all who are redeemed by faith in the death of Christ.

Very simply stated, when a person *believes* that Jesus Christ died for him, God takes that person's faith and counts it as *his death* in Christ.

- God counts him as having died in Christ.
- God credits him as having *already died* in Christ.
- God credits the death of Christ to him so that he never has to die.

Another way to say the same thing is this: God takes the person's faith and . . .

- identifies the person with the death of Christ.
- accepts the death of Christ as the death of the person.

Although these statements may help some to more clearly understand what Paul is saying, there is no clearer statement than the one stated in Scripture: "Christ died for all; therefore, all died [in Him]." The death of Jesus Christ was the representative death for all. His death stands as the death for all men. No person ever has to die. All he has to do is believe that Jesus Christ died for him—truly commit his life to the glorious truth—and God will take his belief and count it as his having already died in Christ.

The point is this: it is the glorious love of Christ that constrains you to stick to the ministry and to serve the Lord so faithfully. You have been given the love of Christ to drive and constrain you to share the message of Christ with a world that is gripped and dying in corruption. (See *The Preacher's Outline & Sermon Bible,*® note, Justification—Ro.5:1; 1 Cor.6:11 for more discussion.)

8. *You are given the hope of the resurrection to sustain you in the ministry.*

> **"Knowing that he which raised up the Lord Jesus shall raise up us also by Jesus, and shall present us with you" (2 Cor.4:14).**
>
> **"For the Lord himself shall descend from heaven with a shout, with the voice of the archangel, and with the trump of God: and the dead in Christ shall rise first: then we which are alive and remain shall be caught up together with them in the clouds, to meet the Lord in the air: and so shall we ever be with the Lord" (1 Th.4:16-17).**
>
> **"Teaching us that, denying ungodliness and worldly lusts, we should live soberly, righteously, and godly, in this present world; looking for that blessed hope, and the glorious appearing of the great God and our Saviour Jesus Christ" (Tit.2:12-13).**

Thought

You serve Christ for *one great reason*: you know that you are to die someday, and you know there is to be a resurrection of the dead. Above all else, the one thing you want is to be with Jesus; therefore, that glorious day of resurrection, the day of full redemption, is ever before your eyes. You suffer and bear all—you continue to preach and teach, to serve and meet the needs of people—all because you know that the day of resurrection is coming. Just as God raised up the Lord Jesus, so God is going to raise you up to be with all those to whom you have ministered.

How do you know this? Because God raised up the Lord Jesus. When God raised up Christ, God demonstrated that it was His will to raise the dead, and that He had the power to raise the dead. You know that you, too, shall be raised, raised to live with Christ forever and ever. This is your great hope, the hope that sustains you in the ministry. As Paul said in giving his great testimony:

> "That I may know him, and the power of his resurrection, and the fellowship of his sufferings, being made conformable unto his death; I might attain unto the resurrection of the dead" (Ph.3:10-11).

CHAPTER 5

What Your Commission and Work as a Minister Are

As a minister, God has given you the greatest commission and work imaginable. Scripture spells out in great detail just what your duties are.

Contents

1. You must challenge and lead people to worship the Lord, the only living and true God, in spirit and in truth.   55

2. You must minister and serve even as Christ ministered and served.   57

3. You must seek and save the lost even as Christ sought and saved the lost.   58

4. You must work and labor for God *right now*: the harvest is ripe and the task is urgent.   59

5. You must preach the Word of God: correcting, rebuking, and exhorting people.   61

6. You must teach. You must instruct—root and ground—people in Jesus Christ and in the Word of God.   67

7. You must edify and build up believers and equip them to do the work of the ministry.   69

8. You must feed believers.   72

9. You must watch over and warn believers.   76

10. You must lead believers into a pure and faultless religion.   78

11. You must do the work of an evangelist. 80

12. You must oversee the administration of the church, set in order the affairs and organization of the church. 81

13. You must build the church first and foremost in the homes, as instructed by Christ. 83

14. You must build up the church as a wise masterbuilder. 87

Chapter 5
What Your Commission and Work as a Minister Are

1. *You must challenge and lead people to worship the Lord, the only living and true God, in spirit and in truth.*

    "But the hour cometh, and now is, when the true worshippers shall worship the Father in spirit and in truth: for the Father seeketh such to worship him. God is a Spirit: and they that worship him must worship him in spirit and in truth" (Jn.4:23-24).

    "Give unto the LORD the glory due unto his name: bring an offering, and come before him: worship the LORD in the beauty of holiness" (1 Chron.16:29).

    "O come, let us worship and bow down: let us kneel before the LORD our maker" (Ps.95:6).

    "O worship the LORD in the beauty of holiness: fear before him, all the earth" (Ps.96:9).

    "Enter into his gates with thanksgiving, and into his courts with praise: be thankful unto him, and bless his name. For the LORD is good; his mercy is everlasting; and his truth endureth to all generations" (Ps.100:4-5).

    "And let us consider one another to provoke unto love and to good works: not forsaking the assembling of ourselves together, as the manner of some is; but exhorting one another: and so much the more, as ye see the day approaching" (Heb.10:24-25).

    "Then saith Jesus unto him, Get thee hence, Satan: for it is written, Thou shalt worship the Lord thy God, and him only shalt thou serve" (Mt.4:10).

Thought

As a minister, you must challenge and lead people to worship God. But note, God wants a very special kind of worship. God dictates exactly how He is to be approached and worshipped: in spirit and in truth. "They that worship him *must* worship Him in spirit and in truth" (Jn.4:24). This is how you must challenge and lead people to worship God: they must come before God and worship God "in spirit and in truth." Note three significant facts in Jn.4:23-24.

First, there has been a change in worship: "The hour cometh, and now is." Christ changed worship. Before Christ, men worshiped God in special places, for example, in temples and before altars. Since Christ, place and locality mean nothing. Christ has opened the door into God's very presence and man can now worship God from anyplace in the universe.

Second, the nature of worship—how we are to worship—is clearly spelled out: man is to worship God in spirit and in truth.

a) To worship God in spirit means to worship God . . .

- with the spiritual drive and ability of one's soul, seeking the most intimate communion and friendship with God.
- with the spiritual core of one's life and being, trusting and resting in God's acceptance and love and care.

b) To worship God in truth means . . .

- to approach God in the right or true way. There is only one way: through His Son Jesus Christ.
- to worship God sincerely and truthfully, not coming half-heartedly with wandering mind and sleepy eyes.

Third, the reason for worship is clearly given: the Father seeks men to worship Him. God desires worship, for He created man to worship and fellowship with Him. Therefore, God seeks men who will worship Him in spirit and truth.

But note Heb.10:25 above. Some had forsaken the church even in the day of the early church. How like some in every generation. The need is just what this verse says: exhort one another, and so much the more, as you see the day approaching. What day? The day of the Lord's return. His return is immediately upon us. Therefore, we must exhort those who have fallen away, lest they miss the salvation of His coming and have to face His judgment.

Genuine believers need each other—the presence, fellowship, strength, encouragement, care, and love of each other. All of this is found when believers come together for worship, found in a very, very special way. You must, therefore, as a minister of God, challenge and lead people to worship God. You must challenge and lead people . . .

- to "give unto the Lord the glory due unto his name"
- to "bring an offering and come before him"
- to "worship the Lord in the beauty of holiness" (1 Chron.16:29).

2. *You must minister and serve even as Christ ministered and served.*

> "But it shall not be so among you: but whosoever will be great among you, let him be your minister; and whosoever will be chief among you, let him be your servant: even as the Son of man came not to be ministered unto, but to minister, and to give his life a ransom for many" (Mt.20:26-28).
>
> "Bear ye one another's burdens, and so fulfil the law of Christ" (Gal.6:2).
>
> "The Spirit of the Lord is upon me, because he hath anointed me to preach the gospel to the poor; he hath sent me to heal the brokenhearted, to preach deliverance to the captives, and recovering of sight to the blind, to set at liberty them that are bruised, to preach the acceptable year of the Lord" (Lk.4:18-19).

Thought

As a minister, you are to fulfill the law of Christ. The law of Christ is the law of ministry and love. Note the verses above and this is clearly seen.

Christ gave and sacrificed Himself to the ultimate degree to reach out to men: He bore the sins of men. You, of course, cannot bear the sins of men; but you can bear the burdens of men. You can . . .

- be compassionate
- encourage
- pray
- forgive
- be warm and tender
- share the promises of God
- sympathize and empathize
- meet needs

- visit and encourage and strengthen
- share the hope of eternal life
- heal the brokenhearted
- give sight to the blind
- set free the bruised
- share the hope of the gospel, in particular with the poor

Note the word "servant" (Mt.20:26-28). It means bond-slave, to be bound to the Lord every moment of life. The idea is not *occasional* service but *constant* service. You are *always* to be *serving and ministering*, regardless of the hour or call or difficulty. As a minister, you are the bond-slave of Christ—His servant every hour of every day—commissioned to meet the needs of people. You are to minister and serve even as Christ ministered and served.

3. *You must seek and save the lost even as Christ sought and saved the lost. (See "You are to be a witness for Christ," pp.30-38.)*

> **"For the Son of man is come to seek and to save that which was lost" (Lk.19:10).**
>
> **"Then said Jesus to them again, Peace be unto you: as my Father hath sent me, <u>even so send I you</u>" (Jn.20:21).**

Thought

As a minister of Christ, your mission is linked with the mission of Christ. Your mission is the very *same mission* as the mission of Christ. Note exactly what Jn.20:21 says:

- God sent Christ on a specific mission.
- Christ sends you on the very same mission.

What is the mission?

> **"The Son of Man is come to seek and to save the lost" (Lk.19:10).**

Man is "lost": separated from God and wandering about without God; cut off from God, perishing and being destroyed; doomed to die and lose eternal life.

You, the minister, are sent forth to seek and save the lost, to seek and proclaim the salvation of God to the lost. You are the prophet and witness of the living Lord.
- Christ is the Way: you point the Way to the lost.
- Christ is the Truth: you proclaim the Truth to the lost.
- Christ is the Life: you share the Life with the lost. Your task as the minister of God is to go forth even as Christ went forth: to seek and save the lost of your community and world.

4. *You must work and labor for God <u>right now</u>: the harvest is ripe and the task is urgent.*

> "Say not ye, There are yet four months, and then cometh harvest? behold, I say unto you, Lift up your eyes, and look on the fields; for they are white already to harvest" (Jn.4:35).

Thought
The heart of Jesus is always upon the harvest of souls. Men focus their hearts upon the world's harvest: the planting of seed and the reaping of grain, the investment of money and the receiving of wages and gain. But the heart of Jesus is upon people, upon the planting of the gospel seed and the reaping of souls for God.

The challenge of Jesus to you, the Lord's minister, is this: "Lift up your eyes, and look on the fields." The challenge is to quit looking down upon the earth and upon the affairs of the world, but *look up* and observe the fields of people streaming across the world.

a) The fields of souls are white *already*: they are ready for harvesting *right now*. Since Christ has come to earth, God has put His Spirit into the world and *supernaturally activated* . . .
- a thirst for God.
- a sense of sin, a conviction of coming short.
- a deep loneliness and emptiness.
- a sense of purposelessness.

- the knowledge that Jesus Christ has come to earth claiming to be the Savior of the world, the very Son of God.

It is absolutely essential that you lift up your eyes and look *now*. If not, the ripe harvest of souls and bodies . . .
- will remain in the fields of the earth.
- will ripen *beyond* being tasteful and useful (be too old, too far gone).
- will rot and be lost forever.
- will fall to the ground and decay.

b) You must lift up your eyes in order to look. You cannot see ahead or around if you do not lift up your eyes and look. The things of the earth have to grow *strangely* dim *before* you can look and see.

c) You must look where you are. Your eyes must see the reality of what is around you. It is the harvest of souls around you that you must look upon and focus your attention upon.

Note: you can look upon foreign fields through the challenge of others. Note another fact: the world is becoming more and more *one neighborhood*. Distance is becoming more and more insignificant. Every believer is becoming more and more responsible for the individual in the foreign land. In fact, a man's country is foreign to everyone else in the world, no matter who he is.

> "For he that soweth to his flesh shall of the flesh reap corruption; but he that soweth to the Spirit shall of the Spirit reap life everlasting. And let us not be weary in well doing: for in due season we shall reap, if we faint not" (Gal.6:8-9).
>
> "But when the fruit is brought forth, <u>immediately</u> he putteth in the sickle, because the harvest is come" (Mk.4:29).
>
> "Therefore said he unto them, The harvest truly is great, but the labourers are few: <u>pray</u> ye therefore the Lord of the harvest, that he would send forth labourers into his harvest" (Lk.10:2).
>
> "And he saith unto them, Follow me, and I will make you fishers of men" (Mt.4:19).

> "Ye have not chosen me, but I have chosen you, and ordained you, that ye should go and bring forth fruit, and that your fruit [souls] should remain: that whatsoever ye shall ask of the Father in my name, he may give it you" (Jn.15:16).
>
> "Let him know, that he which converteth the sinner from the error of his way shall save a soul from death, and shall hide a multitude of sins" (Jas.5:20).
>
> "They that sow in tears shall reap in joy. He that goeth forth and weepeth, bearing precious seed, shall doubtless come again with rejoicing, bringing his sheaves with him" (Ps.126:5-6).

5. *You must preach the Word of God: correcting, rebuking, and exhorting people. (See Chapter 6, "What Your Message—Your Preaching and Teaching—Must Be," p. 91.)*

> "I charge thee therefore before God and the Lord Jesus Christ, who shall judge the quick [living] and the dead at his appearing and his kingdom; preach the word; be instant in season, out of season; reprove, rebuke, exhort with all longsuffering and doctrine" (2 Tim.4:1-2).

Thought

As a minister, you must preach the Word of God. This is the Lord's call to you. Preaching the Word is to be the consuming passion of the minister's life. Note how forcefully this is brought out in this verse:

- "Preach the Word," the Scriptures of the Holy Bible.
- "Be instant in season, out of season": keep a sense of urgency; grasp and make opportunities to preach.
- "Reprove" when preaching.
- "Rebuke" when preaching.
- "Exhort with all longsuffering and doctrine" when preaching.

First, preach the Word. The whole thrust is obsession—the minister is to be obsessed with preaching. Preaching is to burn within your soul; you are to be consumed with preaching, with a burning passion to preach the unsearchable riches of Christ. Why?

- Because preaching is God's chosen method to save men.

    > "**For the preaching of the cross is to them that perish foolishness; but unto us which are saved it is the power of God. . . . For after that in the wisdom of God the world by wisdom knew not God, it pleased God by the foolishness of preaching to save them that believe**" (1 Cor.1:18, 21).

- Because the minister is held accountable to preach.

    > "**For though I preach the gospel, I have nothing to glory of: for necessity is laid upon me; yea, woe is unto me, if I preach not the gospel!**" (1 Cor.9:16).

It is impossible to overemphasize preaching. It is even impossible to fully grasp the importance of preaching. This is the whole thrust of this passage. Just think about the solemn charge and warning that is covered in verse one:

- God and Christ both have their eyes on the minister—to see if he is preaching the Word.
- The minister shall be judged by the Lord Jesus Christ as to whether or not he preached the Word.
- The minister shall face Christ when Christ returns in glory as the conquering Lord—face Him and give an account of his preaching.
- The minister's place and position in the Lord's kingdom will be determined by how faithful he was in preaching the Word.

Therefore, the charge is to preach the Word. Note two very significant points.

a) The word "preach" (kerusso) is the picture of the minister standing before people in all the dignity and authority of God Himself. It is the word that was used of the ambassador who was sent forth by the king to proclaim his message in all the authority and dignity of the king himself.

"This should be the pattern for the preacher today. His preaching should be [with dignity] . . . that dignity which comes from . . . the fact that he is an official herald of the King of kings. It should be . . . [with] authority which will command the respect, careful attention, and proper reaction of the listeners" (Kenneth Wuest. *The Pastoral Epistles.* "Wuest's Word Studies," Vol.2. Grand Rapids, MI: Eerdmans, 1952, p.154).

b) The minister is to preach *"the Word."* What is meant by *"the Word"*?

- "All Scripture"—all Scripture that is given by the inspiration of God (2 Tim.3:16).

The Word means the Scripture, the very Word of God itself. It is "the whole body of revealed truth" (Kenneth Wuest. *The Pastoral Epistles,* Vol.2, p.154). It is the whole counsel of God that comprises what men call *The Holy Bible.* The minister is to preach the Word, the Holy Scripture, the very Word of God Himself. He is not to preach . . .

- his own ideas
- the ideas of other men
- philosophy
- psychology
- self-image
- self-righteousness
- sociology
- science
- educational development
- personal efforts
- ego-boosters
- man-made religion

The great Greek scholar Kenneth Wuest has one of the most challenging descriptions of the word *preach* ever penned by man:

"The word [preach is a] command to be obeyed at once. It is a sharp command as in military language.... The preacher must present, not book reviews, not politics, not economics, not current topics of the day, not a philosophy of life denying the Bible and based upon unproven theories of science, but the Word. The preacher as a herald cannot choose his message. He is given a message to proclaim by his Sovereign. If he will not proclaim that, let him step down from his exalted position" (Kenneth Wuest. *The Pastoral Epistles,* Vol.2, p.154).

Matthew Henry uses striking language:

"It is not their own notions and fancies that they are to preach, but the pure plain Word of God; and they must not corrupt it" (*Matthew Henry's Commentary*, Vol.5. Old Tappan, NJ: Fleming H. Revell, p.848).

"And as ye go, preach, saying, The kingdom of heaven is at hand.... What I tell you in darkness, that speak ye in light: and what ye hear in the ear, that preach ye upon the housetops" (Mt.10:7, 27).

"And he said unto them, Go ye into all the world, and preach the gospel to every creature" (Mk.16:15).

"Go, stand and speak in the temple to the people all the words of this life" (Acts 5:20).

"Preach the word; be instant in season, out of season; reprove, rebuke, exhort with all longsuffering and doctrine" (2 Tim.4:2).

Second, be instant in season, out of season. The word "instant" (epistethi) means to stand and stick to preaching no matter the circumstances, easy or difficult.

Kenneth Wuest says:

"The preacher is to proclaim the Word when the time is auspicious, favorable, opportune, and also when the circumstances seem unfavorable. So few times are still available for preaching that the preacher must take every chance he has to preach the Word. There is no closed season for preaching" (Kenneth Wuest. *The Pastoral Epistles,* Vol.2, p.155).

Matthew Henry says:

> "Do this work with all fervency of spirit. Call upon those under [your] charge to take heed of sin, to do their duty: call upon them to repent, and believe, and live a holy life and this both in season and out of season . . . . We must do it in season, that is, let slip no opportunity; and do it out of season, that is, not shift off the duty, under pretence that it is out of season" (*Matthew Henry's Commentary*, Vol.5, p.848).

William Barclay says:

> "The Christian teacher is to be urgent. The message he brings is literally a matter of life and death. The teacher and the preacher who really get their message across to people are those who have the tone of earnestness in their voice . . . .
>
> "The Christian teacher is to be persistent. He is to urge the claims of Christ 'in season and out of season.' As someone has put it: 'Take or make your opportunity' (*The Letters to Timothy, Titus, and Philemon*. "The Daily Study Bible." Philadelphia, PA: The Westminster Press, 1956, p.234f).

The *Amplified New Testament* says:

> "Keep your sense of urgency (stand by, be at hand and ready, whether the opportunity seems to be favorable or unfavorable, whether it is convenient or inconvenient, whether it be welcome or unwelcome, you as preacher of the Word are to show people in what way their lives are wrong)."

Third, reprove (elegxon). The word means to stir a person to prove himself; to put a person under conviction; to lead a person to see his sin and to feel guilt over it. It means to put a person under conviction of sin and to lead him to confession and repentance.

> "The preacher is to deal with sin, both in the lives of his unsaved hearers and in those of the saints to whom he ministers, and he is to do it in no uncertain tones. The word 'sin' is not enough in the vocabulary of our preaching today" (Kenneth Wuest. *The Pastoral Epistles*, Vol.2, p.155).

Fourth, rebuke (epitimeson). This is a strong word, very strong. It means a sharp, severe rebuke and carries the idea of judgment to come if one does not repent.

"A word of warning and rebuke would often save a brother from many a sin and many a shipwreck. But, as someone has said, that word must always be spoken as 'brother setting brother right.' It must be spoken with a consciousness of our common guilt. It is not our place to set ourselves up as the moral judge of anyone; nonetheless it is our duty to speak that warning word when it needs to be spoken" (William Barclay. *The Letters to Timothy, Titus, and Philemon*, p.236f).

> "**Them that sin rebuke before all, that others also may fear**" (1 Tim.5:20).
>
> "**Holding fast the faithful word as he hath been taught, that he may be able by sound doctrine both to exhort and to <u>convince</u> the gainsayers [opposition]**" (Tit.1:9).
>
> "**These things speak, and exhort, and rebuke with all authority. Let no man despise thee**" (Tit.2:15).

Fifth, exhort with all longsuffering and doctrine. The word "exhort" means to beseech, encourage, comfort, and help. It is not enough to reprove and rebuke people. The minister must encourage and comfort, help and carry the person to Christ. Note how crucial this point is.

a) The minister must "exhort with all longsuffering" (makrothumia). The idea is that the minister patiently endures in exhorting people—no matter the circumstances. He exhorts and exhorts, encourages and encourages. He suffers a long, long time with people . . .

- enduring whatever weaknesses and failings they have.
- enduring whatever evil and injury is done.

The minister suffers a long time without resentment or anger, and he never gives up, for he knows the power of Christ to change lives.

b) The minister "exhorts with all doctrine." He does not teach bits and pieces of God's Word. He does not focus upon subjects . . .

- that are popular.
- that are favorites.
- that arouse curiosity.
- that he thinks are needed.

He focuses upon all the doctrines of God—the whole counsel of God. He exhorts people in all the doctrine of God.

> "But exhort one another daily, while it is called to day; lest any of you be hardened through the deceitfulness of sin" (Heb.3:13).

As a minister, you must preach the Word of God with all the authority of God Himself.

6. *You must teach. You must instruct—root and ground—people in Jesus Christ and in the Word of God.*

> "And he gave some, apostles; and some, prophets; and some, evangelists; and some, pastors and <u>teachers</u>; for the perfecting of the saints, for the work of the ministry, for the edifying of the body of Christ" (Eph.4:11-12).
>
> "These things command and teach" (1 Tim.4:11).
>
> "And the things that thou hast heard of me among many witnesses, the same commit thou to faithful men, who shall be able to teach others also" (2 Tim.2:2).
>
> "Go ye therefore, and teach all nations, baptizing them in the name of the Father, and of the Son, and of the Holy Ghost: teaching them to observe all things whatsoever I have commanded you: and, lo, I am with you alway, even unto the end of the world" (Mt.28:19-20).
>
> "And daily in the temple, and in every house, they ceased not to teach and preach Jesus Christ" (Acts 5:42).

> "And he continued there a year and six months, teaching the word of God among them" (Acts 18:11).
>
> "Whereunto I am ordained a preacher, and an apostle, (I speak the truth in Christ, and lie not;) a teacher of the Gentiles in faith and verity" (1 Tim.2:7).
>
> "Jesus Christ . . . hath abolished death, and hath brought life and immortality to light through the gospel: whereunto I am appointed a preacher, and an apostle, and a <u>teacher</u> of the Gentiles" (2 Tim.1:10-11).

Thought

As a minister, you must teach the Word of God. Teaching is a high calling, one of the greatest of callings. Teaching is ranked second only to the spiritual gifts of apostle and prophet. Every apostle and prophet and pastor has the gift of teaching, but every teacher is not an apostle or prophet or pastor. The gift of teaching bears one of the largest responsibilities given by God; therefore, the teacher will be required to give a strict account to God for his faithfulness in using his gift.

The spiritual gift of teaching is the gift to understand and communicate the Word of God and to edify believers in the truths of God's Word. It involves understanding, interpreting, arranging, and communicating the Word of God. The gift of teaching is given to the believer who commits his life to the Word of God, to sharing its glorious truths with God's people.

As a minister, you must teach. You are called to teach. Teaching people is a great part of your ministry. You must, therefore, be a strong teacher. Note what a strong teacher does:

> "And the things that thou hast heard of me among many witnesses, the same commit thou to faithful men, who shall be able to teach others also" (2 Tim.2:2).

This verse says that a strong teacher has two very basic traits.

a) A strong teacher receives the truth himself. You must live what you teach—believe what you say—experience what you profess. As a minister, you must heed the teaching of other faithful witnesses. As Mt.28:19-20 says, when some other minister or teacher is *going forth* and teaching the things commanded by Christ, you must receive and heed the truth. You must practice the truth—what you have learned—as never before. You must set a blazing example of one who follows the truth of Christ. This is the first task of a strong teacher.

> **"Moreover it is required in stewards, that a man be found faithful" (1 Cor.4:2).**
>
> **"We beseech you, brethren, and exhort you by the Lord Jesus, that as ye have received of us how ye ought to walk and to please God, so ye would abound more and more" (1 Th.4:1).**

b) A strong teacher trains others to teach the truth. You are the link between two generations. You heard the truth and received it. You must now transmit and pass the truth on to others. Why? So that they in turn will pass it on down to future generations. This is the second trait of a strong teacher.

Note one other significant fact about a strong teacher. He commits the truth to *faithful believers*. A *faithful* believer is a person . . .

- who *believes* in Christ and in the Word of God.
- who is loyal, reliable, dependable, and trustworthy.

Naturally, a person who does not believe in God or in God's Word cannot be said to be faithful to God. He is unfaithful and disloyal. God cannot trust or rely upon him.

The point is this: a strong teacher will not commit the truth to an unfaithful person. The strong teacher will look for faithful people and commit the truth to them.

7. *You must edify and build up believers and equip them to do the work of the ministry.*

> **"And he gave some, apostles; and some, prophets; and some, evangelists; and some, pastors and teachers; for the perfecting of the saints, for the work of the ministry, for the edifying of the body of Christ: till we all come in the unity of the faith, and**

of the knowledge of the Son of God, unto a perfect man, unto the measure of the stature of the fulness of Christ" (Eph.4:11-13).

"But he that prophesieth speaketh unto men to edification, and exhortation, and comfort" (1 Cor.14:3).

"How is it then, brethren? when ye come together, every one of you hath a psalm, hath a doctrine, hath a tongue, hath a revelation, hath an interpretation. Let all things be done unto edifying" (1 Cor.14:26).

"Again, think ye that we excuse ourselves unto you? we speak before God in Christ: but we do all things, dearly beloved, for your edifying" (2 Cor.12:19).

"Let no corrupt communication proceed out of your mouth, but that which is good to the use of edifying, that it may minister grace unto the hearers" (Eph.4:29).

"Preach the word; be instant in season, out of season; reprove, rebuke, exhort with all longsuffering and doctrine" (2 Tim.4:2).

"Holding fast the faithful word as he hath been taught, that he may be able by sound doctrine both to exhort and to convince the gainsayers" (Tit.1:9).

"These things speak, and exhort, and rebuke with all authority. Let no man despise thee" (Tit.2:15).

Thought

As a minister, your task is to equip believers to do the work of the ministry. The word "perfecting" (katartizo) means to equip for service and ministry. This is critical to see, for you—the minister—are not to be the only one going about doing the work of the ministry. In fact, your *primary task* is to be an equipper, a person who makes disciples and prepares others to serve Christ. Note another critical point: the very purpose for equipping laymen is so that the body of Christ, the church, may be built up. This is a significant point, for it means that the church cannot be built up without the members themselves doing the work of the ministry. All believers within a church must be involved in the work of the ministry.

This is your task as a minister of God: to edify believers and equip them to minister to the needy and lost of the world.

Note: what you are to do is clearly spelled out. Three things are said.

a) You must work to bring about a perfect unity among God's people. The minister of God is called . . .

- to bring peace and reconciliation to the church.
- to lead people into perfect harmony and oneness of spirit.
- to shepherd people out of cliques, and from divisiveness, murmuring, grumbling, griping, and all the other sins that militate against a perfect unity.

> "Now I beseech you, brethren, by the name of our Lord Jesus Christ, that ye all speak the same thing, and that there be no divisions among you; but that ye be perfectly joined together in the same mind and in the same judgment" (1 Cor.1:10).
>
> "Finally, brethren, farewell. Be perfect, be of good comfort, be of one mind, live in peace; and the God of love and peace shall be with you" (2 Cor.13:11).
>
> "Finally, be ye all of one mind, having compassion one of another; love as brethren, be pitiful, be courteous" (1 Pt.3:8).

b) You must work to bring about the knowledge of the Son of God.

> "Then said Jesus to those Jews which believed on him, If ye continue in my word, then are ye my disciples indeed; and ye shall know the truth and the truth shall make you free" (Jn.8:31-32).
>
> "And this is life eternal, that they might know thee the only true God, and Jesus Christ, whom thou hast sent" (Jn.17:3).
>
> "That I may know him, and the power of his resurrection, and the fellowship of his sufferings, being made conformable unto his death" (Ph.3:10).
>
> "That ye might walk worthy of the Lord unto all pleasing, being fruitful in every good work, and increasing in the knowledge of God" (Col.1:10).

c) You must work to bring about a perfect man, a man who measures up to the stature of Christ Himself—to the fulness of His stature.

> "When I was a child, I spake as a child, I understood as a child, I thought as a child: but when I became a man, I put away childish things" (1 Cor.13:11).
>
> "But strong meat belongeth to them that are of full age, even those who by reason of use have their senses exercised to discern both good and evil" (Heb.5:14).
>
> "Therefore leaving the principles of the doctrine of Christ, let us go on unto perfection; not laying again the foundation of repentance from dead works, and of faith toward God" (Heb.6:1).

8. *You must feed believers.*

> "He saith unto him the third time, Simon, son of Jonas, lovest thou me? Peter was grieved because he said unto him the third time, Lovest thou me? And he said unto him, Lord, thou knowest all things; thou knowest that I love thee. Jesus saith unto him, Feed my sheep" (Jn.21:17).
>
> "Take heed therefore unto yourselves, and to all the flock, over the which the Holy Ghost hath made you overseers, to feed the church of God, which he hath purchased with his own blood" (Acts 20:28).
>
> "Feed the flock of God which is among you, taking the oversight thereof, not by constraint, but willingly; not for filthy lucre [gain, a profit], but of a ready mind; neither as being lords over God's heritage, but being ensamples to the flock" (1 Pt.5:2-3).
>
> "And I will give you pastors according to mine heart, which shall feed you with knowledge and understanding" (Jer.3:15; cp. Jer.23:4; Ezk.34:23).

Thought

As a minister, this exhortation is to you, and it is direct and forceful. It is as clear as can be: "Feed the flock of God." Note

1 Pt.5:2-3 above. The word "feed" (poimanate) is an all inclusive word that covers all the duties of the minister. It means not only to preach and teach the Word of God, but to tend and shepherd the flock. It means to act like a shepherd, to carry out the duties of a shepherd. The duties of the shepherd are severalfold:

- to feed the sheep even if he has to gather them in his arms and carry them to the pasture.
- to guide the sheep to the pasture and away from the rough places and precipices.
- to seek and save the sheep who get lost.
- to protect the sheep. The true shepherd is even willing to sacrifice his life for the sheep.
- to restore the sheep who go astray and return.
- to reward the sheep for obedience and faithfulness.
- to keep the sheep separate from the goats.

Note another significant fact: the flock is *the flock of God*; it is not the flock of the minister. Ministers are only undershepherds to God. But they are to be undershepherds: they are to tend the flock of God, to look after and care for the flock. God is the Chief Shepherd, but this does not mean that you can leave the care of the flock up to God as though He is going to automatically care for the flock. God looks after the flock through the undershepherds whom He chooses. This is the way He shepherds. Therefore, you are important; you are to feed and tend and shepherd the flock of God. And Scripture pulls no punches about the fact: Scripture lays down exactly how you are to go about feeding the flock.

a) You, the minister, must take the oversight of the flock willingly, not by force. This does not mean that you do not feel the constraint of God and His love in your ministry. You do; in fact, all ministers are to sense the constraint of God. Paul forcefully declared the fact:

> **"Necessity is laid upon me; yea, woe is unto me, if I preach not the gospel!" (1 Cor.9:16).**
> **"For the love of Christ constraineth us" (2 Cor.5:14).**

But the point is this: you should not have to be forced and coerced to minister. You should willingly feed the flock of God. You must willingly do the will of God. You should never have to be constrained or coerced to minister to God's people.

The great tragedy is this: many have been called by God into the ministry, called to feed His flock, but they refused. Why?

- Some felt unworthy and inadequate.
- Some felt it would cost them too much.
- Some felt it required too much sacrifice.
- Some did not want to bear the reproach of the ministry.
- Some felt the demands and duties and expectations were too much to bear.

On and on the list could go, but Scripture is clear. If you have been called into the ministry by God, you must not reject His call. You must not have to be constrained and coerced to do God's will. You must willingly minister and feed the flock of God.

> **"Jesus saith unto them, My meat is to do the will of him that sent me, and to finish his work" (Jn.4:34).**
>
> **"So being affectionately desirous of you, we were willing to have imparted unto you, not the gospel of God only, but also our own souls, because ye were dear unto us" (1 Th.2:8).**

b) You, the minister, must not take the oversight of the flock for personal profit and gain, but with a ready and eager mind. The Greek says that no person is to enter the ministry for "filthy lucre" (medeais-chrokerdos), that is, for base gain or for some soiled and dirty advantage. No person should ever enter the ministry . . .

- just as a profession.
- strictly as a means of livelihood.
- solely as a means to serve mankind.

- because people say he has the gifts for it.
- because people say he would make a good minister.
- because family and friends encourage him to enter the ministry.

All of these reasons usually surround a person's entrance into the ministry. But they must never be *the reasons* why a person enters the ministry and cares for God's people. The ministry is a *call from God*, and no person dare enter the ministry without a personal call to the ministry. But note: when the call comes, the person is to have a ready mind. He is to minister to God's people; he is to readily feed the flock of God.

> **"Then Peter began to say unto him, Lo, we have left all, and have followed thee" (Mk.10:28).**
>
> **"So likewise, whosoever he be of you that forsaketh not all that he hath, he cannot be my disciple" (Lk.14:33).**
>
> **"I have coveted no man's silver, or gold, or apparel" (Acts 20:33).**
>
> **"Let no man seek his own, but every man another's wealth" (1 Cor.10:24).**

c) You, the minister, must not take the oversight of the flock as a lord, but by being an example. Note: the flock of God is called God's heritage (kleron). This is the word that was used of Israel in the Old Testament. It means that the Jews were the people who were set apart and allotted and assigned to God. They were His very special allotment and assignment, the people charged to His care and oversight. This is the picture painted of the minister and the flock of God. God has given you a very special heritage or allotment and assignment: you have been assigned to feed the heritage of God, the very flock that belongs to God Himself.

Now note how you are to lead God's flock. You are not to lord it over them, but you are to lead them by example. You . . .

- are not to be a dictator, but an example.
- are not to preach one thing and do something else.

You are to lead people by living for Christ. You are to preach and teach Christ, but you are to first of all live a pure and righteous life just like Christ lived. You are to live exactly what you preach. You are to be a pattern and model for Christ, a pattern and model of just what God wants His people to be.

"For I have given you an example, that ye should do as I have done to you" (Jn.13:15).

"In all things showing thyself a pattern of good works: in doctrine showing uncorruptness, gravity, sincerity" (Tit.2:7).

9. *You must watch over and warn believers.*

"Obey them that have the rule over you [the ministers], and submit yourselves: for they watch for your souls, as they that must give account, that they may do it with joy, and not with grief: for that is unprofitable for you" (Heb.13:17).

"I have set watchmen upon thy walls, O Jerusalem, which shall never hold their peace day nor night: ye that make mention of the LORD, keep not silence" (Is.62:6).

"Son of man, I have made thee a watchman unto the house of Israel: therefore hear the word at my mouth, and give them warning from me" (Ezk.3:17; cp. Jer.6:17).

"But if the watchman see the sword come, and blow not the trumpet, and the people be not warned; if the sword come, and take any person from among them, he is taken away in his iniquity; but his blood will I require at the watchman's hand. So thou, O son of man, I have set thee a watchman unto the house of Israel; therefore thou shalt hear the word at my mouth, and warn them from me. When I say unto the wicked, O wicked man, thou shalt surely die; if thou dost not speak to warn the wicked from his way, that wicked man shall die in his iniquity; but his blood will I require at thine hand. Nevertheless, if thou warn the wicked of his way to turn from it; if he do not turn from his way, he shall die in his iniquity; but thou hast delivered thy soul" (Ezk.33:6-9).

Thought

As a minister, you are God's watchman. This is a picture from the Old Testament. The watchmen were the men appointed by the king or general . . .

- to guard the headquarters of the general and his army.
- to guard the city and its citizens.

The watchman stood on the walls of the city or either on a hilltop that gave him the clearest view possible. His duty was to watch, guard, protect, and sound the warning of any approaching danger.

You, the minister, are God's watchman. Your duties as God's watchman are clearly spelled out in the above verses.

a) As God's watchman, you are to watch over the souls of God's people (Heb.13:17). You must watch over their . . .

- welfare
- love
- purity
- growth
- peace
- knowledge
- holiness
- joy
- faith

You must guard them against all temptations and trials. You must protect their spirits and strengthen them as much as possible to stand against all sickness, disease, accidents, and sufferings.

b) As God's watchman, you must never hold your peace day or night (Is.62:6).

- You are to continually proclaim the Lord, making mention of Him. You are never to keep silent.
- You are to continually cry out before the Lord in behalf of God's people.
- You are to cry out before God in prayer: that God will remember His promises to protect, deliver, and provide for His people. You are never to keep silent in prayer: you are to be a watchman of prayer before God.

c) As God's watchman, you are the watchman over His house, the church—over all of His dear people (Ezk.3:17). As the watchman over His house, your duties are twofold:

- To hear the Word of God that has come from God's very own heart and mouth.
- To warn people of coming attacks and judgment.

d) As God's watchman, you must blow the trumpet of warning. You must warn the people about the sword of coming . . .

- temptations
- trials
- death
- judgment
- doom

Note what happens if you warn the people:

- You are counted faithful by God and your soul is delivered from death, from any accountability.
- The wicked have the chance to be saved and delivered from death.

But note what happens if you do not warn the people. Two things will happen:

- The wicked persons shall die in their sin.
- You will be held accountable for the death of the wicked. Note Ezk.33:6-9. The idea is that you yourself will be condemned to death.

The point is this: you are God's watchman. You are to watch and proclaim the Word of God; to warn of coming temptation, trial, death, judgment, and doom. You were called by God for this very purpose: to be a watchman and warn the people.

10. *You must lead believers into a pure and faultless religion.*

> **"Pure religion and undefiled before God and the Father is this, To visit the fatherless and widows in their affliction, and to keep himself unspotted from the world" (Jas.1:27).**

Thought
As God's minister, you are to lead believers to practice pure religion. What is pure religion? It can be summarized as two things.

a) A person must visit the fatherless and widows in their affliction. This certainly would apply to visiting all who have need within a community, those who are . . .

- orphaned
- fatherless
- widowed
- motherless
- shut-in
- lonely
- newcomers
- grieved
- lost or unsaved
- bedridden

Whatever the need, God expects you to visit them. He expects you to reach all within your community, and the task is not really all that difficult, not in a country where a church is in every community. Just think of a church within a community being surrounded by rows of houses. You and the members can easily visit every home by simply setting up several visitation hours and simply going house to house. As you go, all you have to do is share that you are visiting for Christ and the church. You want them to know that you are available if they ever need your help. Letting the community know that you really care will cause many to call upon the believers of the church when the hour of crisis strikes, and it will strike, for it strikes us all. In addition to this, every church should have a corps of genuine believers who can share Christ with the lost. Now note:

> "Then shall the King say unto them on his right hand, Come, ye blessed of my Father, inherit the kingdom prepared for you from the foundation of the world: for I was an hungered, and ye gave me meat: I was thirsty, and ye gave me drink: I was a stranger, and ye took me in: naked, and ye clothed me: I was sick, and ye visited me: I was in prison, and ye came unto me" (Mt.25:34-36).
>
> "We then that are strong ought to bear the infirmities of the weak, and not to please ourselves" (Ro.15:1).

> "Bear ye one another's burdens, and so fulfil the law of Christ" (Gal.6:2).
>
> "Remember them that are in bonds, as bound with them; and them which suffer adversity, as being yourselves also in the body" (Heb.13:3).

b) Pure religion is keeping yourself unspotted from the world. Pure religion does not become corrupted with false beliefs or with false religion. It holds to the purity of the gospel and to the purity of God's Word. Pure religion does not focus upon form and ritual and ceremony. It focuses upon the power of God to change lives eternally and it reaches out to change people's lives by visiting them.

Pure religion does not become morally corrupt; it does not become entangled with the affairs and pleasures of this world. True religion stirs people to separate themselves from the things of this world, from things that arouse their fleshly desires and cravings. True religion stirs people to keep themselves unspotted from the lust of the eyes, the lust of the flesh, and the pride of life—all of this world. This is a necessary preparation if a person is to conquer the temptations and sins of this world.

> "Wherefore come out from among them, and be ye separate, saith the Lord, and touch not the unclean thing; and I will receive you, and will be a Father unto you, and ye shall be my sons and daughters, saith the Lord Almighty" (2 Cor.6:17-18).
>
> "Love not the world, neither the things that are in the world. If any man love the world, the love of the Father is not in him. For all that is in the world, the lust of the flesh, and the lust of the eyes, and the pride of life, is not of the Father, but is of the world" (1 Jn.2:15-16).
>
> "And have no fellowship with the unfruitful works of darkness, but rather reprove them" (Eph.5:11).

11. *You must do the work of an evangelist. (See point 3, "You must seek and save the lost," p.69.)*

> "And he gave some, apostles; and some, prophets; and some, <u>evangelists</u>; and some, pastors and teachers" (Eph.4:11).
>
> "But watch thou in all things, endure afflictions, do the work of an evangelist, make full proof of thy ministry" (2 Tim.4:5).

Thought

As a minister, you must do the work of an evangelist. This does not mean that you are to become a travelling or professional evangelist. It means that your work is to be evangelistic—you are to seek to win souls in all that you do. You are to share the love of God in all your preaching and teaching and in everything else you do. The very thrust of your ministry is to be that of reconciling people to God, that of sharing the glorious news of God's love: that God saves people through His Son, the Lord Jesus Christ.

12. *You must oversee the administration of the church, set in order the affairs and organization of the church.*

    > "For this cause left I thee in Crete, that thou shouldest <u>set in order</u> the things that are wanting, and ordain elders in every city, as I had appointed thee" (Tit.1:5).
    >
    > "Then the twelve called the multitude of the disciples unto them, and said, It is not reason that we should leave the word of God, and serve tables. Wherefore, brethren, look ye out among you seven men of honest report, full of the Holy Ghost and wisdom, whom we may <u>appoint over this business</u>. But we will give ourselves continually to prayer, and to the ministry of the word" (Acts 6:2-4).
    >
    > "But as God hath distributed [gifted] to every man, as the Lord hath called every one, so let him walk. And so <u>ordain</u> I in all churches" (1 Cor.7:17).
    >
    > "The rest will I set in order when I come" (1 Cor.11:34).
    >
    > "Feed the flock of God which is among you, taking the <u>oversight</u> thereof, not by constraint, but willingly; not for filthy lucre, but of a ready mind" (1 Pt.5:2).

Thought
As a minister, you must oversee the administration of the church, set its affairs and organization in order. Note Titus 1:5 above. Two administrative duties are being assigned to the minister (Titus).

First, you must set in order the things that are defective and left undone. No matter the church, there are still some defects and some things to be done. Every church still has a long way to go before it reaches the full stature of what it should be before its Lord. But tragically, too many churches have two serious defects and flaws: they are not adequately organized for ministry and they have allowed false teaching in their ranks. As a result they are not reaching people for Christ and, in some cases, they are facing terrible division and the destruction of their testimony.

Second, you must ordain and set up whatever leadership is needed to carry on the ministry of the church (cp. Acts 6:2-4 above). If you cannot look after every member of the church yourself, then three things are essential.

a) You and the church must secure more help. You must seek out persons who love the Lord and people, and who sense the hand of God upon them, sense His calling them to minister and care for others.

b) You and the church must be willing to quit demanding so much of yourselves. You and the church must accept the ministry of other men who are also called to minister to the flock of God.

c) You must be willing to call the whole church together, to work cooperatively within a democratic process. This is exactly what the apostles themselves did. If they followed the rule of democracy in organizing the church, how much more should you and all the other ministers of God? Note: the committee or body of apostles had met and discussed the problem and need before coming to the church. A great deal of administration, of levels of leadership, is seen in this passage:

- The committee of the apostles.
- The deacons (cp. 1 Tim.3:8-13).

- The church, the body of believers.

Note why you must make sure the church is organized and operated orderly and efficiently: so that you can give yourself to prayer and to the ministry of the Word. Your primary call is . . .

- to bathe yourself, your people, and the worldwide mission of Christ in prayer.
- to always be ministering the Word of God to people by comforting, encouraging, challenging, growing, and seeking their conversion.

Your church is to be orderly—efficiently organized—so that you can be effective and bear fruit in your ministry.

13. *You must build the church first and foremost in the homes, as instructed by Christ.*

> **"And he sent them to preach the kingdom of God, and to heal the sick . . . .And whatsoever house ye enter into, there abide, and thence depart" (Lk.9:2, 4).**
>
> **"Use hospitality one to another without grudging" (1 Pt.4:9).**

Thought

As a minister, you must center the church first and foremost in the homes of believers. The church cannot and must not be centered in what we call church buildings. Why? Six things give us the answer.

First, the method Christ chose for reaching the world was the method of home evangelism. Note Lk.9:2, 4 above. The disciple was to carefully investigate and search out a receptive family and home. He was to make that home the center of his ministry. Note several things about this method.

a) It emphasizes the family, making it the very hub of ministry.

b) It stresses stability, security, and settledness. Nothing on earth is to be any more secure and stable than the family. By placing the center of ministry in the home, the Kingdom of God becomes secure and stable.

c) It centers preaching and ministering in the community, right where people live and walk. It makes the presence of Christ visible to all in day to day living.

d) It serves as the center from which the message can move out in an ever widening circle, spreading from family to family.

The most ideal form of evangelism is probably this method given by Christ: a selected home and family serving as the center of witness within a community or town.

Second, the early church was centered in the homes of believers. In fact, there were no church buildings until about two hundred years after Christ. Note some of the references to a home-centered church in Scripture.

> "And daily in the temple, and in <u>every house</u>, they ceased not to teach and preach Jesus Christ" (Acts 5:42).
>
> "And how I kept back nothing that was profitable unto you, but have showed you, and have taught you publicly, and from <u>house to house</u>" (Acts 20:20).
>
> "Likewise greet the church that is <u>in their house</u>. Salute my well beloved Epaenetus, who is the firstfruits of Achaia unto Christ" (Ro.16:5).
>
> "The churches of Asia salute you. Aquila and Priscilla salute you much in the Lord, with the church that is in <u>their house</u>" (1 Cor.16:19).
>
> "Salute the brethren which are in Laodicea and Nymphas, and the church which is <u>in his house</u>" (Col.4:15).
>
> "And to our beloved Apphia, and Archippus our fellowsoldier, and to the church <u>in thy house</u>" (Phile.2; cp. Acts 12:12; 16:40).

Third, the early believers had to open their homes and show hospitality to one another or else the church would have had difficulty surviving. The reasons are these:

- When believers were persecuted and forced to flee to other cities, they had no place to live (cp. Acts 8:1-4).
- When missionaries and evangelists travelled about, they needed a place to stay, and many of them were poor. The

inns were just too dirty and immoral; therefore, room and board had to be provided for them in the homes of believers.
- When the jobs of Christians required them to travel, they needed homes to stay in because of the unsuitability of the inns.

Hospitality was an absolute essential for the early church, and it is an absolute essential within the church today. Why? For love and care and ministry and close fellowship. It is almost impossible to maintain a loving and caring church and a dynamic ministry unless believers are fellowshipping together in their homes. In fact, Christ taught that we are to use our homes as centers of Christian love, fellowship, and outreach. This is a fact that is often unknown or ignored (see *The Preacher's Outline & Sermon Bible,*® notes—Lk.9:4; 10:5-6).

Note: we are to open our homes without grudging, that is, without murmuring or complaining (1 Pt.4:9). We are to willingly and cordially open our homes, open them joyfully expecting great things of God.

What would happen if you began to set up a home within every community for Christ, a home that was a center for love, fellowship, worship, and outreach? May God touch the hearts of many ministers and churches to adopt the very method laid down by Christ Himself (see *The Preacher's Outline & Sermon Bible,*® outline and notes—Lk.9:4; 10:5-6).

- The bishop or minister must be given to hospitality.

    "A bishop then must be blameless, the husband of one wife, vigilant, sober, of good behaviour, <u>given to hospitality</u>, apt to teach" (1 Tim.3:2).
    "But a [bishop must be a] <u>lover of hospitality</u>, a lover of good men, sober, just, holy, temperate" (Tit.1:8).

- All believers must open their doors—even to strangers in need.

    "Be not forgetful to entertain strangers: for thereby some have entertained angels unawares" (Heb.13:2).

- All believers must use hospitality as a means to minister and use it without grumbling.

   "Given to hospitality" (Ro.12:13).
   "Use hospitality one to another without grudging" (1 Pt.4:9).

- Widows in particular are to use hospitality as a means to minister.

   "Well reported of for good works; if she have brought up children, if she have lodged strangers, if she have washed the saints' feet, if she have relieved the afflicted, if she have diligently followed every good work" (1 Tim.5:10).

Fourth, a home-centered church is the only way the world can ever be permanently reached for Christ. Political and legal change often lead to oppression or confiscation of church property. And as long as the world stands, there will be political and legal changes and oppression that affect church property—sometimes drastically—even in democracies.

The point is this: when the church is centered within the homes of the world, changes within the state and government do not affect the church as much as a building-centered church.

Fifth, the cost of building and maintaining church properties is enormous and always will be. Why? Because the church must stand on its own, independent of the state and government. The church must not become entangled with the governments and secular institutions of the world, for they can make demands and restrict the message of the gospel.

Sixth, the enormous and extravagant cost of buildings and church properties consumes money, high amounts of money, money that often should be used to send the gospel around the world. Many believers—especially those in industrialized societies—will argue this. But when you and I have been chosen to be the ministers and leaders of Christ in proclaiming the gospel to the whole world—when you and I stand before God in the day of judgment—it will be impossible for God to overlook the extravagant church buildings when so many people suffer so much and have never heard a clear-cut presentation of the gospel. Many of us—ministers and lay leaders alike—will stand condemned and have to suffer the terrible judgment of God. We will have failed just as the rich young ruler did: failed to give all we are and have to the poor and needy of the world. God help us—for Christ and His cause—in seeking and saving the lost and in ministering to the needy of the world.

14. *You must build up the church as a wise masterbuilder.*

> "According to the grace of God which is given unto me, as a wise masterbuilder, I have laid the foundation, and another buildeth thereon. But let every man take heed how he buildeth thereupon. For other foundation can no man lay than that is laid, which is Jesus Christ" (1 Cor.3:10-11).

Thought
The word "masterbuilder" (archtekton) means the superintendent or architect of the building project. Paul says that he was the one who planned the church at Corinth. He was the one who laid the foundation, who began and superintended (managed) the founding of the church. Note five things in the Scripture above.

a) As a minister, you are a masterbuilder because of the "grace of God," not because of any personal ability or merit. The word "grace" means far more than just being called to minister in a church; it means to be enabled, empowered, and equipped to do the job. It was God's power, God's gifts, God's abilities that were given to Paul to do the job God had called him to do. Paul was only the instrument through which God built the church. The same is true of you.

Now note a crucial factor: Paul was not talking about a building. He was talking about people. The church is not a building; the church is a body of people who truly believe in Jesus Christ. God gives His minister the grace—the strength, power, and ability—to reach people for Jesus Christ and to *assemble them together* into a body to worship God and to honor His Son, Jesus Christ. Where the church meets together does not matter. The believers can meet in a home, a hut, a cave, a field, a back yard, a public building, or a church building. What matters is that they are one in their . . .

- trust in the Lord.
- belief and worship of God.
- purpose and mission to reach their neighbors and the world with the message of God's great love.

b) As a minister, you are to be a "wise masterbuilder." The word "wise" means skillful. You are not to approach the task and project of building the church unthoughtfully. You are to think long and hard; you are to keep your mind upon the task. You are not to allow the pleasures of the world to distract you; nor are you to allow the desires of your own flesh, which sometimes ache for less demanding work, to interfere. Paul knew what God had called him to do, to plan and establish churches all over the world. This he did as a "*wise*" architect and building superintendent. As a minister of Christ, you are to be a "wise masterbuilder."

c) Others built upon Paul's work in Corinth. When Paul left Corinth, God raised up others to labor and to continue building the church. They would include . . .

- the ministers
- the leaders
- the teachers
- the members who served and carried on the ministry of the church in order to build it. This should include all members of a church, for all members are certainly to be building the church through their witness and service for the Lord. Every member is either building or destroying the testimony and strength of a church.

Think about an amazing fact: every church has had a person who was the master builder, the architect, the founder of the church. Someone surrendered himself to go forth for God. Someone gave himself up to God to become a masterbuilder, an architect, a pioneer, a builder of churches for God.

The all important question is: Where are the men and women today who will surrender their lives to God? Who will be the masterbuilders? Who will go forth and build churches for God? The need is desperate: people need to be reached and assembled together under the love and mission of Christ.

> **"He saith unto them, But whom say ye that I am? And Simon Peter answered and said, Thou art the Christ, the Son of the living God. And Jesus answered and said unto him, Blessed art thou, Simon Barjona: for flesh and blood hath not revealed it unto thee, but my Father which is in heaven. And I say also unto thee, That thou art Peter, and upon this rock I will build my church; and the gates of hell shall not prevail against it"** (Mt.16:15-18).

Another important question is this: How many ministers are building up—really building up—the church? How many are building wisely and skillfully upon the foundation that has already been laid? Are you? Am I? How many other ministers are building wisely and skillfully upon Jesus Christ?

d) As a minister, note the clear warning—let every minister *take heed* how he builds upon the foundation of the church. The foundation has been laid, and it is strong. It shall never be moved. It is now to be built upon, but everyone in the church—minister and layman alike—must take heed how he builds upon it.

e) As a minister, there is only one foundation upon which you can build a true church: the foundation of Jesus Christ Himself. All other foundations are as *sinking sand*. They cannot stand up against the storms of life. No minister—no matter who he is—can lay any other foundation that can last. All other foundations will crumble and be destroyed forever. What does it mean to say that Christ is the only foundation?

- It means that Christ Himself, His person, is the only foundation upon which men can build their lives.

> **"Jesus saith unto him, I am the way, the truth, and the life: no man cometh unto the Father, but by me"** (Jn.14:6).

"Neither is there salvation in any other: for there is **none other name** under heaven given among men, whereby we must be saved" (Acts 4:12).

- It means that the teaching or doctrine of Christ is the only foundation upon which men can build their lives.

    "Whosoever heareth these sayings of mine, and doeth them, I will liken him unto a wise man, which built his house upon a rock" (Mt.7:24).
    "Simon Peter answered him, Lord, to whom shall we go? thou hast the words of eternal life" (Jn.6:68).
    "Verily, verily, I say unto you, If a man keep my saying, he shall never see death" (Jn.8:51).

- It means that Jesus Christ is the only foundation upon which men can build a true church.

    "He saith unto them, But whom say ye that I am? And Simon Peter answered and said, Thou art the Christ, the Son of the living God. And Jesus answered and said unto him, Blessed art thou, Simon Barjona: for flesh and blood hath not revealed it unto thee, but my Father which is in heaven. And I say also unto thee, That thou art Peter, and upon this rock I will build my church; and the gates of hell shall not prevail against it" (Mt.16:15-18).
    "This is the stone which was set at nought of you builders, which is become the head of the corner. Neither is there salvation in any other: for there is none other name under heaven given among men, whereby we must be saved" (Acts 4:11-12).
    "And are built upon the foundation of the apostles and prophets, Jesus Christ himself being the chief corner stone; in whom all the building fitly framed together groweth unto an holy temple in the Lord" (Eph.2:20-21).

CHAPTER 6

What Your Message—Your Preaching and Teaching—Must Be

God wants to reveal Himself to the world; He longs for all men to know Him, to know Him personally. This was the very reason God created man, that man might know Him personally. Consequently, your first duty is to share the Word of God—His message, His revelation—with the world. What you preach and teach is, therefore, of critical importance to God. As a minister of Christ, Scripture has far more to say to you about your preaching and teaching than it does about any other subject. (See both Chapters VI and VII.)

Contents

A. YOU AND YOUR MESSAGE	93
1. You must hold fast to sound doctrine and you must preach and teach sound doctrine.	93
2. You must preach and teach the Word of God, the Holy Scripture.	95
3. You must proclaim Jesus Christ and Him crucified.	99
4. You must proclaim that Jesus Christ was buried and raised from the dead.	106
5. You must preach and teach the kingdom of God and of heaven.	110
6. You must not mishandle the Word of God.	114

B. You and Your Preaching and Teaching ... 116
1. You must make absolutely sure that you live what you preach and teach. ... 116
2. You must preach the gospel with a sense of urgency. ... 120
3. You must preach in the power of God's Spirit, not with the persuasive thoughts and ideas of men. ... 122
4. You must preach and teach to please God, not men. You must not tone down the gospel and use flattering words in order to secure support. ... 124
5. You must not glory in yourself; you must glory only in the cross. You must not seek worldly popularity and recognition, nor seek to make a good impression and attract attention to yourself. ... 127
6. You must not preach yourself—lift yourself up—but preach Christ Jesus the Lord. ... 131
7. You must be consistent and teach over a long period of time. ... 133

CHAPTER 6

What Your Message—Your Preaching and Teaching—Must Be

A. YOU AND YOUR MESSAGE

1. *You must hold fast to sound doctrine and you must preach and teach sound doctrine.*

    > "Hold fast the form of sound words, which thou hast heard of me, in faith and love which is in Christ Jesus" (2 Tim.1:13).
    > "But speak thou the things which become sound doctrine" (Tit.2:1).

    Thought
    As a minister, the first thing you must do is hold fast to *sound doctrine* (2 Tim.1:13). The word "sound" (hugiainonton) is interesting. It means healthy and health-giving. You must hold fast to sound, health-giving words, that is, to words that will make you and your people sound and healthy. What *words* will make you and your people sound and healthy? The words just covered by the Scripture:

    - the words of the gospel (2 Tim.1:8).
    - the words of salvation (2 Tim.1:9).
    - the words about Jesus Christ, the glorious message that He has abolished death and brought life and immortality to man (2 Tim.1:9-10).
    - the words that Paul himself taught, the words that he taught to Timothy and to the believers of the early church (2 Tim.1:13).

    Simply stated, you are to hold fast to the Holy Scriptures, to the very Word of God Himself. The Word of God alone can bring health and life to the human soul. Note what the verse says (2 Tim.1:13).

    a) You must hold fast to sound words in faith. That is, you must believe in Christ, surrender your heart and life to Him, and you must be loyal to Christ. If you do not believe the words and message about Christ—if you do not have *faith in Christ*—then you are not holding fast to sound words. The very first sign that a person is clinging to sound words is his faith in Christ. If a person does not believe in Christ, he is believing a false doctrine, a false philosophy of life, and will thereby perish. The only words that can bring health and soundness to your people are the words of Christ—the life-giving words of His salvation. You must hold fast to sound words by believing in Christ Jesus, the only Savior who has brought the life-giving words of God to earth. This is the only way you can bring true health and soundness to your precious people.

b) You must hold fast to sound words in *love*. It is not enough to believe in the sound words about Christ; you must also do what Christ did: love everyone regardless of who they are or what they have done. A person who truly believes the gospel believes in Christ, and he loves both Christ and those for whom Christ died and came to save.

The point is this: it is impossible to truly believe Christ and His gospel without loving Christ and His Word. If you truly love Christ and His Word, then you do what Christ did: you see the people of the world through the eyes of Christ and you love everyone even as Christ loved everyone. You hold fast to sound words in love: you seek to share the words of health and soundness with all men. You want all men to know the sound words of salvation that bring health and soundness to the human soul.

"Take heed unto thyself, and unto the doctrine; continue in them: for in doing this thou shalt both save thyself, and them that hear thee" (1 Tim.4:16).

Second, you must preach and teach sound doctrine (Tit.2:1). This is in contrast to the false teachers discussed in the Book of Titus. As stated above, the word "sound" means wholesome and healthy. Therefore, *sound doctrine* means the doctrines and teachings of God's Word—the wholesome and healthy teachings of God's Word in contrast to the diseased teachings of false teachers. The teachings of false teachers will only implant a cancerous disease into the human heart and result in death and destruction. Therefore, the exhortation is urgent. The health and destiny of God's people and of the church are at stake. You must preach and teach sound doctrine—the teachings of God's Word. You must not preach and teach your own ideas or opinions, nor the latest fads of theology. You must not add anything to the Word of God nor take anything away from it. You must take the teachings of God's Word in all their soundness and preach and teach them.

> "Charge some that they teach no other doctrine, neither give heed to fables and endless genealogies [godly heritage and traditions], which minister questions, rather than godly edifying which is in faith: so do" (1 Tim.1:3-4).

2. *You must preach and teach the Word of God, the Holy Scripture.*

> "I charge thee therefore before God, and the Lord Jesus Christ, who shall judge the quick [living] and the dead at his appearing and his kingdom; preach the word; be instant in season, out of season; reprove, rebuke, exhort with all longsuffering and doctrine" (2 Tim.4:1-2).

> "Paul also and Barnabas continued in Antioch, teaching and preaching the word of the Lord, with many others also" (Acts 15:35).

> "And he continued there a year and six months, teaching the word of God among them" (Acts 18:11).

Thought
As a minister, the eyes of God and of Christ are watching you. You are "[ever] *before* God, and the Lord Jesus Christ." Why? To see if you are preaching and teaching the Word of God. Note 2 Tim.4:1-2 above. This is exactly what is being said. The thrust of this great passage is the two previous verses:

> "All scripture is given by inspiration of God, and is profitable for doctrine, for reproof, for correction, for instruction in righteousness: that the man of God may be perfect, thoroughly furnished unto all good works" (2 Tim.3:16-17).

Therefore, "I charge you . . . preach the word" (2 Tim.4:1-2). You must preach the Word, for God and Christ are watching: their eyes are upon you. They are watching to see if you preach the Word. You are not to be preaching your own ideas nor the ideas of other men. The message of the gospel is not the message of human philosophy, psychology, sociology, or education. It is not the message of self-image and personal development. As helpful as these subjects may be, they are not the gospel; they are not the Word of God.

What is the Word of God? The Word is the glorious gospel of our salvation. The Word is the Scripture which we hold in our hands and study and teach to all who will listen and heed. The Word of God is . . .

- the very revelation of God Himself, the record of what God wants us to know, the record that is recorded in the Holy Scriptures, the Holy Bible (2 Tim.3:16-17).
- the unbelievable love of God that tells us about Jesus Christ, the Son of God, who came to earth to save man from the sin, suffering, and death of this world (Jn.3:16; Ro.5:1-5; 5:6-11).
- the great mercy of God that He has poured out upon us through the death of His Son, the Lord Jesus Christ (Eph.2:4-7).
- the coming resurrection and judgment of all men (Mt.25:31-46; Jn.5:28-30; 1 Cor.15:1-58).

This is the Word of God. This is the Word you are to preach. This is the Word you are to proclaim from the housetops ever so boldly and courageously. No matter the trials or the threats of men, you are to "preach the Word"—the Word of the living God.

> **"Having therefore obtained help of God, I continue unto this day, witnessing both to small and great, saying <u>none other things</u> than those which the prophets and Moses did say should come" (Acts 26:22).**

Now, note 2 Tim.4:1-2 again: there are three strong reasons why you must preach the Word of God.

a) The Lord Jesus Christ shall judge the living and the dead. If you are living when He returns, He is going to judge you. If you die before He returns, He is going to judge you. The idea is twofold.

- First, He is going to judge you as to whether or not you preached. If He calls you to preach and you do not preach, you shall be judged and condemned.

- Second, He is going to judge you as to whether or not you preached the Word. If you preach the ideas of men instead of God's Word, you shall be judged and condemned. If you preach a mixture of men's ideas and God's Word, you shall be judged and condemned. William Barclay states it well:

> "Some day Timothy's work will be tested, and that test will be carried out by none other than Jesus Christ Himself. A Christian's work [is] not to satisfy men, but to satisfy Jesus. He must do every task in such a way that he can take it and offer it to Christ. He is not concerned with either the criticism or the verdict of men. The one thing he covets is the 'Well done!' of Jesus Christ" (The Letters to Timothy, Titus, and Philemon, p.232f).

"For the Son of man shall come in the glory of his Father with his angels; and then he shall reward every man according to his works" (Mt.16:27).

"And he commanded us to preach unto the people, and to testify that it is he which was ordained of God to be the Judge of quick [living] and dead" (Acts 10:42).

"For we must all appear before the judgment seat of Christ; that every one may receive the things done in his body, according to that he hath done, whether it be good or bad" (2 Cor.5:10).

b) The Lord Jesus Christ shall appear in glory. He is returning to earth and nothing is going to stop His return. This is seen in the word "appearing" (epiphaneian). It means the glorious and visible appearance of the Lord Jesus (Kenneth Wuest. *The Pastoral Epistles*, p.153). The history of the word is found in the appearance of the great Roman Emperor, especially when he was scheduled to visit a city. Thorough preparations were made: buildings and streets were scrubbed and cleaned; people worked hard to prepare themselves and their city for their coming king. They were excited about his coming and focused their attention and energy upon his coming. As a minister, this is exactly what you must do: you must preach the Word, keeping your mind upon the return of the Lord Jesus Christ. You must be prepared for His return, and you prepare by preaching the Word. The conquering Lord is returning; if you fail to preach the Word, you will stand before Him unprepared—embarrassed and ashamed. If you fail to be subjected to Him now—fail to preach His Word—you shall be subjected and judged by Him.

> "Therefore be ye also ready: for in such an hour as ye think not the Son of man cometh" (Mt.24:44).
> "So that ye come behind in no gift; waiting for the coming of our Lord Jesus Christ" (1 Cor.1:7).
> "That thou keep this commandment without spot, unrebukeable, until the appearing of our Lord Jesus Christ" (1 Tim.6:14).

c) The Lord Jesus Christ shall set up His kingdom forever and ever. As a true minister of God, you shall be a citizen of the Lord's kingdom. Your position and rank—the amount of responsibility assigned you in that kingdom—will be based upon your faithfulness in this world. Therefore, you must preach the Word faithfully. You must keep your eye upon the kingdom of Christ even as Christ is keeping His eye upon your faithfulness. "So live and so work that you will rank high in the roll of citizens of the Kingdom when the Kingdom comes" (William Barclay. *The Letters to Timothy, Titus, and Philemon*, p.234).

> "And I appoint unto you a kingdom, as my Father hath appointed unto me; that ye may eat and drink at my table in my kingdom, and sit on thrones judging the twelve tribes of Israel" (Lk.22:29-30).

3. *You must proclaim Jesus Christ and Him crucified.*

> "And I, brethren, when I came to you, came not with excellency of speech or of wisdom, declaring unto you the testimony of God. For I determined not to know any thing among you, save Jesus Christ, and him crucified" (1 Cor.2:1-2).
>
> "But we preach Christ crucified, unto the Jews a stumblingblock, and unto the Greeks foolishness" (1 Cor.1:23).
>
> "Then Philip went down to the city of Samaria, and preached Christ unto them" (Acts 8:5).
>
> "Then Philip opened his mouth, and began at the same scripture, and preached unto him Jesus" (Acts 8:35).

Thought

As a minister, you must proclaim Jesus Christ and Him crucified. The phrase "I determined" (ekrina) means to have decided, to have made a decision. Paul made a *deliberate decision*, a *strong determination* to preach only Jesus Christ and Him crucified. His theme was not . . .

- Jesus the great model for men.
- Jesus the great teacher.
- Jesus the great man of purpose.
- Jesus the great example.
- Jesus the great martyr.

The message of Paul was Jesus Christ, *His Person as the Son of God*, who was made unto us "wisdom, and righteousness, and sanctification, and redemption" (1 Cor.1:30-31). The message of Paul was Jesus Christ and Him *crucified*. Paul declares, "I determined not to know anything among you, save Jesus

Christ, and him crucified" (1 Cor.2:2). This is an emphatic, forceful statement:

- The thrust of Paul's preaching was the death of Jesus Christ.
- The theme of Paul's preaching was the death of Jesus Christ.
- The message of Paul's preaching was the death of Jesus Christ.
- The principle of Paul's preaching was the death of Jesus Christ.
- The heart of Paul's preaching was the death of Jesus Christ.

You, too, must know nothing but Jesus Christ and Him crucified. You must do as Paul did: concentrate on the death of Jesus Christ. The reason is clearly seen when we look at what Scripture says about the death of our Lord (see **Jesus Christ**, Death, *The Preacher's Outline & Sermon Bible,*® Vol.14—Master Outline & Subject Index for more discussion.)

- It is by the death of Jesus Christ that you are cleansed and freed from all sin.

    "**For this is my blood of the new testament, which is shed for many for the remission of sins**" (Mt.26:28).
    "**Who his own self bare our sins in his own body on the tree, that we, being dead to sins, should live unto righteousness: by whose stripes ye were healed**" (1 Pt.2:24; cp. Jn.1:29; 1 Cor.15:3; Heb.9:22; 9:26; 9:28; 1 Jn.1:7; 3:5).

- It is by the death of Jesus Christ that you are accepted and reconciled to God and have peace with God.

    "**To the praise of the glory of his grace, wherein he hath made us accepted in the beloved. In whom we have redemption through his blood, the forgiveness of sins, according to the riches of his grace**" (Eph.1:6-7).
    "**And, having made peace through the blood of his cross, by him to reconcile all things unto himself; by him, I say, whether they be things in earth, or things in heaven**" (Col.1:20).

- It is by the death of Jesus Christ that you are justified.

    "**Much more then, being now justified by his blood, we shall be saved from wrath through him**" **(Ro.5:9).**

- It is by the death of Jesus Christ that you are eternally redeemed.

    "**In whom we have redemption through his blood, even the forgiveness of sins**" **(Col.1:14).**

    "**For there is one God, and one mediator between God and men, the man Christ Jesus; who gave himself a ransom for all, to be testified in due time**" **(1 Tim.2:5-6; cp. Ro.3:24-25; Heb.9:12; 1 Pt.1:18; Rev.5:9).**

- It is by the death of Jesus Christ that you are delivered from death.

    "**Our Saviour Jesus Christ, who hath abolished death, and hath brought life and immortality to light through the gospel**" **(2 Tim.1:10).**

    "**But we see Jesus, who was made a little lower than the angels for the suffering of death, crowned with glory and honour; that he by the grace of God should taste death for every man**" **(Heb.2:9).**

- It is by the death of Jesus Christ that you are delivered from condemnation.

    "**Who is he that condemneth? It is Christ that died, yea rather, that is risen again, who is even at the right hand of God, who also maketh intercession for us**" **(Ro.8:34).**

- It is by the death of Jesus Christ that you are delivered from the curse of the law, that is, from death and separation from God.

    "**Christ hath redeemed us from the curse of the law, being made a curse for us: for it is written, Cursed is every one that hangeth on a tree**" **(Gal.3:13).**

> "But when the fulness of the time was come, God sent forth his Son, made of a woman, made under the law, to redeem them that were under the law, that we might receive the adoption of sons" (Gal.4:4-5).

- It is by the death of Jesus Christ that you are delivered from the judgment and wrath to come.

    > "And to wait for his Son from heaven, whom he raised from the dead, even Jesus, which delivered us from the wrath to come" (1 Th.1:10).
    >
    > "For God hath not appointed us to wrath, but to obtain salvation by our Lord Jesus Christ, who died for us, that, whether we wake or sleep, we should live together with him" (1 Th.5:9-10).

- It is by the death of Jesus Christ that you are delivered from this present evil (corruptible and dying) world.

    > "Who gave himself for our sins, that he might deliver us from this present evil world, according to the will of God and our Father" (Gal.1:4).

- It is by the death of Jesus Christ that Satan's power over death and the world is broken and destroyed.

    > "Having spoiled principalities and powers [Satan and his demonic forces], he made a show of them openly, triumphing over them in it [the cross]" (Col.2:14-15).
    >
    > "Forasmuch then as the children are partakers of flesh and blood, he also himself likewise took part of the same; that through death he might destroy him that had the power of death, that is, the devil; and deliver them who through fear of death were all their lifetime subject to bondage" (Heb.2:14-15; Rev.12:11).

- It is by the death of Jesus Christ that you are healed.

    > "But he was wounded for our transgressions, he was bruised for our iniquities: the chastisement of our peace was upon him; and with his stripes we are healed" (Is.53:5).

- It is by the death of Jesus Christ that you are given all things.

    "He that spared not his own Son, but delivered him up for us all, how shall he not with him also freely give us all things?" (Ro.8:32).

- It is by the death of Jesus Christ that those without strength are saved.

    "For when we were yet without strength, in due time Christ died for the ungodly" (Ro.5:6).

    "And through thy knowledge [spiritual liberty] shall the weak brother perish, for whom Christ died?" (1 Cor.8:11).

- It is by the death of Jesus Christ that the ungodly are saved.

    "For when we were yet without strength, in due time Christ died for the ungodly" (Ro.5:6).

- It is by the death of Jesus Christ that sinners are saved.

    "But God commendeth his love toward us, in that, while we were yet sinners, Christ died for us" (Ro.5:8).

- It is by the death of Jesus Christ that the enemies of God are saved.

    "For if, when we were enemies, we were reconciled to God by the death of his Son, much more, being reconciled, we shall be saved by his life" (Ro.5:10).

- It is by the death of Jesus Christ that the unjust are saved.

    "For Christ also hath once suffered for sins, the just for the unjust, that he might bring us to God, being put to death in the flesh, but quickened by the Spirit" (1 Pt.3:18).

- It is by the death of Jesus Christ that all men are drawn to Christ.

    "And I, if I be lifted up from the earth, will draw all men unto me" (Jn.12:32).

- It is by the death of Jesus Christ that you have access into the holy presence of God.

    "Having therefore, brethren, boldness to enter into the holiest by the blood of Jesus, by a new and living way, which he hath consecrated for us, through the veil, that is to say, his flesh" (Heb.10:19-20).

- It is by the death of Jesus Christ that the great love of God is revealed to you.

    "And walk in love, as Christ also hath loved us, and hath given himself for us an offering and a sacrifice to God for a sweetsmelling savour" (Eph.5:2; cp. Ro.5:8).

- It is by the death of Jesus Christ that you are freed from a self-centered life and live for Christ.

    "And that he died for all, that they which live should not henceforth live unto themselves, but unto him which died for them, and rose again" (2Cor.5:15).

    "I am crucified with Christ: nevertheless I live; yet not I, but Christ liveth in me: and the life which I now live in the flesh I live by the faith of the Son of God, who loved me, and gave himself for me" (Gal.2:20; cp. 2 Cor.4:10-11; 1 Pt.4:1).

- It is by the death of Jesus Christ that you are enabled to live a righteous life.

    "For ye are bought with a price [the death of Christ]: therefore glorify God in your body, and in your spirit, which are God's" (1 Cor.6:20).

    "For he hath made him to be sin for us, who knew no sin; that we might be made the righteousness of God in him" (2 Cor.5:21; cp. 1 Pt.2:24).

- It is by the death of Jesus Christ that you are taught to love and sacrifice your life for others.

> "And walk in love, as Christ also hath loved us, and hath given himself for us an offering and a sacrifice to God for a sweetsmelling savour" (Eph.5:2).
>
> "Hereby perceive we the love of God, because he laid down his life for us: and we ought to lay down our lives for the brethren" (1 Jn.3:16).

- It is by the death of Jesus Christ that your *conscience* is genuinely cleared so that you can serve God and bear fruit.

  > "Who gave himself for us, that he might redeem us from all iniquity, and purify unto himself a peculiar people, zealous of good works" (Tit.2:14).
  >
  > "How much more shall the blood of Christ, who through the eternal Spirit offered himself without spot to God, purge your conscience from dead works to serve the living God?" (Heb.9:14).

- It is by the death of Jesus Christ that you know the power of God.

  > "For the preaching of the cross is to them that perish foolishness; but unto us which are saved it is the power of God" (1 Cor.1:18).

- It is by the death of Jesus Christ that you are enabled to purge out your old sins.

  > "Purge out therefore the old leaven, that ye may be a new lump, as ye are unleavened. For even Christ our passover is sacrificed for us" (1 Cor.5:7).

- It is by the death of Jesus Christ that you are reconciled to men.

  > "But now in Christ Jesus ye who sometimes were far off are made nigh by the blood of Christ. For he is our peace, who hath made both one, and hath broken down the middle wall of partition between us . . . . That he might reconcile both unto God in one body by the cross, having slain the enmity thereby . . . . For through him we both have access by one Spirit unto the Father" (Eph.2:13-14, 16, 18).

- It is by the death of Jesus Christ that Christ gained the right to be exalted as the Lord of the dead and the living.

    "For to this end Christ both died, and rose, and revived, that he might be Lord both of the dead and living" (Ro.14:9).

    "Looking unto Jesus the author and finisher of our faith; who for the joy that was set before him endured the cross, despising the shame, and is set down at the right hand of the throne of God" (Heb.12:2; cp. Ph.2:8-11; Heb.1:3).

- It is by the death of Jesus Christ that the church of God was purchased.

    "Take heed therefore unto yourselves, and to all the flock, over the which the Holy Ghost hath made you overseers, to feed the church of God, which he hath purchased with his own blood" (Acts 20:28).

    "Christ also loved the church, and gave himself for it" (Eph.5:25).

God has done so much for you through the cross—so much for both believers and unbelievers. This is the reason you must know nothing but Jesus Christ and Him crucified, the reason you must focus your preaching and teaching upon the death of Christ. The death of our Lord must consume your life and ministry, for His death is our salvation and life, and the only hope for a world lost in corruption and death.

4. *You must proclaim that Jesus Christ was buried and raised from the dead.*

    "For I delivered unto you first of all that which I also received, how that Christ died for our sins according to the scriptures; and that he was buried, and that he <u>rose again</u> the third day according to the scriptures" (1 Cor.15:3-4).

    "Remember that Jesus Christ of the seed of David was raised from the dead according to my gospel" (2 Tim.2:8).

Thought

As a minister, you must proclaim the burial and resurrection of Jesus Christ. Note three crucial facts declared in 1 Cor.15:3-4 above.

a) The burial of Jesus Christ is important, for it proves two significant things.
- It proves that Jesus Christ died. A man is not buried unless he is dead.
- It proves the resurrection. The empty tomb is evidence that Christ arose from the dead.

b) Jesus Christ arose from the dead. The resurrection of Jesus Christ assures the believer that he too shall be raised from the dead.
- The resurrection of Christ proves that *God is*: that He does exist and care for the earth. There is no power on earth that can raise a man from the dead. Only a Supreme, eternal power and Person can do that. Only God can give life to dead matter and to the dust of the earth. The very fact that Jesus Christ was raised from the dead proves that God exists and cares for this earth.
- The resurrection of Christ proves that Jesus Christ is who He claimed to be, the Son of God Himself. It proves that Jesus Christ was sent to earth to live a sinless life and to secure the Ideal righteousness for man. It proves that He was sent to die and to arise from the dead for man.

  "**And declared to be the Son of God with power, according to the spirit of holiness, by the resurrection from the dead**" **(Ro.1:4).**
  "**Which [God's mighty power] he wrought in Christ, when he raised him from the dead, and set him at his own right hand in the heavenly places**" **(Eph.1:20).**

- The resurrection of Christ proves that Jesus Christ is the Savior of the world. It proves that Christ is the very One whom God sent to earth to save men from death and to give them life, both now and eternally.

"Who was delivered for our offences, and was raised again for our justification" (Ro.4:25).

"That if thou shalt confess with thy mouth the Lord Jesus, and shalt believe in thine heart that God hath raised him from the dead, thou shalt be saved" (Ro.10:9).

"By which [the gospel] also ye are saved, if ye keep in memory what I preached unto you, unless ye have believed in vain. For I delivered unto you first of all that which I also received, how that Christ died for our sins according to the scriptures; and that he was buried, and that he rose again the third day according to the scriptures" (1 Cor.15:2-4).

- The resurrection of Christ proves that Jesus Christ is "the Spirit of life." It proves that Christ is the very energy and force of life, the very power and Being of life; and it proves that He can give the same "Spirit of life" to men. He can raise men from the dead, even as He arose from the dead.

    "But if the Spirit of him that raised up Jesus from the dead dwell in you, he that raised up Christ from the dead shall also quicken your mortal bodies by his Spirit that dwelleth in you" (Ro.8:11; cp. Ro.8:2).

    "For if we believe that Jesus died and rose again, even so them also which sleep in Jesus will God bring with him" (1 Th.4:14).

    "Blessed be the God and Father of our Lord Jesus Christ, which according to his abundant mercy hath begotten us again unto a lively [living] hope by the resurrection of Jesus Christ from the dead, to an inheritance incorruptible, and undefiled, and that fadeth not away, reserved in heaven for you" (1 Pt.1:3-4; cp. 1 Pt.3:18).

c) Jesus Christ "rose again . . . according to the Scripture."

- Jesus Christ said that Jonah was a type of His resurrection.

> "For as Jonas was three days and three nights in the whale's belly; so shall the Son of man be three days and three nights in the heart of the earth" (Mt.12:40).

- The Gospel of John says that the resurrection was predicted in the Old Testament. Jesus Christ rebuked the disciples for not believing the predictions of His death and of His return to glory (resurrection).

    > "Then he said unto them, O fools, and slow of heart to believe all that the prophets have spoken: ought not Christ to have suffered these things, and to enter into his glory? And beginning at Moses and all the prophets, he expounded unto them in all the scriptures the things concerning himself" (Lk.24:25-27).
    > "For as yet they knew not the scripture, that he must rise again from the dead" (Jn.20:9).

- Paul proclaimed the Old Testament predictions concerning the resurrection of Christ.

    > "Having therefore obtained help of God, I continue unto this day, witnessing both to small and great, saying none other things than those which <u>the prophets and Moses did say</u> should come: that Christ should suffer, and that he should be the first that should rise from the dead, and should show light unto the people, and to the Gentiles" (Acts 26:22-23).

- Peter proclaimed the Old Testament prophecies predicting the Lord's resurrection.

    > "Wherefore he saith also in another psalm, Thou shalt not suffer thine Holy One to see corruption. For David, after he had served his own generation by the will of God fell on sleep, and was laid unto his fathers and saw corruption: but he, whom God raised again, saw no corruption" (Acts 13:35-37).

- Psalm 16:10 is a clear prediction of the Lord's resurrection.

  "For thou wilt not leave my soul in hell; neither wilt thou suffer thine Holy One to see corruption" (Ps.16:10).

- All the Old Testament predictions of the Messiah's eternal reign are prophecies of His resurrection. This is clear, for He could reign eternally only if He was raised from the dead. (See *The Preacher's Outline & Sermon Bible,*® note, **Jesus Christ, Davidic Heir**—Lk.3:24-31 for the prophecies and their fulfillment.)

Note the implication of this fact for all believers. No man can live forever unless he (the basic elements of his body) is raised from the dead, for all men are doomed to die. Therefore, all the prophecies concerning believers living forever can be fulfilled only if we are raised from the dead. You must, therefore, as the minister of God, proclaim the glorious resurrection of Jesus Christ.

5. *You must preach and teach the kingdom of God and of heaven.*

    "And as ye go, preach, saying, The kingdom of heaven is at hand" (Mt.10:7).

    "Now after that John was put in prison, Jesus came into Galilee, preaching the gospel of the kingdom of God, and saying, The time is fulfilled, and the kingdom of God is at hand: repent ye, and believe the gospel" (Mk.1:14-15).

    "And he said unto them, I must preach the kingdom of God to other cities also: for therefore am I sent" (Lk.4:43).

    "And it came to pass afterward, that he went throughout every city and village, preaching and showing the glad tidings of the kingdom of God: and the twelve were with him" (Lk.8:1).

    "And he sent them to preach the kingdom of God, and to heal the sick" (Lk.9:2).

    "But when they believed Philip preaching the things concerning the kingdom of God, and the

name of Jesus Christ, they were baptized, both men and women" (Acts 8:12).

"And now, behold, I know that ye all, among whom I have gone preaching the kingdom of God, shall see my face no more" (Acts 20:25).

"And when they had appointed him a day, there came many to him into his lodging; to whom he expounded and testified the kingdom of God, persuading them concerning Jesus, both out of the law of Moses, and out of the prophets, from morning till evening" (Acts 28:12).

"Preaching the kingdom of God, and teaching those things which concern the Lord Jesus Christ, with all confidence, no man forbidding" (Acts 28:31).

"For the kingdom of God is not meat and drink; but righteousness, and peace, and joy in the Holy Ghost" (Ro.14:17).

Thought
As a minister, you must preach and teach the kingdom of God and of heaven. Note what Christ says: "And as ye go, preach, saying, The kingdom of heaven is at hand" (Mt.10:7). Your message is a given message, given by the Lord Himself. You are not to proclaim your own ideas nor the ideas of others. You are to preach the message *given* by the Lord. No matter the generation, the message needed is the message of God's kingdom and of heaven. The message needs to be repeated time and again for every generation:

- It is the same yesterday, today and forever (Heb.13:8).
- It was the message of Christ (Mt.4:17, 23).
- It was the message of John (Mt.3:2).
- It was the message of the apostles and ministers of Christ.

What is the kingdom of God? It is the same thing that any kingdom is: the country of a king and the rule and reign of a king. The kingdom of God is . . .

- heaven, where God presently rules and reigns over all who are there.

- the future kingdom or universe that will be recreated and perfected eternally. God is going to rule and reign over a perfect universe sometime in the future. His rule and reign are going to be perfectly executed over all the universe and over all dimensions and worlds.
- the present rule and reign of God in hearts and lives upon earth.

a) You must preach that the kingdom of God exists now, right now. A person can enter God's kingdom today: he can open up his heart and let Christ rule and reign in His life now. Therefore, you must preach the kingdom now.

- You must preach that God wants to enter hearts and lives now.
- You must preach that a person can enter the kingdom only when he humbles himself before God as a small child.

   "**Suffer the little children to come unto me, and forbid them not: for of such is the kingdom of God**" **(Mk.10:14).**

- You must preach that a person has to be born again to enter the kingdom of God.

   "**Jesus answered and said unto him, Verily, verily, I say unto thee, Except a man be born again, he cannot see the kingdom of God**" **(Jn.3:3).**

- You must preach that sinners enter the kingdom before the proud and the self-righteous religionists.

   "**Verily I say unto you, That the publicans and the harlots go into the kingdom of God before you**" **(Mt.21:31).**
   "**Verily I say unto you, Whosoever shall not receive the kingdom of God as a little child, he shall not enter therein**" **(Mk.10:15).**

- You must preach that the kingdom is a spiritual, life-changing blessing.

   "**For the kingdom of God is not meat and drink; but righteousness, and peace, and joy in the Holy Ghost**" **(Ro.14:17).**

- You must preach that the kingdom is to be the first thing sought by believers.

    "But seek ye first the kingdom of God, and his righteousness; and all these things shall be added unto you" (Mt.6:33).

- You must preach that the kingdom of God which is presently on earth includes many persons who make a false profession. They profess to live a godly and righteous life, but they do not. They do not allow God to rule and reign in their lives.

    "Another parable put he forth unto them, saying, The kingdom of heaven is likened unto a man which sowed good seed [good men] in his field: but while men slept, his enemy came and sowed tares [evil men] among the wheat, and went his way" (Mt.13:24-25).

b) You must preach that God's eternal kingdom is coming in the future—coming soon.

- You must preach that God is going to rule and reign in a perfect universe for all eternity.

    "But the day of the Lord will come as a thief in the night; in the which the heavens shall pass away with a great noise, and the elements shall melt with fervent heat, the earth also and the works that are therein shall be burned up. Seeing then that all these things shall be dissolved, what manner of persons ought ye to be in all holy conversation and godliness, looking for and hasting unto the coming of the day of God, wherein the heavens being on fire shall be dissolved, and the elements shall melt with fervent heat? Nevertheless we, according to his promise, look for new heavens and a new earth, wherein dwelleth righteousness" (2 Pt.3:10-13).

    "And I saw a new heaven and a new earth: for the first heaven and the first earth were passed away" (Rev.21:1).

    "Then cometh the end, when he shall have delivered up the kingdom to God, even the Father; when he shall have put down all rule and all authority and power" (1 Cor.15:24).

- You must preach that God is going to perfect believers, that He is going to create a perfect body for them and give them a perfect life.

"Now this I say, brethren, that flesh and blood cannot inherit the kingdom of God; neither doth corruption inherit incorruption. Behold, I show you a mystery: We shall not all sleep, but we shall all be changed, in a moment, in the twinkling of an eye, at the last trump: for the trumpet shall sound, and the dead shall be raised incorruptible, and we shall be changed. For this corruptible must put on incorruption, and this mortal must put on immortality" (1 Cor.15:50-53; cp. Ph.3:20-21).

"And God shall wipe away all tears from their eyes; and there shall be no more death, neither sorrow, nor crying, neither shall there be any more pain: for the former things are passed away. And he that sat upon the throne said, Behold, I make all things new. And he said unto me, Write: for these words are true and faithful" (Rev.21:4-5).

6. *You must not mishandle the Word of God.*

"Therefore seeing we have this ministry, as we have received mercy, we faint not; but have renounced the hidden things of dishonesty, not walking in craftiness, <u>nor handling the word of God deceitfully</u>; but by manifestation of the truth commending ourselves to every man's conscience in the sight of God" (2 Cor.4:1-2).

Thought

As a minister, you must live a life of honesty and integrity, and you must not mishandle the Word of God, not under any circumstance. Note four significant points in the above passage.

a) You must renounce dishonesty, "the hidden things of dishonesty." The word "dishonesty" (aischunes) means shame, disgrace, scandal. The hidden or secret things that shame and disgrace men, that cause scandals, are to have no part in your life. You are to renounce all secret and hidden . . .

- immorality
- desires
- thoughts
- feelings
- covetousness
- ambitions
- greed
- methods

You must live an *open and above-board life,* a life of honesty and integrity. This is the only way you can preach and teach a pure gospel.

b) You are not to "walk in craftiness" (panourgiai). The word means trickery, cunning, cleverness, shrewdness, evil design. It means a man who will do anything and use any means to get what he wants. Note: you are not to "walk" this way; you are not to walk using and misusing people, circumstances, events, and things for your own end. As a minister of God, you are to walk as Jesus walked.

c) You are not to handle "the Word of God deceitfully" (dolountes). The word "deceitful" means to falsify, adulterate, corrupt, deceive, ensnare. "The Word *of God"* has come from God, not man. The author of the Word of God is God. God is the *Authority* of the Word of God. You are only the *spokesman* for God; therefore, you are . . .

- not to falsify the Word of God.
- not to adulterate the Word of God.
- not to corrupt the Word of God.
- not to deceive or ensnare people by mishandling the Word of God.

You are not *to add* the ideas, traditions, philosophies, or speculations of men to the Word of God. Neither are you to take away portions of Scripture, denying their validity as the Word of God; nor are you to neglect, ignore, or keep silent about some part of God's Word. You are not to distort the Word of God in any form or fashion.

d) You must proclaim the truth honestly, openly, and purely. You are to be true to the truth of God as revealed in God's Word. You are to be both humble and receptive before God in your study and prayer life. You are not to be wise in your own conceits. And when you go before people, you are to proclaim and teach the truth as God's Word reveals it.

B. YOU AND YOUR PREACHING AND TEACHING

1. *You must make absolutely sure that you live what you preach and teach.*

> "**Thou therefore which teachest another, teachest thou not thyself? thou that preachest a man should not steal, dost thou steal? Thou that sayest a man should not commit adultery, dost thou commit adultery? thou that abhorrest idols, dost thou commit sacrilege? Thou that makest thy boast of the law, [the Word] through breaking the law dishonourest thou God? For the name of God is blasphemed among the Gentiles through you, as it is written**" (Ro.2:21-24).
>
> "**Not every one that saith unto me, Lord, Lord, shall enter into the kingdom of heaven; but he that doeth the will of my Father which is in heaven. Many will say to me in that day, Lord, Lord, have we not prophesied in thy name? and in thy name have cast out devils? and in thy name done many wonderful works? And then will I profess unto them, I never knew you: depart from me, ye that work iniquity**" (Mt.7:21-23).
>
> "**They profess that they know God; but in works they deny him, being abominable, and disobedient, and unto every good work reprobate**" (Tit.1:16).

Thought

As a minister, you must live what you preach and teach. Scripture is direct and pointed about the matter. Note the Scripture above (Ro.2:21-24), the five frank and straightforward questions asked of you as a minister:

a) "You who teach others, do you not teach yourself?" The question is for you and for all other ministers and teachers of the Word. You claim to know some truths about morality and about how people should live and behave. You often share these truths with your church and with believers, children, friends, and others. When you share and teach, do you not listen to the truth? Do you not teach yourself? What right do you have to tell others how to live if you do not live that way? This is the sin of hypocrisy, a sin committed by too many ministers.

> "Even so ye also outwardly appear righteous unto men, but within ye are full of hypocrisy and iniquity" (Mt.23:28).
>
> "And why call ye me, Lord, Lord, and do not the things which I say?" (Lk.6:46).
>
> "My little children, let us not love in word, neither in tongue; but in deed and in truth" (1 Jn.3:18).

b) "You who say that a person should not steal, do you steal?" Do you take from others; do you . . .

- steal money?
- steal by not paying your bills?
- steal by ordering books and other things and then not paying for them?
- steal while shopping?
- steal time or other things from your church and ministry?
- steal from your neighbor or fellow ministers?
- steal from your family?

If you steal, what right do you have to say that others should not steal—that everyone else should not have the right to take what they want from whom they want? If enough people began to take what they wanted when they wanted, then the world would exist in utter chaos. If you say that men should not steal, why do you steal? This is the sin of some ministers.

Stealing is a sin that leads to utter chaos. Because of its devastating effect, it is one of the ten commandments, and note: it is so important a commandment, it is repeated time and again.

> "Thou shalt not steal" (Ex.20:15; Lev.19:11; Dt.5:19; Mt.19:18; Ro.13:9).

> "Let him that stole steal no more: but rather let him labour, working with his hands the thing which is good, that he may have to give to him that needeth" (Eph.4:28).

c) "You who say that a person should not commit adultery, do you commit adultery?" You preach and teach that people should be pure brides and spouses, pure husbands and wives, and you want a pure son and daughter. But do you live purely? What are you looking at and watching, reading and hearing? Do you . . .

- look a second time?
- read pornographic books, magazines, and novels?
- have lustful thoughts?
- harbor sexual thoughts?
- have an illicit relationship?
- dress in a manner exposing your body?
- watch and support television and films that have scenes of immorality or even suggest immorality?

Regardless of man's denial, we do what we think; and our thoughts come from what we see and watch, read and hear. Therefore, if you look and watch, read and listen to sexual suggestions, your thoughts center upon fleshly desires. This is the reason for the breakdown of morals in society. If you say a man should not commit adultery, do you commit adultery? Do you commit it in your mind? This is a major sin among some ministers. Christ knew this; therefore, He said . . .

> "Ye have heard that it was said by them of old time, Thou shalt not commit adultery: but I say unto you, That whosoever looketh on a woman to lust after her hath committed adultery with her already in his heart" (Mt.5:27-28).

d) "You who abhor idols, do you commit sacrilege?" The word "sacrilege" (hierosuleo) means to violate one's commitment to God and to rob from God. It means to consider something more important than God, something so important that it *requires* . . .

- the commitment that you owe God.
- the tithes and offerings that you owe God.

You say that you worship God and abhor idols. But ask yourself: do you take what belongs to God—your commitment, your time, your energy, your tithes—and give it to something else? Do you make something else more important than God; do you make it an idol? This is one of the major sins of some ministers.

> "**Take heed to yourselves, that your heart be not deceived, and ye turn aside, and serve other gods, and worship them**" (Dt.11:16).
>
> "**I am the LORD: that is my name: and my glory will I not give to another, neither my praise to graven images**" (Is.42:8).
>
> "**Little children, keep yourselves from idols**" (1 Jn.5:21).

e) "You who boast and take pride in the law [the Bible], through breaking the law do you not dishonor God?" The answer is clear.

- You do dishonor God when you talk about His Word yet break His commandments.
- You do dishonor God before men, causing His name to be blasphemed and cursed.

When you boast in God's Word yet break His commandments, you give great occasion for the world and its people to take the name of God and . . .

- blaspheme
- mock
- curse
- deny
- reproach
- insult
- ridicule
- profane

Many a person is doomed because of the hypocrisy of some ministers. This is one of the terrible sins of a hypocritical minister.

As a minister, you must be responsible; you must live up to your profession. Scripture demands this of all believers, especially of ministers:

> "He that saith he abideth in him ought himself also so to walk, even as he walked" (1 Jn.2:6).

The word "walk" is continuous action. It means to *walk in Christ and to keep on walking* in Him. In fact, the word "ought" means debt, constraint, and obligation. As a minister, you profess Christ; you claim to know God. Therefore, you are in debt to Christ. You are obligated to walk as Christ walked. How did Christ walk upon earth? He walked . . .

- believing and trusting God
- worshipping and praying to God
- fellowshipping and communing with God
- giving and sacrificing all He was and had to God
- seeking and following after God
- teaching and telling others about God
- loving and caring for others just as God said to do
- obeying and keeping all of God's commandments

This is the responsible man, the man you are to be. You are to do just what Christ did: believe and trust God, worship and pray to God—you are to walk in the very footsteps of Christ, doing exactly what Christ did. This is your duty and obligation as a minister: you are to live what you preach and teach. If you are not living for Christ—living what you preach and teach—then you must confess and repent immediately, for Christ and for the sake of your own soul, lest you become a castaway.

2. *You must preach the gospel with a sense of urgency.*

> "For though I preach the gospel, I have nothing to glory of: for necessity is laid upon me; yea, woe is unto me, if I preach not the gospel!" (1 Cor.9:16).

Thought

As a minister, you must preach the gospel with a sense of urgency. You must sense—be gripped with—a compulsion to preach the gospel. Why? There are three reasons.

a) You are obligated, duty-bound, to preach the gospel. Note what Paul says: a God-given "necessity [epikeitai] was laid upon" him to preach the gospel. The word "necessity" means to be pressed, compelled, constrained, required, duty-bound to preach the gospel. God had called Paul to preach the gospel; therefore, it was his charge, his work, his business, his call in life. He could not do otherwise: he was compelled to preach. His preaching was not a matter of choice; he had not chosen to be a preacher. His preaching was a matter of duty. If he did not preach, he would be disobeying God and would miss the very purpose for his life upon earth.

As a minister, you must preach the gospel with a sense of urgency, lest you miss your purpose in life.

b) You are held accountable by God to preach the gospel. If you fail to preach, you will face the judgment and woe of God. The word "woe" means this: when Paul stood before God, he would have to face *some terrible* . . .

- regret
- distress
- disaster
- denunciation
- grief

No person—not a *single* person—who has ever been called by God is exempt from this coming judgment. This is made clear.

If Paul preached the gospel willingly, he had a reward. But if he preached unwillingly, "a dispensation of the gospel [was still] committed to him" (1 Cor.9:17). This simply means he was *still responsible* to preach the gospel even if he did it unwillingly or if he refused to do it. The word "dispensation" (oikonomia) means a stewardship, a trust. The steward was the manager of a large household or estate. The minister of God is the manager of God's household and estate (the church and the world).

Once God has called you to preach, the stewardship and trust of preaching are yours. Whether you follow through and preach does not matter; you are still responsible for preaching. There is no release from the call and duty. You will stand accountable for preaching the gospel or you will stand accountable for not preaching the gospel.

As a minister, you must preach the gospel with urgency or else face the judgment and woe of God.

c) You must preach the gospel with urgency because of the enslavement of sin, death, and judgment to come. Death and judgment are two appointments that every person must keep. There is no escape from either appointment. The only hope of escape—of living forever and of being delivered from the wrath of God—is the gospel of the Lord Jesus Christ. The destiny of every person is death and judgment—eternal death and judgment—unless they have been saved by God's Son, the Lord Jesus Christ.

As the minister of Christ, you must preach the gospel with the greatest of urgencies, preach it so that men can understand and be saved from sin, death, and judgment to come.

"**And as it is appointed unto men once to die, but after this the judgment**" **(Heb.9:27).**

3. *You must preach in the power of God's Spirit, not with the persuasive thoughts and ideas of men.*

"**And my speech and my preaching was not with enticing words of man's wisdom, but in demonstration of the Spirit and of power: that your faith should not stand in the wisdom of men, but in the power of God**" **(1 Cor.2:4-5).**

Thought
As a minister, you must preach in the power of God's Spirit. You must not preach—you must not seek to reach people—with the attractive, persuasive thoughts and ideas of men. Note several points in the verses above.

a) A distinction is made between daily *speech* or ordinary conversation and *preaching*. Paul's daily conversations focused upon Jesus Christ just as his preaching did. He is saying what he has already stressed: he was determined not to know anything among people except "Jesus Christ and Him crucified" (p.101).

What a dynamic example! Your life and conversation is to focus upon Jesus Christ—every day, all day long. When possible and *whenever opportunity can be made*, the theme of your conversation should be Jesus Christ and Him crucified...

- at home
- at work
- at play
- at meals
- in preaching
- in teaching
- in discussing
- in sharing

> **"For we cannot but speak the things which we have seen and heard" (Acts 4:20).**

b) The word "enticing" (peithois) means persuasive, plausible. Your witnessing and preaching are not to be based upon the enticing, persuasive, plausible arguments of man's wisdom and philosophy.

c) The word "demonstration" (apodeixei) means to show forth with the most rigorous evidence and proof. The idea is that the evidence is presented so strongly that the truth is clearly seen.

d) The only way your witness and preaching can be proclaimed so strongly is through the Holy Spirit and His power. The gospel of salvation can be convincing only when the Holy Spirit and His power demonstrates it. Only the Holy Spirit can *convict, convince,* and *convert* a person to live for God.

Only the Holy Spirit can impart life to a person. Therefore, as the minister of God, you must surrender your life to the Spirit of God. You must be filled with the presence, fulness, and power of the Holy Spirit.

> **"And when he [the Holy Spirit] is come, he will reprove the world of sin, and of righteousness, and of judgment: of sin, because they believe not on me; of righteousness, because I go to my Father, and ye**

see me no more; of judgment, because the prince of this world is judged" (Jn.16:8-11).

e) Your preaching must have one objective and one objective only: to lead people to faith in the Lord Jesus Christ. You must do just what the Scripture above says: you must not place the faith of people in the wisdom of men, but in the power of God's Spirit (1 Cor.2:5). The wisdom of men cannot save man. Only the power of God can. It is of no value whatsoever for a man to just acknowledge . . .

- that Jesus Christ lived, that He was an historical person.
- that Jesus Christ is the Savior, that He is truly the Son of God.
- that other religions and positions are not true.

A person's salvation cannot stand in the human knowledge and wisdom of men. Human arguments and appeals may seem rational and logical, but they have no spiritual power. No person—no speech and no preaching—can convert a human soul and impart eternal life to it. Only God can do such a thing. Therefore, you must speak and preach under the influence and power of God's Spirit.

Anything short of God's Spirit places a person's faith in the knowledge and wisdom of men. The crying need is for God's ministers and God's people to be controlled by God's Spirit so that God can demonstrate His power through them to a lost and dying world.

> **"But ye shall receive power, after that the Holy Ghost is come upon you: and ye shall be witnesses unto me both in Jerusalem, and in all Judaea, and in Samaria, and unto the uttermost part of the earth" (Acts 1:8).**
>
> **"And with great power gave the apostles witness of the resurrection of the Lord Jesus: and great grace was upon them all" (Acts 4:33).**

4. *You must preach and teach to please God, not men. You must not tone down the gospel and use flattering words in order to secure support.*

> "But as we were allowed of God to be put in trust with the gospel, even so we speak; not as pleasing men, but God, which trieth our hearts. For neither at any time used we flattering words, as ye know, nor a cloak of covetousness; God is witness" (1 Th.2:4-5).

Thought
You must always preach and teach to please God, not men. You must never tone down the gospel nor use flattering words in order to secure the approval and support of people. Most people do not want to hear . . .

- about sin and judgment.
- about the utter necessity of men to depend upon the death of Christ in order to be saved.
- about the demand that a person commit *all he is and has* to Christ in order to meet the needs of a desperate world.

The preaching of the truth is not always popular, not with a carnal and unbelieving people. Therefore, when you are thrown in the midst of a people who are worldly, you can be tempted to tone down your message to please the people. The temptation can be especially strong if your livelihood is at risk.

However, note what Paul says; he gives two glorious testimonies.

a) Paul makes a clearcut statement: he sought only to please God, not men. You, too, must seek to please God and not men. There are two strong reasons why.

- First, God is the Person who has trusted you with the gospel, not men. God owns the gospel, and He is the Person who has called you to proclaim the gospel. Men had nothing to do with the formulation of the gospel nor with calling you. God will take care of you as you preach the gospel. God has called you to preach; therefore, you are God's. Consequently, you can trust God to take care of you if men react against the gospel and attack you.

- Second, God alone will try your heart and judge you. You are to stand and give an account for your ministry someday, and you are to stand before God, not before men. Men might be able to cause some difficulty for you on earth, but God will cause difficulty for you through all eternity if you abuse or oppose the gospel of God.

b) Paul makes another clearcut statement: he did not preach and teach for what he could get out of it. Neither should you nor any other minister.

- The word "flattery" (kolakeias) always means the kind of flattery that is given in order to get something out of people (William Barclay. *The Letters to the Philippians, Colossians, and Thessalonians.* "The Daily Study Bible." Philadelphia, PA: The Westminster Press, 1957, p.221). Paul did not flatter people in order to secure their friendship, following, or support. He of course commended people, and his letters in the New Testament show that he commended them quite often. But he did it truthfully, always covering the weak areas that people needed to strengthen as well as their strong and commendable areas. As a minister of the Lord, you must commend people, but only truthfully. You must never flatter people to secure their support or following nor to increase your livelihood.

- The word "covetousness" shows that Paul was accused of being in the ministry out of greed; that he had chosen the ministry to earn a livelihood, to make money. Emphatically, Paul denies this and says that his lifestyle proves it. He declares that the church knows the truth and that God is witness to the truth.

  You must never use the ministry as a cloak of covetousness for what you can get out of it. Your purpose for being in the ministry is not to make money, not even to earn a livelihood. Your purpose is to preach and teach the gospel of the Lord Jesus Christ.

As a minister, you must never tone down the gospel because you fear reaction and the loss of livelihood, income, or some upcoming raise in salary. You must always preach and teach to please God, not men.

5. *You must not glory in yourself; you must glory only in the cross. You must not seek worldly popularity and recognition, nor seek to make a good impression and attract attention to yourself.*

> "Nor of men sought we glory, neither of you, nor yet of others" (1 Th.2:6).
>
> "As many as desire to make a fair show [good impression] in the flesh, they constrain you to be circumcised [to follow religious rituals and ceremonies]; only lest they should suffer persecution for the cross of Christ. For neither they themselves who are circumcised keep the law; but desire to have you circumcised, that they may glory in your flesh [boast in you as a convert]" (Gal.6:12-13).
>
> "But God forbid that I should glory, save in the cross of our Lord Jesus Christ, by whom the world is crucified unto me, and I unto the world" (Gal.6:14).
>
> "For we preach not ourselves, but Christ Jesus the Lord; and ourselves your servants for Jesus' sake" (2 Cor.4:5).

Thought
Paul is straightforward; he pulls no punches in what he says: he did not seek the glory, prestige, honor, or recognition of people (1 Th.2:6^a). Note two significant points.

a) As a minister, you must not glory in yourself. You must do as Paul says he did: you must not seek the glory, prestige, honor, or recognition of people. Paul was not out to be recognized as a great preacher or good minister. He was not seeking to be recognized as a leader or as a man of position. But the great tragedy is this: some ministers do glory in themselves; they do seek to make a good showing and impression in the flesh. Some do seek worldly popularity and recognition.

Note Galatians 6:12 above. This is a much needed lesson for the minister of God. False ministers had infiltrated the churches of Galatia. They opposed both Paul and the gospel he preached. Their major stress was that a person had to undergo the basic ritual of religion, that of circumcision (baptism, confirmation, church membership, etc.). They made circumcision necessary for salvation. If a person was circumcised, he was well on his way to being saved. Paul attacked this position and made a strong charge against false teachers. He charged them with being driven by worldly motives. Keep in mind that he was dealing with false teachers and ministers *within the church*. What he had to say is a strong lesson for teachers of every generation.

First, the false teachers sought to gain the approval of their peers and to escape persecution. They sought the favor of men over the favor of God. Many of the earliest ministers of the gospel were priests who saw Jesus Christ as the Savior of the world. However, they accepted Him only as an addition to the law. They said that Jesus Christ came primarily to show how God wants us to live; therefore, He only added to the law. The law was still important in approaching God: we were to approach God through both the law and Jesus Christ. Therefore, it was unpopular in the ministry of that day to proclaim that *Christ alone was the way to God*. The ministers who proclaimed Christ alone were persecuted through ridicule, mockery, abuse, and rejection. A minister who preached salvation through the cross of Christ alone was thought to be destroying both the law and established religion. Therefore, the ministers of established religion persecuted the ministers of the cross. As a result, it took real courage to stand up and proclaim the truth. Most chose the easy way out and went along with the established ministry in order to avoid the persecution.

You—all of us as ministers of God—need to ask yourself: Do I go along with the *established and popular religion of the world* instead of proclaiming the truth of Jesus Christ and His Word? Do I fear the ridicule, rejection, and abuse of the cross? How often am I tempted to tone down the message of the cross to keep from offending some in the congregation? Do I have to fear reaction if I proclaim the simple message of salvation in the cross of Christ alone? Do I have to fear reaction from my peers and denominational leaders?

Second, the false teachers sought to make a good showing by adding to their statistical numbers (Gal.6:13). Note exactly what Scripture says: they wanted to have people circumcised so that they could boast in their numbers. Their interest was not so much in teaching people to obey the Lord and the law as it was in building up their own security. They wanted recognition through the appearance of a *growing ministry*. They sought the approval and acceptance of people more than the welfare of the people. Their primary concern was the appearance of a growing ministry so that they could secure their own livelihood and position with the people.

People are impressed with increased numbers on statistical growth. Everyone knows this, both religious and lay leaders. As a result, you must guard against the temptation to stress growth in baptisms, church attendance, Bible study, programs, or activities. You must guard against stressing increased numbers, for increased numbers can lead to glorying in oneself. Increased numbers . . .

- build image
- boost egos
- convey success
- enlarge reputation
- secure position
- increase opportunity
- point to gifts and abilities
- stress charisma
- open doors
- help to increase income
- attract attention

b) As a minister, you must glory in one thing and in one thing only: in the cross of Christ (Gal.6:14). The cross of Christ is the *only glory or boast* of a true minister of God, for there is no approach to God other than the cross.

God accepts a person only if he comes to Him by way of the cross. There is no other way to become acceptable to God. Therefore, the true minister has no other message, no other truth of which to boast. Note why: because the cross crucifies the world to you and you to the world. What does this mean?

First, the cross crucifies the world to you. The world has all kinds of attractions that appeal to you, and your flesh sometimes desires the attractions. There are such attractions as . . .

- position
- sex
- power
- pleasure
- acceptance
- honor
- recognition
- food
- money
- possessions

The list could go on and on to include every appealing attraction on earth, but what is the end of all lustful cravings? Deterioration, decay, death, and a sense of judgment. Even man himself ages, dies, and decays. There is nothing on earth that lasts and lives eternally. If you wish to live forever, someone with omnipotent power has to restructure this world. Someone has to destroy the world and remake it, everything in it, including your flesh. The glorious news is that God has done this very thing. God has shown that He loves this world, and He has demonstrated His love in the most perfect way possible. How?

God sent His Son into the world to *die for you* and to free you from this world. When Jesus Christ died upon the cross, He bore the penalty of your transgressions. He took the law's condemnation of death against you and bore the condemnation for you. Therefore, if you believe that Jesus Christ died for you—believe to the point that you truly follow Christ—you shall be saved from this world of death. God declares that He will count you as having been crucified with Christ. You never have to die. When the moment comes for you to pass from this world into the next, God will transfer you right into His presence to live eternally. It will all happen within the blinking of an eye. Because you believe Christ—truly believe and follow Him—you will never die, never taste or experience death.

This is what is meant by the world being crucified to you. *You never have to go the way of the world*, that is, the way of sin, corruption, death, and judgment.

- Jesus Christ died to deliver you from the world, and all its bondages including the bondage of death.
- The Spirit of Jesus Christ (the Holy Spirit) lives within you to give you the power to overcome the world in all its corruptible attractions. Through the Spirit of God, you have the power to conquer the lusts of the flesh.

Second, the cross crucifies you to the world. What does this mean? When you die to the world, you turn away from the attractions and pleasures of the world; therefore, you become unattractive to the world. Worldly men do not like what they see, for you are rejecting the lifestyle and pleasures of the world. Consequently, the worldly want nothing to do with you. They want you out of their way. They want you as nonexistent, as a dead person to them. Therefore, when you come to the cross of Christ, the cross crucifies you to the world and its ways. You are no longer attractive to the world.

The point is this: as a minister of God, you must glory in the cross of Christ, not in yourself. God has given you everything in the cross of Christ, both life now and eternally—both deliverance from the lusts of this world and from the condemnation of the flesh, death, and judgment to come. Therefore, you must not seek worldly popularity and recognition, not seek to make a good impression nor to attract attention to yourself. You must glory in Christ and in Him alone.

6. *You must not preach yourself—lift yourself up—but preach Christ Jesus the Lord.*

> **"For we preach not ourselves, but Christ Jesus the Lord; and ourselves your servants for Jesus' sake" (2 Cor.4:5).**

Thought

The ministry demands servitude—that you be a servant to Jesus Christ and to others. Note two striking points in the Scripture above.

a) You must preach Christ, not yourself.

- You do not preach to build yourself up in the eyes of people.
- You do not preach your own ideas, notions, thoughts, opinions, or philosophy
- You do not preach to impress people with your charisma, ability, fluency, speech, or leadership.

You preach Jesus Christ and Him alone. Note what you preach: "Christ Jesus as Lord." In the Greek, there is no definite article (the). The message of the gospel is that "Christ Jesus is Lord."

- *Christ* means the Messiah, the Messianic Savior promised by God from the beginning of history.
- The Messiah is *Jesus*, the carpenter from Nazareth.
- Jesus is *Lord*, the Lord God Himself.

> **"God hath made that same Jesus, whom ye have crucified, both Lord and Christ" (Acts 2:36).**
> **"And straightway he preached Christ in the synagogues, that he is the Son of God" (Acts 9:20).**
> **"That if thou shalt confess with thy mouth the Lord Jesus, and shalt believe in thine heart that God hath raised him from the dead, thou shalt be saved" (Ro.10:9).**

b) You must serve men, not yourself. Note the word "servant" (doulos): it means bondslave. You are to be a slave to others, serving and ministering to them. You are to be as devoted to people as a slave is to his master, as ready to help them and to meet their needs as a slave would be required to do by his master. Note why: for Jesus' sake. What does this mean?

Jesus became our servant or slave. He sacrificed Himself every day and He did it for us. He struggled to overcome the world and the flesh for our sakes, to conquer sin and lust, to gain freedom from the enslaving bondages and habits of life. Jesus Christ suffered daily and then sacrificed Himself in the ultimate sense by dying and bearing our punishment for us. He gave Himself for our sakes, became a slave to us in order to save us. Therefore, as the Lord's minister, you are to become a servant to men; you are to sacrifice yourself in serving men for the sake of Jesus Christ. You are to do this because Jesus Christ did it for you. No higher service can be done than to serve others for the sake of Christ, the sake of Him who loved you and gave Himself for you.

> **"Whosoever will be great among you, shall be your minister: and whosoever of you will be the chiefest, shall be servant of all" (Mk.10:43-44).**
>
> **"If I then, your Lord and Master, have washed your feet; ye also ought to wash one another's feet" (Jn.13:14).**
>
> **"Bear ye one another's burdens, and so fulfil the law of Christ" (Gal.6:2).**

7. *You must be consistent and teach over a long period of time.*

> **"And when he [Barnabas] had found him [Paul], he brought him unto Antioch. And it came to pass, that [for] a <u>whole year</u> they assembled themselves with the church, and taught much people. And the disciples were called Christians first in Antioch" (Acts 11:26).**
>
> **"And he continued there a <u>year and six months</u>, teaching the word of God among them" (Acts 18:11).**

Thought
You must be consistent and teach over a long period of time. It takes much time to teach the Word of God to people. Your teaching and teaching style are unique: no one else can preach and teach the Word of God quite like you. God has given you the spiritual gift—the spiritual ability—to teach the Word of God in your own unique way. When you teach the Word, some people—not everyone, but some—are able to understand the Word as never before. Therefore, you must be consistent and stay where you are and teach for a long period of time.

Note three facts in Acts 11:26:

a) The purpose for the church meeting together was to be taught about the Lord.

b) "Many people" were taught, not just a few. Many hungered to learn the truth. Not everyone hungered for the truth, but many did. And Paul and Barnabas taught those who hungered. You, too, must teach all who hunger—many or few—within your church.

c) The ministers and the people met consistently for a whole year. They met for intensive training in the Word of God.

Note Acts 18:11 where Paul gave intensive training for eighteen months to the believers in Corinth.

Remember: the believers usually met most nights as well as on Sunday for preaching and teaching. You will have to meet with your people consistently and over a long period of time in order to make the contribution God wants you to make in their lives.

CHAPTER 7

What Your Duty as a Minister Toward False Teaching Must Be

As a minister of Christ, you face false teaching at every turn of life. The world—both the secular and the religious world—is bombarded with false teaching. What does Scripture say about false teaching? What is your duty as a minister toward false teaching? Scripture is very clear in its instructions to you as you deal with false teaching.

Contents

A. YOU AND FALSE TEACHERS OR HERETICS	137
1. You must make sure you are genuine, that you yourself are not a false teacher—not a ravenous wolf in sheep's clothing.	137
2. You must test yourself: Do you believe—really confess and preach—that Jesus Christ has come in the flesh: that God actually sent His Son to earth to save the world?	140
3. You must ask yourself: Am I really truthful? Do I honestly believe and confess that Jesus is the Christ, the Messiah, the Son of God?	145
4. You must not depart from the faith.	147
5. You must guard against those who resist the truth.	151
6. You must guard against those who deny the only Lord God and our Lord Jesus Christ.	152

7. You must reject heretics, false teachers.	154
8. You must reject those who do not teach the words of Christ and the doctrine of godliness.	156
B. You and Other Gospels	162
1. You must not pervert the gospel of Christ nor preach any other gospel.	162
2. You must not bring destructive heresies into the church, heresies that deny the Lord and His death for man.	167
3. You must not preach another Jesus, a Jesus other than the Jesus proclaimed by Scripture and true ministers.	171
C. You and False Doctrine and Teaching	175
1. You must not teach the traditions, ideas, and commandments of men as doctrine.	175
2. You must not be carried away with different kinds of teachings. You must not preach or teach the fables, myths, speculations, ideas, and false doctrines of men.	177
3. You must turn away from empty talk and the opposition of false science and false knowledge.	180
4. You must guard against the false teaching of religion and of the state.	183
5. You must not preach man's empty ideas and discussions—questionable things—but love and faith and the need for a pure conscience.	185

CHAPTER 7
What Your Duty as a Minister Toward False Teaching Must Be

A. YOU AND FALSE TEACHERS OR HERETICS

1. *You must make sure you yourself are genuine, that you yourself are not a false teacher—not a ravenous wolf in sheep's clothing.*

    > "**Beware of false prophets, which come to you in sheep's clothing, but inwardly they are ravening wolves**" **(Mt.7:15).**

    Thought
    This thought may be offensive to some ministers, but we must constantly examine ourselves. Every-one of us—you, me, and all other ministers—must make sure we are genuine, that we are not false teachers—not ravenous wolves in sheep's clothing. These are the words of our Lord Himself (Mt.7:15).

    Now, to make this personal, let each one of us ask ourselves: "Am I sure that I am a genuine minister of Christ? Am I sure that I am not a false teacher, not a ravenous wolf in sheep's clothing? We must always remember this: every false prophet or teacher claims to be a minister and to be representing and teaching the truth. But he is not a true minister nor does he teach the truth of God, not the truth of the only living and true God, not the truth which God has revealed in His Son and in His Holy Word. It is this that makes him a false teacher. Note exactly what Christ says:

    > "**False prophets . . . come to you [God's people] in sheep's clothing, but inwardly they are ravening wolves**" **(Mt.7:15).**

    a) False teachers appear in sheep's clothing, that is, they appear to be committed to Christ just like true ministers and believers. They profess to know Christ and behave like Christians. They claim to be called ministers, and they hold the position of ministers within churches and use Bible verses or texts for their messages. They appear to be messengers of light (2 Cor.11:13-15). They appear harmless, innocent, and good. They start out as excellent examples of society, but they lack two things: a life and a testimony changed by the Word of God.

> **"For such are false apostles, deceitful workers, transforming themselves into the apostles of Christ. And no marvel; for Satan himself is transformed into an angel of light. Therefore it is no great thing if his ministers also be transformed as the ministers of righteousness; whose end shall be according to their works" (2 Cor.11:13-15).**

b) False teachers are ravening wolves: they are anything but sheep.

- Some false teachers are just like wolves in that they may not be aware they are *not* what they should be. They go about doing what they know to do, not knowing that what they do is corrupt and evil (Mt.7:17). They appear as sheep, but consume all they can in order to fill whatever appetite—personal conviction or doctrine—they have.

- Some false teachers are just like wolves in that they are out for self and personal gain: ego, recognition, fame, prestige, position, livelihood, career, and comfort. They are concerned primarily with realizing their own motives and purposes and with pushing their own thoughts and formulas for succeeding in life.

- Some false teachers are just like wolves in that they want a pack in which to move and with which to identify. They want a following to acknowledge their lead in intelligence and creativity or knowledge and ability. They appear as sheep, but they howl their own formulas (false gospels), crying aloud: "This is the way; walk in it." When possible, they use all the media they can: screen, radio, journals, magazines, books, newspapers, pamphlets, and tracts.

c) False teachers preach heresies. They proclaim justice, morality, righteousness, and good. They teach mental and emotional and physical strength; self-image, self-improvement, and positive thinking—all the high ideals and commendable ideas of men. But they never preach the true gospel of the living Lord.

> "I marvel that ye are so soon removed from him that called you into the grace of Christ unto another gospel: which is not another; but there be some that trouble you, and would pervert the gospel of Christ. But though we, or an angel from heaven, preach any other gospel unto you than that which we have preached unto you, let him be accursed. As we said before, so say I now again, If any man preach any other gospel unto you than that ye have received, let him be accursed. For do I now persuade men, or God? or do I seek to please men? for if I yet pleased men, I should not be the servant of Christ" (Gal.1:6-10; cp. Is.56:10-11; Jer.23:1-40; 50:6; Ezk.34:2-3; Jn.10:12).

d) Inwardly false prophets are wolves, real wolves, knowingly or unknowingly. They may appear as sheep, but they are wolves.

- They have not confessed the *Lord Jesus*: that God has raised Him from the dead.

  > "That if thou shalt confess with thy mouth the Lord Jesus, and shalt believe in thine heart that God hath raised him from the dead, thou shalt be saved. For with the heart man believeth unto righteousness; and with the mouth confession is made unto salvation" (Ro.10:9-10).

- They have not "put off the old man" of the world.

  > "That ye put off concerning the former conversation [behavior] the old man, which is corrupt according to the deceitful lusts" (Eph.4:22).

- They have not been "renewed in the spirit of their mind" nor "put on the new man."

  > "And be renewed in the spirit of your mind; and that ye put on the new man, which after God is created in righteousness and true holiness" (Eph.4:23-24).

> "And have put on the new man, which is renewed in knowledge after the image of him that created him" (Col.3:10).
>
> "Therefore if any man be in Christ, he is a new creature: old things are passed away; behold, all things are become new" (2 Cor. 5:17).

- They have not been put into the ministry by God. (Note especially 1 Tim.1:12: the fact that God counts the men whom He chooses as trustworthy.)

> "And I thank Christ Jesus our Lord, who hath enabled me, for that he counted me faithful, putting me into the ministry" (1 Tim.1:12).

e) A false prophet sometimes does not know he is false. He is *deceiving* because he is *being deceived*.

> "But evil men and seducers shall wax worse and worse, deceiving, and being deceived" (2 Tim.3:13).
>
> "In whom the god of this world hath blinded the minds of them which believe not, lest the light of the glorious gospel of Christ, who is the image of God, should shine unto them" (2 Cor.4:4. Cp. 2 Tim.3:1-15.)

As a minister of Christ, you must constantly make sure you are genuine and remaining true to Christ. You must never become a false prophet, a ravenous wolf, out for yourself.

2. *You must test yourself: Do you believe—really confess and preach—that Jesus Christ has come in the flesh: that God actually sent His Son to earth as a man to save the world?*

> "Beloved, believe not every spirit, but try the spirits whether they are of God: because many false prophets are gone out into the world. Hereby know ye the Spirit of God: Every spirit that confesseth that Jesus Christ is come in the flesh is of God: and every spirit that confesseth not that Jesus Christ is come in the flesh is not of God: and this is that spirit of antichrist, whereof ye have heard that it should

come; and even now already is it in the world" (1 Jn.4:1-3).

"For many deceivers are entered into the world, who confess not that Jesus Christ is come in the flesh. This is a deceiver and an antichrist" (2 Jn.7).

Thought
As a minister, your confession and preaching are to be tested and examined by believers. This is reason enough for us to test and examine ourselves.

What is it that makes a teacher true or false? Jesus Christ. What a man believes about Jesus Christ makes the teacher true or false. What a man confesses about Jesus Christ exposes his spirit, a spirit of truth or a spirit of error. And note what it is about Jesus Christ that exposes a teacher: the incarnation. That is, did Jesus Christ—God's own Son—come in the flesh or not?

a) The true spirit, the Spirit of God Himself, confesses that Jesus Christ did come in the flesh, that the incarnation is true. If a minister or teacher has the Spirit of God dwelling in him, then he confesses the incarnation, the wonderful truth that God did become Man and did come to earth to save man. The Spirit of God *cannot confess* anything other than the truth; therefore, every teacher who has the Spirit of God will confess the same truth. He cannot confess anything else because the Spirit of God Himself dwells within him. If he confesses anything else, then the spirit within him is not the Spirit of God. Now note the confession in detail, exactly what it is that a true teacher confesses: "Jesus Christ is come in the flesh."

- The true teacher confesses *Jesus*. The name *Jesus* means *Savior*. It is believing that Jesus Christ did come from God to save man, to be the Savior of the world.

- The true teacher confesses *Christ*. The name *Christ* means *Messiah*, the Anointed One of God. It is believing that Jesus Christ is the promised Messiah of Scripture; that He is the fulfillment of all the prophecies of Scripture; that He is the Anointed Savior sent from God to earth.

- The true teacher confesses that Jesus Christ is the *Son of God*; that God did send His Son *out of* (ek) heaven, out of the spiritual world and dimension into this world; that God sent His Son in human flesh to save man in fulfillment of Scripture. It means that Jesus Christ fulfilled the Scripture predicting the coming death, resurrection, and exaltation of the Messiah. Simply stated, it means that Jesus Christ is the Son of God who came to earth to save man.

This is the confession of the true minister, true teacher, and of every true believer. We must always remember that a true minister and a true teacher are indwelt by the Spirit of God Himself. Therefore, the true minister and the true teacher *will always* confess the incarnation, the wonderful truth that "Jesus Christ is come in the flesh."

> "Therefore the Lord himself shall give you a sign; Behold, a virgin shall conceive, and bear a son, and shall call his name Immanuel" (Is.7:14).
>
> "For unto us a child is born, unto us a son is given: and the government shall be upon his shoulder: and his name shall be called Wonderful, Counsellor, The mighty God, The everlasting Father, The Prince of Peace" (Is.9:6).
>
> "And, behold, thou shalt conceive in thy womb, and bring forth a son, and shalt call his name JESUS" (Lk.1:31).
>
> "And the Word was made flesh, and dwelt among us, (and we beheld his glory, the glory as of the only begotten of the Father,) full of grace and truth" (Jn.1:14).
>
> "And without controversy great is the mystery of godliness: <u>God was manifest</u> [revealed] in the flesh, justified in the Spirit, seen of angels, preached unto the Gentiles, believed on in the world, received up into glory" (1 Tim.3:16).
>
> "Forasmuch then as the children are partakers of flesh and blood, he also himself likewise took part of the same; that through death he might destroy him that had the power of death, that is, the devil;

and deliver them who through fear of death were all their lifetime subject to bondage" (Heb.2:14-15).

b) The false spirit denies that Jesus Christ is come in the flesh. He denies the incarnation. He does not believe that God took on human flesh and became a man.

- The false teacher does not believe that Jesus Christ is the Savior of the world. He may accept Jesus Christ as a great teacher and a great religious leader, perhaps the greatest, but he does not believe that Jesus Christ is *the Savior*. He believes that there are other ways to God, that other people who believe in God will be as acceptable to God as a follower of Jesus Christ.

- The false teacher does not believe that Jesus is the Christ, the promised Messiah and Anointed One from God. He does not believe that the Scriptures are the inspired Word of God. He accepts them only as the writings of great religious people of the past; therefore, there are no prophetic promises of a Messiah, no promise of a coming Savior. To the false teacher, Jesus Christ is only a great religious teacher, only one way to reach God. He is not *the Anointed One* sent from God to save all men. He is not the only way to God.

- The false teacher does not believe that Jesus Christ has *come from God*. He does not believe that Jesus Christ is the Son of God, that Jesus Christ came out of heaven, out from the spiritual world and dimension. He does not believe that God sent His Son into the world in human flesh as a man. Again, the false teacher believes that Jesus Christ is only a man just like all other men—a great man, perhaps the greatest, perhaps the man who got closer to God than any other man. Nevertheless, to the false teacher Jesus Christ was only a man who taught us how to worship and serve God. The false teacher would say . . .

    - that Jesus Christ was not sinless. He lived close to God, but no man can achieve sinlessness.
    - that Jesus Christ died, but not as a substitute for man's sins. He died as a great martyr showing us how we

should face death and how we should be willing to die for the great cause of righteousness.

- that the resurrection of Jesus Christ did not take place. It is only a picture of the spiritual truth that man can live in God's presence.

Now, note the fatal mistake of the false teachers: to deny that Jesus Christ has come in the flesh is to deny that man can ever be saved beyond this world. Why? Because man can never know for sure that God exists nor can he know how to reach God if He does exist. No person has ever seen God or heaven, and no person ever will, not by physical and material technology. This physical world cannot penetrate or cross over into the spiritual world and dimension, no matter what some persons may claim. If man is ever to know God and the spiritual world, then God has to come to earth and reveal the truth to us. There is no other way. Therefore, to deny that God sent His Son into the world is to deny that we can ever be saved.

There is another fact that needs to be noted as well, that of perfection. God is perfect and man is imperfect. Therefore, God could never let man penetrate or cross over into perfection. Why? Because man's imperfection would affect the perfect world of God. Heaven would no longer be heaven; it would no longer be perfect if God allowed imperfect beings to enter it. No matter what some people may claim about penetrating heaven, they have not. Imperfection just cannot cross over into perfection. The fatal mistake of false teachers is just that, *fatal*—fatal and eternally dooming. The consequences of denying the incarnation of Jesus Christ are terrible. If Jesus Christ has not come in the flesh, then it means . . .

- that God has not loved us enough to reveal Himself to us (1 Jn.1:2).

- that God has not loved us enough to send us the Word of life (1 Jn.1:1).

- that God has not loved us enough to show us eternal life (1 Jn.1:2).

- that there is no eternal life (1 Jn.1:2).

- that there is no fellowship with God, not for sure (1 Jn.1:3).
- that the message of hope and of Scripture are not true, not for sure (1 Jn.1:3).
- that there is no joy beyond this life, not for sure, no fulness of joy (1 Jn.1:4).
- that Jesus Christ is not our Advocate (1 Jn.2:2).
- that there is no forgiveness of sin (1 Jn.1:9; 2:2).
- that there is no perfect sacrifice for sin (1 Jn.2:2).

On and on the list could go, but the point is clearly seen. The false teacher destroys the hope of salvation and of eternity with God. We are left without hope and without God in this world unless God has loved us, loved us so much that He sent His Son Jesus Christ into this world. Jesus Christ is the crux of the message of the gospel. Note that the spirit of the false teacher is the spirit of antichrist (see *The Preacher's Outline & Sermon Bible,*® outline and notes—1 Jn.2:18-23). If a teacher confesses that Jesus Christ is come in the flesh, he is a true teacher. If not, he is a false teacher who promotes the very spirit of antichrist.

> **"Beloved, believe not every spirit, but try the spirits" (1 Jn.4:1).**
>
> **"But whosoever shall deny me before men, him will I also deny before my Father which is in heaven" (Mt.10:33).**
>
> **"Whosoever therefore shall be ashamed of me and of my words in this adulterous and sinful generation; of him also shall the Son of man be ashamed, when he cometh in the glory of his Father with the holy angels" (Mk.8:38).**

3. *You must ask yourself: Am I really truthful? Do I honestly believe and confess that Jesus is the Christ, the Messiah, the Son of God?*

> **"Who is a liar but he that denieth that Jesus is the Christ? He is antichrist, that denieth the Father and the Son. Whosoever denieth the Son, the same hath not the Father: (but) he that acknowledgeth the Son hath the Father also" (1 Jn.2:22-23).**

Thought

As a minister of Christ, you must be truthful to yourself and to people. Do you honestly believe and confess that Jesus is the Christ, the Messiah, the Son of God?

The false teacher is antichrist: he stands against Christ. He is a person who denies that Jesus is the Messiah, the very Son of God whom God had promised to send as the Savior of the world. Two terrible things are said about this person (note the above verse): first, he is a liar; and second, he denies the Father if he denies the Son, the Lord Jesus Christ. Why is this so? How is it that a person denies God if he denies Christ? The answer is twofold.

First, if a person denies that God sent His Son into the world, then his image of God differs entirely from the God who is the Father of Jesus Christ. God has sent His Son into the world. Therefore, if we picture a *god* in our minds that did not send His Son, then our image of God differs entirely from the true and living God. The true and living God is love, perfect love. Therefore, He has loved man perfectly. God has done the greatest thing that can be done for man: He has sent His only Son into the world to save man by dying for man's sins. No greater love could ever be demonstrated for man. Therefore, if a man says that God did not send His Son into the world—that Jesus Christ is not the Son of God—then that man is thinking of some *god* other than the Father of the Lord Jesus Christ.

- By denying Jesus Christ, the man denies the Father.
- By denying the Son, the man does not have the Father, not the Father of the Lord Jesus Christ. He is separated from the Father, standing against and opposed to both God and His Son, the Lord Jesus Christ. The man is doomed, for he has denied that God loves the world enough to send His Son to save the world.

Second, any person who denies Jesus Christ is denying the New Testament. Why? Because the New Testament says time and again that Jesus Christ is the Son of God, the one Person who reveals God the Father to the world. Just a few of the verses are these (the whole Gospel of John was written for the very purpose of *revealing the Son of God* to the world):

> "All things are delivered unto me of my Father: and no man knoweth the Son, but the Father; neither knoweth any man the Father, save the Son, and he to whomsoever the Son will reveal him" (Mt.11:27).
>
> "Jesus cried and said, He that believeth on me, believeth not on me, but on him that sent me. And he that seeth me seeth him that sent me" (Jn.12:44-45).
>
> "Jesus saith unto him, I am the way, the truth, and the life: no man cometh unto the Father, but by me" (Jn.14:6).
>
> "Jesus saith unto him, Have I been so long time with you, and yet hast thou not known me, Philip? he that hath seen me hath seen the Father; and how sayest thou then, Show us the Father? Believest thou not that I am in the Father, and the Father in me? the words that I speak unto you I speak not of myself: but the Father that dwelleth in me, he doeth the works" (Jn.14:9-10).

The point is clear: any person who denies Jesus Christ is denying the Father of Jesus Christ, God Himself, the only living and true God. Any person who denies that Jesus Christ is the Son of God is a false teacher, a forerunner of the antichrist.

4. *You must not depart from the faith.*

> "Now the Spirit speaketh expressly, that in the latter times some shall <u>depart from the faith</u>, giving heed to seducing spirits, and doctrines of devils; speaking lies in hypocrisy; having their conscience seared with a hot iron" (1 Tim.4:1-2).

Thought

As a minister, you must not depart from the faith. God has called you to preach and teach the glorious gospel of His dear Son. This you must do: you must never turn away from your calling. You must never commit apostasy; you must not become an apostate.

But note the above Scripture: the Holy Spirit clearly warns that some ministers will turn away. And note where they come from: from within the church. There was a time when they actually held to the faith, a time when they believed and taught the

Word of God. But they turned away from the Word of God and from God's Son, the Lord Jesus Christ, who alone can save us.

As stated in the verse, this is a warning from the Spirit of God Himself. Therefore, it is a warning that every minister must heed. The Spirit of God gives three warnings.

a) As a minister, you must not give attention to seducing spirits and teachings of devils. There are all kinds of evil spirits throughout the world, spirits that are set on seducing and deceiving you. They are set on leading you to follow them and their ideas and teachings. They do all they can to turn you away from the doctrine and faith of Christ. And note: the method they use is not a frontal attack, not a clear or loud declaration against the truth. They mix some truth with error. Their method is to . . .

- seduce
- lure
- persuade
- deceive
- entice
- charm
- delude
- attract
- appear as light and truth

> "For such are false apostles [representatives of Christ], deceitful workers, transforming themselves into the apostles of Christ. And no marvel; for Satan himself is transformed into an angel of light. Therefore it is no great thing if his ministers also be transformed as the ministers of righteousness; whose end shall be according to their works" (2 Cor.11:13-15).
>
> "For there are many unruly and vain talkers and deceivers, specially they of the circumcision [religionists]: whose mouths must be stopped, who subvert whole houses, teaching things which they ought not, for filthy lucre's sake [personal gain, livelihood]" (Tit.1:10-11).

b) You must not speak lies in hypocrisy. Very simply, you must not teach something different from what the Scripture says. There are some who know they are not teaching what Scripture says. In fact, they take pride in their stand against what they call "a literal interpretation" of Scripture. They even mock and poke fun at those who believe and hold to the truth of Scripture. But note what is so often overlooked:

- "Speaking lies" means speaking and teaching what is contrary to Scripture. This is exactly what Scripture is declaring. In the eyes of Scripture, a lie is a teaching that is contrary to the teaching of Scripture.
- "In hypocrisy" means the teacher knows that he is teaching contrary to Scripture. He claims to be a minister or teacher of God, Christ, and the Word (Scripture); and yet he teaches something contrary to what Scripture says. A hypocrite is a person who claims to be one thing but he is something else.

The point is this: you must not be a person who speaks lies in hypocrisy. The false teacher denies, refutes, or ignores what Scripture says and he knows it; yet he claims to be a minister or teacher of Christ and the gospel. This is the minister who is an instrument or tool of some seducing and deceptive spirit, a minister who teaches the doctrines of evil spirits. As the minister of Christ, you must never be a hypocrite. You must not speak lies in hypocrisy. You must never allow yourself to turn away from the faith.

> "Now I beseech you, brethren, mark them which cause divisions and offences contrary to the doctrine which ye have learned; and avoid them. For they that are such serve not our Lord Jesus Christ, but their own belly; and by good words and fair speeches deceive the hearts of the simple" (Ro.16:17-18).
>
> "Beware lest any man spoil you through philosophy and vain deceit, after the tradition of men, after the rudiments [elementary notions and teachings] of the world, and not after Christ" (Col.2:8).
>
> "They profess that they know God; but in works they deny him, being abominable, and disobedient, and unto every good work reprobate" (Tit.1:16).

William Barclay has an excellent statement on men becoming tools of Satan and of evil spirits.

"It was from these evil spirits and demons that this false teaching came. But though it came from the demons, it came through men.... Now here is the threatening and the terrible thing. We know that God and God's Spirit are everywhere looking for men to use. God is always searching for men who will be His instruments, His weapons, His tools in the world. But here we come face to face with the terrible fact that the forces of evil are also looking for men to use. Just as God seeks men for His purposes, the forces of evil seek men for their purposes. Here is the terrible responsibility of manhood. Man can accept the service of God, or the service of the devil. Man can become an instrument of the Supreme Good or the Supreme Evil. Men are faced with the eternal choice—to whom are we to give our lives, to God or to God's enemy? Are we to decide to be used by God, or are we to decide to be used by the devil?" (*The Letters to Timothy, Titus, and Philemon,* p.107).

c) You must guard your conscience lest it become seared, that is cauterized, hardened, and insensitive. It does not bother most false teachers to teach contrary to the truth of Scripture. They can ignore and deny the Scripture and present their own ideas and it does not bother them at all. They are totally insensitive to the pricking and convictions of God's Spirit. They have no conscience and no remorse about twisting the Scriptures and the truth about Christ. They are completely past feeling any kind of movement from God's Spirit.

You must not let this happen to you. You are the minister of Christ. You must not allow any teaching in your life that would harden your conscience. You must never turn away from the faith.

> **"For the heart of this people is waxed gross, and their ears are dull of hearing, and their eyes have they closed; lest they should see with their eyes, and hear with their ears, and understand with their heart, and should be converted, and I should heal them" (Acts 28:27).**

> "For if after they have escaped the pollutions of the world through the knowledge of the Lord and Saviour Jesus Christ, they are again entangled therein, and overcome, the latter end is worse with them than the beginning. For it had been better for them not to have known the way of righteousness, than, after they have known it, to turn from the holy commandment delivered unto them. But it is happened unto them according to the true proverb, The dog is turned to his own vomit again; and the sow that was washed to her wallowing in the mire" (2 Pt.2:20-22).
>
> "Happy is the man that feareth always: but he that hardeneth his heart shall fall into mischief" (Pr.28:14).

5. *You must guard against those who resist the truth.*

> "Now as Jannes and Jambres withstood Moses, so do these [false teachers] also resist the truth: men of corrupt minds, reprobate concerning the faith. But they shall proceed no further: for their folly shall be manifest unto all men, as theirs also was" (2 Tim.3:8-9).

Thought
There are corrupt ministers and teachers who resist the truth. Why? Because their *minds are corrupted*, that is, their understanding of the gospel is twisted, distorted, and depraved. They do not follow the glorious news and power of the death and resurrection of the Lord Jesus Christ.

Note the reference to Jannes and Jambres, two religious leaders in Egypt. They opposed Moses when he went to Pharoah to deliver Israel out of slavery. They stood toe to toe with Moses and resisted the truth, but in the end they were destroyed (cp. Ex.7:1; 8:7; 9:11). The two men are not named in the Old Testament, but they are mentioned in other Jewish religious writings. Their names were apparently well known to all Jews.

William Barclay clearly describes the resistance to the truth of the gospel:

"The Christian leader will never lack his opponents. There will always be those who prefer their ideas to God's ideas. There will always be those who wish to exercise power and influence over people and who will stoop to any means to do so. There will always be those who have their own twisted ideas of the Christian faith, and who wish to win others to their mistaken belief. But of one thing Paul was sure—the days of the deceivers were numbered. Their falsity would be demonstrated; and they would receive their own appropriate place and reward" (*The Letters to Timothy, Titus, and Philemon*, p.223).

Note the end of corrupt ministers. Their corrupt teaching and religion will be exposed. In the end all false teachers and their teaching will be tracked down and exposed. God will catch and expose every corrupt minister. It will happen when the Lord Jesus Christ returns. Corrupt ministers and their corrupt teaching will *proceed no further*. As a God-called minister, you must guard against those who resist the truth.

> **"And to you who are troubled rest with us, when the Lord Jesus shall be revealed from heaven with his mighty angels, in flaming fire taking vengeance on them that know not God, and that obey not the gospel of our Lord Jesus Christ: who shall be punished with everlasting destruction from the presence of the Lord, and from the glory of his power" (2 Th.1:7-9).**

6. *You must guard against those who deny the only Lord God and our Lord Jesus Christ.*

> **"For there are certain men crept in unawares [unnoticed, unknowingly], who were before of old ordained to this condemnation, ungodly men, turning the grace of our God into lasciviousness, and denying the Lord God, and our Lord Jesus Christ" (Jude 4).**

Thought

As a God-called minister, you must guard against those who deny our only Master and Lord, Jesus Christ. Your only Master and Lord is Jesus Christ; therefore, you are to serve and obey Him and Him alone. Note three points in the above verse.

a) False teachers creep into the church unknowingly. They are *not God-called* teachers. They choose to teach in the church as a profession or as a way to serve people and to teach the morals and virtues of life. The idea is that they entered the church unnoticed. They did not believe in Jesus Christ, that He is the Son of God who came to earth to save man. Therefore, they do not belong in the church. But they joined it for the benefit and opportunities it brought them. They accepted the teachings of Christ, believed that He was a great religious leader, but they denied His deity.

> **"For such are false apostles, deceitful workers, transforming themselves into the apostles of Christ. And no marvel; for Satan himself is transformed into an angel of light. Therefore it is no great thing if his ministers also be transformed as the ministers of righteousness; whose end shall be according to their works" (2 Cor.11:13-15).**

b) False teachers are ordained to judgment. They reject Jesus Christ; therefore, judgment is waiting for them. God has ordained from the beginning of time that all unbelievers shall be judged. And both Jesus Christ and Scripture teach that the judgment for false teachers is to be far more severe than for other persons.

> **"I marvel that ye are so soon removed from him that called you into the grace of Christ unto another gospel: which is not another; but there be some that trouble you, and would pervert the gospel of Christ. But though we, or an angel from heaven, preach any other gospel unto you than that which we have preached unto you, let him be accursed. As we said before, so say I now again, If any man preach any other gospel unto you than that ye have received, let him be accursed" (Gal.1:6-9).**

c) False teachers are ungodly. They do not live like God; they are different from God. They have a different lifestyle than what God would have if He was walking upon earth. God is perfect, moral, pure, just, and loving. But false teachers are not moral, pure, just, or loving. They are deceptive, leading people away from the love and purity of God, the love and purity revealed in His Son, the Lord Jesus Christ. They do not teach the truth of God's love and purity demonstrated in Christ. They profane God and the truth of His love and godliness.

> **"For the wrath of God is revealed from heaven against all ungodliness and unrighteousness of men, who hold the truth in unrighteousness" (Ro.1:18).**

7. *You must reject heretics, false teachers.*

> **"A man that is an heretic after the first and second admonition reject; knowing that he that is such is subverted, and sinneth, being condemned of himself" (Tit.3:10-11).**

Thought
As a minister of Christ, you must reject heretics, those who forsake the truth of Christ and of God's Word. The Greek word "heretic" (hairetikos) is interesting. It means to take for oneself; to choose for oneself. Therefore, a heretic is a person who chooses what he is to believe, who takes false teaching as his own. He rejects all authority no matter what it is: God, Christ, the Word of God, the church, man. He himself chooses what he is to believe. He and he alone is his authority; he and he alone determines truth—what is and what is not truth. Note two significant points.

First, this heretic is in the church; he associates with believers. This is the picture of most heretics. Few reject all the teachings of Christ and of the Bible. Most heretics remain in the church, holding to some basic teachings but rejecting those doctrines they do not like. The Scripture is clear: you and the church *are to reach out* to the heretic or false teacher. He is not to be lambasted, rejected, and expelled from the church. An attempt is to be made to reach him for Christ. In fact, Scripture says two strong attempts are to be made to reach him. He is to be shown love and care and admonished to repent and confess the truth of Christ and His Word. But note: there is a limit. On the third try, if he does not repent he is to be rejected, that is, expelled from the church. He is not to be allowed to lead other believers astray. (See *The Preacher's Outline & Sermon Bible,*® outline and notes—Mt.18:15-20 for more detailed discussion on church discipline as taught by Christ.)

Second, the heretic is "subverted" (ektrepo). This means he is twisted and has turned away from the truth of Christ and His Word. Note that the heretic sins. The idea is that he sins greatly. Therefore, he condemns himself. He has chosen the path of unbelief, and he will be condemned for his unbelief.

> "He that believeth on him is not condemned: but he that believeth not is condemned already, because he hath not believed in the name of the only begotten Son of God" (Jn.3:18).

The point is clear to the thinking and honest minister, and honesty is as necessary as the willingness to think about the issue. A person who uses the scissors of self-opinion and cuts up Christ and the Word of God—casting away some of the teachings concerning Him and His Word—is considered a heretic by the Bible. It does not matter who he is: preacher, teacher, or layman. This is the person called a heretic by the Bible. If he turns or twists himself out of the truth of Christ and Scripture, he is a heretic. Therefore, he is to be approached in love and admonished on two specific occasions. If he rejects the two admonitions, he should be approached a third time, and then rejected if he still refuses to repent. He should be rejected and expelled even if he is a minister and teacher in the church.

A striking and tragic question is this—a question that God will surely answer in that great and terrible day of judgment: How many millions of people have been led astray within our churches by false teachers, those whom the Bible calls heretics—those who have turned away from the truth of Christ and of His Word?

> "Moreover if thy brother shall trespass against thee, go and tell him his fault between thee and him alone: if he shall hear thee, thou hast gained

thy brother. But if he will not hear thee, then take with thee one or two more, that in the mouth of two or three witnesses every word may be established. And if he shall neglect to hear them, tell it unto the church: but if he neglect to hear the church, let him be unto thee as an heathen man and a publican" (Mt.18:15-17).

"But there were false prophets also among the people, even as there shall be false teachers among you, who privily [quietly, secretly] shall bring in damnable heresies, even denying the Lord that bought them, and bring upon themselves swift destruction" (2 Pt.2:1).

8. *You must reject those who do not teach the words of Christ and the doctrine of godliness.*

"If any man <u>teach otherwise</u>, and consent not to wholesome words, even the words of our Lord Jesus Christ, and to the doctrine which is according to godliness; he is proud, knowing nothing, but doting about questions and strifes of words, whereof cometh envy, strife, railings, evil surmisings, perverse disputings of men of corrupt minds, and destitute of the truth, supposing that gain is godliness: from such withdraw thyself" (1 Tim.6:3-5).

Thought

As a minister of Christ, you must reject those who do not teach the words of Christ and the doctrine of godliness. You are the minister of Christ, His representative upon earth; therefore, you must oppose and reject those who teach a different doctrine. This is a terrible indictment. Imagine being in the pulpit of a Christian church and claiming to be a teacher of the Lord Jesus Christ, yet not teaching His words. How many of us are guilty of this indictment? How many of us are guilty of teaching a different doctrine? Two reasons are given as to why the false teacher teaches a different doctrine.

First, the false teacher does not *consent* to the words of our Lord Jesus Christ. The word "consent" (proserchomai) means *approach* and has the sense of "attaching oneself to" Christ (Daniel Guthrie. *The Pastoral Epistles.* "Tyndale New Testament Commentaries." Grand Rapids, MI: Eerdmans, 1972, p.110f). The false teacher is just not willing to attach himself to the *Lord Jesus Christ.*

- He is not willing to confess that Jesus is the *Lord God* from heaven, the very Son of God Himself.
- He is not willing to confess that Jesus is the Christ, the Messiah and Savior of the world.

Second, the false teacher does not consent to the teachings of godliness.

- He is not willing to accept the righteousness of God revealed in Jesus Christ.
- He is not willing to separate himself from the world nor to set his life wholly apart unto God.

One or both of these reasons are why the false teacher does not teach the wholesome words of Christ, but rather chooses to teach a different doctrine and way of life. He has committed his life to the *profession* of the ministry . . .

- as a way to serve mankind.
- as a way to earn a livelihood.

But he is not committed to represent Christ and His Word. As a result, the person is called a false teacher by both the Holy Scriptures and Christ. The above Scripture says four things about the false teacher.

a) The false teacher is proud (tetuphotai). The word means *puffed up* and conceited. But note: the word includes the idea of folly; it lacks good sense. Rejecting the evidence that Jesus is the Lord—the Lord Jesus Christ—is the height of pride and folly. Such rejection just lacks good sense (source unknown).

The false teacher takes pride . . .

- in his views and ideas.
- in his rejection of certain portions of the Bible.
- in his knowledge that some of the stories and events in the Bible are what he calls fables or myths.

- in his intellectual ability to dissect the truth from the falsehood about Christ.
- in his enlightenment—that he knows better than to believe in such things as the miracles, deity, virgin birth, incarnation, resurrection, ascension, and the personal return of Christ to earth.
- in his new and novel concepts and ideas about Christ.

The list could go on and on, but all ministers have detected this pride in discussions with other ministers. And, tragically, we have all been guilty of feeling pride over our own ideas. William Barclay has an excellent comment on the pride of the false teacher:

> "His first characteristic is conceit. His first aim is self-display. His desire is not to display Christ, but to display himself. There are still preachers and teachers who are more concerned to gain a following for themselves than for Jesus Christ. They are more concerned to press their own views upon people than they are to bring to men the word of God. When people meet together for worship they are not concerned to listen to what any man thinks; they are eager to hear what God says. The great preacher and teacher is not a purveyor of his own ideas; he is an echo of God" (*The Letters to Timothy, Titus, and Philemon*, p.146).

b) The false teacher has a sick interest in controversial questions. When preparing to preach and teach, the false teacher does not rely upon the primary source, the Word of God. He relies upon secondary sources, that is, books *about* the Bible.

The Bible is not the basis for his life nor for his preaching and teaching. The false teacher rejects the primary source (the Bible), and turns to secondary sources *about* the Bible. In some cases, he does not even know how to study the Bible. His interest lies . . .

- in trying to *discover* the truth in the Bible, not in proclaiming the truth of the Bible.
- in *questioning* what is true and not true instead of living out what the Bible says.

The result, of course, is what we so often see written in the faces and minds of the false teacher and those who sit under him: many thoughts and moments of . . .

- disturbance and lack of peace
- wondering if God really does exist
- emptiness and lack of purpose
- wondering if there is really any meaning to religion and worship
- questioning life and lacking meaning in life
- wondering if there really is a world or life beyond this earth

Why? Because what the human heart craves is God and His Word, the knowledge and assurance of Him and His guidance.

This is only reasonable and to be expected, for God—the Creator and Giver of life—is bound to have put within man a deep, natural hunger for Him and His Word. Therefore, what the human heart craves, even the heart of the false teacher, is not controversial questions and arguments over the "words of our Lord Jesus Christ" or of the Bible. What the heart craves is to hear from God, to hear the *authoritative proclamation of the Word of God itself.*

c) The false teacher has a corrupt mind and is destitute of the truth. His mind is corrupt in this very thing: it is not centered upon teaching the "words of our Lord Jesus Christ and the doctrine . . . of godliness" (the Word of God, the Scriptures, the Bible. 1 Tim.6:3). His mind . . .

- focuses upon the doctrines and theologies of men.
- focuses upon the psychologies and philosophies of men.
- focuses upon man's own energy and self-improvement, upon building up man's ego and self-image.
- focuses upon the latest religions or theological ideas.
- focuses upon the popular religious discussions that please and tickle men's ears.

The point is this: the false teacher does not focus upon the truth, the Word of God. He is destitute and empty of the truth. He does not possess nor teach the truth. He is bankrupt when it comes to the truth. However, note: what the false teacher teaches often helps us do better: it often helps to build our ego and self-image and to achieve more in this life. Some self-help preaching is just like some self-help programs, clinics, and seminars conducted all across the nation: they are excellent in so far as they go. But they have one serious flaw: *they do not go far enough*. They do not show . . .

- that God is really with us and looking after us as we walk upon earth.
- that Jesus Christ has really died for our sins and risen to give us life—life that goes on forever.
- that God has really forgiven our sins and accepted us in Christ.
- that when we die, God will immediately transfer us into His presence to live with Him forever.

This kind of absolute, intense assurance is missing in the false teacher and in anyone else whose mind is not focused upon "the words of our Lord Jesus Christ and the doctrine . . . of godliness," that is, the Word of God (1 Tim.6:3).

d) The false teacher thinks religion leads to gain. This means at least three things.

- Some false teachers *are concerned* with morality and virtue and with man being the best and achieving the most that he can. They believe in God, not necessarily in Christ, but in God. Therefore, they know the answer to making man and his world better is religion. Hence, they commit their lives to God and religion, to getting men to do the works of religion and to living more righteous and moral lives. They want people to be good and to do good. They think that "godliness is gain," that it helps and benefits man and his world.

  Note that the false teacher is right on this point: the moral teaching of religion—living moral and upright lives—is good for man. But as pointed out above, works and self-help ministers do not go far enough. They do not focus upon God's Son, the Lord Jesus Christ. And God will never accept anyone who *does not honor* His Son, for God has only one Son who is begotten of Him, only one Son whom He loves with the *most perfect love* eternally possible.

- Some false teachers enter the ministry as a profession and as a means to make a living. They probably have some concern for the religious welfare of people, but the major consideration in choosing to enter the ministry was this: they thought it would be a good and commendable profession and provide a good livelihood for them and their present or future family.
- Some false teachers have commercialized religion. This false teacher is "out for profit. He looks on his teaching and preaching, not as a vocation, but as a career. He is in the business, not to serve others, but to advance himself" (William Barclay. *The Letters to Timothy, Titus, and Philemon*, p.148).

The exhortation of Scripture to the minister is clear, direct, and forceful: "from such withdraw." We must not sit under, associate, or have anything to do with the person who is a false minister and teacher. The church is not the place for professionalism nor for the doctrine of human effort and works (humanism).

Man-centered and self-help teaching is helpful, but it does not belong in the pulpit of God's church; it belongs in the conference rooms and halls of the secular world. The church must be kept pure and free in proclaiming the gospel and the supreme love of God demonstrated in His Son, the Lord Jesus Christ. If the human race fails to keep the pure Word of God flowing from the pulpits of God's church, then the human race is doomed. Why? Because when we die, that will be it. We shall be separated from God eternally. For God will only accept us if we approach Him in Christ. Therefore, the critical hour for man will always be when he sits under the preaching of the Word of God—the preaching of "the words of our Lord Jesus Christ and the doctrine . . . of godliness." When man hears the Word of God preached, he must respond and do as God says.

> "Now I beseech you, brethren, mark them which cause divisions and offences contrary to the doctrine which ye have learned; and avoid them. For they that are such serve not our Lord Jesus Christ, but their own belly [desires, ambitions]; and by good words and fair speeches deceive the hearts of the simple" (Ro.16:17-18).
>
> "Having a form of godliness, but denying the power thereof: from such turn away" (2 Tim.3:5).
>
> "If there come any unto you, and bring not this doctrine, receive him not into your house, neither bid him God speed: for he that biddeth him God speed is partaker of his evil deeds" (2 Jn.10-11).

B. YOU AND OTHER GOSPELS

1. *You must not pervert the gospel of Christ nor preach any other gospel.*

    > "I marvel that ye are so soon removed from him that called you into the grace of Christ unto another gospel: which is not another; but there be some that trouble you, and would pervert the gospel of Christ. But though we, or an angel from heaven, preach any other gospel unto you than that which we have preached unto you, let him be accursed. As we said before, so say I now again, If any man preach any other gospel unto you than that ye have received, let him be accursed" (Gal.1:6-9).
    >
    > "For I know this, that after my departing shall grievous wolves enter in among you, not sparing the flock. Also of your own selves shall men arise, speaking perverse things, to draw away disciples after them" (Acts 20:29-30).

Thought

As a God-called minister, you must not pervert the gospel of Christ nor preach any other gospel. This is critical, an absolute essential. The very souls of people are at stake. This is a strong warning, but Paul had no choice. Paul had to be strong in writing these words, for Christ had taught that the value of a single soul was worth more than *all the wealth* of the world.

> "For what shall it profit a man, if he shall gain the whole world, and lose his own soul? Or what shall a man give in exchange for his soul?" (Mk.8:36-37).

Forcefully and powerfully, Paul warns us—all of us who are ministers—God has only one message: the gospel of Christ. It is God's gospel and God's gospel alone that must be preached, taught, and heeded. Three warnings are issued.

a) You must not preach and teach "another gospel." The word "another" (heteron) means a different kind of gospel, not just a difference in emphasis or spirit (A.T. Robertson. *Word Pictures in the New Testament*, Vol.4. Nashville, TN: Broadman Press, 1931, p.276). It means a different kind of gospel that presents . . .

- a different Jesus
- a different grace
- a different way to be saved
- a different God
- a different picture of God's love

But note what Scripture declares: there is *not another gospel*. There is no other gospel; there is only one true gospel by which men can become acceptable to God, and that is the gospel of God Himself revealed in the death of His Son, even "the grace of Christ" (Gal.1:6).

You must never preach another gospel. There is only one true gospel, the gospel of our Lord Jesus Christ.

> "For God so loved the world, that he gave his only begotten Son, that whosoever believeth in him should not perish, but have everlasting life" (Jn.3:16).
>
> "Then Simon Peter answered him, Lord, to whom shall we go? thou hast the words of eternal life" (Jn.6:68).
>
> "I said therefore unto you, that ye shall die in your sins: for if ye believe not that I am he, ye shall die in your sins" (Jn.8:24).

> "Neither is there salvation in any other: for there is none other name under heaven given among men, whereby we must be saved" (Acts 4:12).
>
> "For I determined not to know any thing among you, save Jesus Christ, and him crucified" (1 Cor.2:2).
>
> "For other foundation can no man lay than that is laid, which is Jesus Christ" (1 Cor.3:11).

b) You must not pervert the gospel of Christ. The word "pervert" (metastrepsai) means to turn about, to change completely, to distort. You must not take the gospel of God's love as demonstrated in His Son, Jesus Christ, and change it. In Paul's day, the false teachers claimed to be Christians, followers of Christ. They even believed with Paul . . .

- that God loved the world and sent His Son into the world.
- that Jesus Christ was the Son of God who actually came to earth.
- that Jesus Christ died and arose from the dead.

However, the false teachers were adding to and taking away from the gospel; they were twisting its meaning and making it say something entirely different from the Scripture Paul preached. They distorted the gospel by saying . . .

1) That God did show His love for the world by sending His Son, but He sent His Son in particular for the religious person (the Jew and the religionist). They were saying that God loves the world, but He especially loves the people who live religious lives. (Note how this makes God show favoritism and partiality and opens the door for caste systems and prejudice.)

2) That Jesus Christ did come to earth; however, it was not to secure a perfect righteousness for men, but to show men how to live a good life that pleases God and merits God's approval.

3) That Jesus Christ did die for man; however, He did not die for man's sin. He died to show man how he should be willing to die for God's cause.

4) That the death of Jesus Christ is not sufficient by itself; it cannot stand alone; it is not enough to make man acceptable to God. More is needed than the raw love of God and the pure grace of Christ.

5) That a person was saved and secure if he underwent the ritual that had been the main ritual of believers down through the centuries: circumcision (church membership, baptism, confirmation, etc.).

6) That a person must work to keep the law of God and certain church ceremonies and rituals, rules and regulations.

Note how devastating the false teaching was: believers were troubled, that is, disturbed, bewildered, perplexed, confused. They were not only turning away from the gospel, but from God Himself and from the glorious grace of Christ (Gal.1:6).

Note a shocking fact: how close false teaching within the church is to the truth! How a little addition here and a little subtraction there distorts the purity of the gospel! You must guard against adding your own ideas to the gospel of God. You must never pervert nor twist the gospel of Christ.

> **"In vain they do worship me, teaching for doctrines the commandments of men" (Mt.15:9).**
>
> **"For I know this, that after my departing shall grievous wolves enter in among you, not sparing the flock. Also of your own selves shall men arise, speaking perverse things, to draw away disciples after them" (Acts 20:29-30).**
>
> **"We are not as many, which corrupt the word of God" (2 Cor.2:17).**

c) You will be accursed if you preach a false gospel. No matter who you are, what position you hold, and what you claim, you will be accursed if you hold to a false gospel. This is a strong statement, but it is clearly understandable. The gospel is the means by which men are saved out of the grip of sin, death, and condemnation. Without the gospel no person is saved—no person can become acceptable to God—no person can inherit eternal life. Scripture is clear about the matter and warns you and all other ministers. Note how clear Scripture declares the fact.

1) The gospel is greater than the apostle Paul himself. This is a striking statement, for remember who Paul was: probably the most committed servant of God who has ever lived. He had ventured forth as a pioneer into the heathen areas of the world to reach people with the gospel of Christ, the good news that men could be delivered from sin and death and live forever. He loved the Galatians so much that he had risked all he was and had for their sake. To some Paul must have been a giant, and he must have been held ever so dear to their hearts. But note what Paul says: if he returned to them preaching any other gospel, he was to be accursed. The Galatians were not to receive him no matter how much they esteemed him: they were to reject him. The gospel in all its simplicity and purity was far more important than Paul himself.

2) The gospel is greater than the angels from heaven. Even if an angel came from heaven and began to preach another gospel, he was to be rejected, for he too would be accursed. The glorious message of the gospel is far more important than even the angels in heaven.

3) The gospel is greater than any man (Mt.15:9). If any man preach *any other gospel*, he is to be accursed. The gospel is far more important than any man.

4) The preachers of false gospels shall suffer the judgment of a double curse. The word "accursed" (anathema) means just that: to be accursed, doomed to destruction, given over to eternal punishment, placed under the wrath of God. The idea is that of eternal death. This is clear from Paul's use of the word elsewhere where he applies it to himself: "I could wish that myself were *accursed* from Christ for my brethren. . . . " (Ro.9:3). Paul was a Jew; he was saying that he loved his Jewish brothers so much that he would gladly suffer eternal punishment for their salvation (the very same love that Christ had demonstrated for all men).

This is one of the most severe warnings in all of Scripture, and note to whom it is given: to you and to all other ministers. Lehman Strauss points out that every person who does not love the Lord Jesus Christ shall be accursed. The false teacher shall suffer God's eternal wrath. (Lehman Strauss. *Devotional Studies in Galatians and Ephesians.* Neptune, NJ: Loizeaux Brothers, 1957, p.21.)

> "Beware of false prophets, which come to you in sheep's clothing, but inwardly they are ravening wolves. Ye shall know them by their fruits. Do men gather grapes of thorns, or figs of thistles? ... Every tree that bringeth not forth good fruit is hewn down, and cast into the fire" (Mt.7:15-16, 19).
>
> "Many will say to me in that day, Lord, Lord, have we not prophesied in thy name? and in thy name have cast out devils? and in thy name done many wonderful works? And then will I profess unto them, I never knew you: depart from me, ye that work iniquity" (Mt.7:22-23).
>
> "Ye serpents, ye generation of vipers, how can ye escape the damnation of hell?" (Mt.23:33).

2. *You must not bring destructive heresies into the church, heresies that deny the Lord and His death for man.*

> "But there were false prophets also among the people, even as there shall be false teachers among you, who privily [quietly, secretly] shall bring in damnable heresies, even denying the Lord that bought them [by His death], and bring upon themselves swift destruction" (2 Pt.2:1).

Thought
As a minister of Christ, you must not bring destructive heresies into the church that deny the Lord and His death for man. Note the Scripture: you must not *secretly* teach destructive heresies, *secretly* introduce or bring in destructive teaching. *Bring in where?* Into the church, right among believers. False teachers are not out in the world, but they are within the church. They have joined the church and they have been outstanding members long enough to become teachers and preachers within the church. They hold leadership positions from which they can

teach their destructive heresies. Note that the word "heresies" (haireseis) is plural. What are the heresies being referred to? Any teaching that goes contrary to the Scripture, that is, the Word of God or the Bible. This is clearly what is meant, for the exhortation has just been given: "Take heed to the word of prophecy, to the Scripture" (cp. 2 Pt.1:19-21).

> "[Scripture is the] more sure word of prophecy; whereunto ye do well that ye take heed . . . for the prophecy came not in old time by the will of man: but holy men of God spake as they were moved by the Holy Ghost" (2 Pt.1:19, 21).

The point is this: any teaching that is contrary to God's Word is a destructive heresy. It destroys God's purpose for the church, and it destroys the lives of people within the church. Teachings that are contrary to God's Word are destructive and there is no escaping the fact. No matter how personable a person may be, no matter how much we may like him, if he is teaching a destructive heresy, he is destroying the church and the lives of people. William Barclay states it well:

> "A heretic [is] . . . a man who believes what he wishes to believe instead of accepting the truth of God which he must believe.
>
> "What was happening in the case of Peter's people was that certain men, who claimed to be prophets, were insidiously persuading men to believe the things they wished to be true rather than the things which God has *revealed* as true. They did not set themselves up as opponents of Christianity. Far from it. Rather they set themselves up as the *finest fruits of Christian thinking*. Insidiously, unconsciously, imperceptible, so gradually and so subtly that they did not even notice it, people were being lured away from God's truth to *men's private opinions*, for that is what heresy is" (*The Letters of James and Peter*. "The Daily Study Bible." Philadelphia, PA: The Westminster Press, 1958, p.374). (Italics are added by us for emphasis.)

a) The most tragic heresy of all is denying the Lord who bought us. Jesus Christ has bought us, and He has paid the supreme price to buy us. He gave all that He is and has—

even His life—in order to buy us out of sin and death. We owe our lives to Him; we owe everything to Him. The picture is that of a servant: we owe Christ our minds and hearts, our duty and service. Therefore, to deny Him is to deny our Lord and Master. And we know what happens to the servant who denies his Lord and Master: swift destruction. No matter who you are, no matter how high a position you hold or how influential you are, if you deny your Master, you bring swift destruction upon yourself. What does it mean to deny Christ?

- It means to deny that Jesus Christ is the Son of God: that He left heaven above and came to earth as Man (the God-Man) to reveal God's great love for man.
- It means to deny that Jesus Christ is the Savior of the world: that He lived a perfect and sinless life and secured the perfect righteousness for man.
- It means to deny that Jesus Christ died *for man*: that He took man's sin upon Himself and bore the judgment, condemnation, and punishment for man.
- It means to deny that Jesus Christ arose from the dead and conquered death for man.
- It means to deny that Jesus Christ is seated at the right hand of God to receive all the worship, glory, honor, and praise of the universe.

The list could go on and on to include all that the Scripture teaches about Christ. To deny any teaching of Scripture about Christ is to deny Christ. This is the very point that Scripture is making: you must take heed to the Scriptures . . .

- for the Scriptures have been given by God Himself, and there are false teachers among us (2 Pt.1:21).

Remember: false teachers are in the church. They are the preachers and teachers who profess Christ and say they are following Christ and building up His church. But what they are preaching and teaching is a complete denial of Him, and it is destroying the church.

"But whosoever shall deny me before men, him will I also deny before my Father which is in heaven" (Mt.10:33).

"Whosoever therefore shall be ashamed of me and of my words in this adulterous and sinful generation; of him also shall the Son of man be ashamed, when he cometh in the glory of his Father with the holy angels" (Mk.8:38).

"Who is a liar but he that denieth that Jesus is the Christ? He is antichrist [against Christ], that denieth the Father and the Son" (1 Jn.2:22).

b) False teachers shall be destroyed swiftly. Note: they bring destruction upon themselves. They are responsible for their own actions. They do not have to teach false doctrine; they make the choice to teach it. They could teach the truth [the Holy Scriptures], but they make a deliberate choice to teach contrary to what God has said. Therefore, they bring swift destruction upon themselves. The idea of swift is both certain and quick. When the judgment comes, there will be no discussion about the matter—no questioning, no leniency, no mercy, no love. There will be pure justice, exactly what they deserve—no more, no less—and the justice will be swift, immediate judgment and destruction.

- The word "destruction" (apoleian) means to lose one's well being; to be ruined; to be wasted; to perish; to be destroyed; to suffer perdition.

You must never allow this to happen to you. You must never turn away from Christ and begin preaching destructive heresies. You must never deny the Lord and His death for man.

"He that believeth on the Son hath everlasting life: and he that believeth not the Son shall not see life; but the wrath of God abideth on him" (Jn.3:36).

"Of how much sorer punishment, suppose ye, shall he be thought worthy, who hath trodden underfoot the Son of God, and hath counted the blood of the covenant, wherewith he was sanctified, an unholy thing, and hath done despite unto the Spirit of grace?" (Heb.10:29).

3. *You must not preach another Jesus, a Jesus other than the Jesus proclaimed by Scripture and true ministers.*

> "For if he that cometh preacheth another Jesus, whom we have not preached, or if ye receive another spirit, which ye have not received, or another gospel, which ye have not accepted...such are false apostles, deceitful workers, transforming themselves into the apostles of Christ. And no marvel; for Satan himself is transformed into an angel of light, therefore it is no great thing if his ministers also be transformed as the ministers of righteousness; whose end shall be according to their works" (2 Cor.11:4, 13-15).

Thought

As a minister, you must fear the preaching of another Jesus. This is always a danger that confronts the minister. Note five significant points in the above passage.

a) False ministers preach another Jesus. It is not another Christ (Messiah) that they preach, but another Jesus. That is, they are mixed up about who Jesus the carpenter was and who Jesus the Son of God is. They are confused about the humanity of Jesus. They are teaching that...

- Jesus was only a good man who lived as men should live.
- Jesus was only a great teacher who taught man how to live.
- Jesus was only a wonderful martyr who showed men how they should die.

They stress the humanity of Jesus and ignore or deny His deity.

Note what Scripture says: men can receive another spirit other than the Spirit of God, and they can receive another gospel other than the gospel of the Lord Jesus Christ (2 Cor.11:4). There are other spirits and gospels who seek after the loyalty of men; therefore, you and the church must be on guard against the preaching of another Jesus.

b) False ministers are disguised as the ministers of Christ, but they are deceitful workers.

- They are religious workers, workers who serve in religion.
- They are false ministers: they claim to be ministers of Christ, but they are not.
- They transform themselves (meta-shematizomenoi) into ministers of Christ. The word means to fashion, to change one's outward appearance. They pose as "gentlemen of the cloth," but they are nothing but cloth (A.T. Robertson. *Word Pictures in the New Testament*, Vol.4, p.259). They are false ministers.
- They are religious workers who deceive and mislead people away from Christ:
  - into false beliefs and doctrine.
  - into new ideas and positions.
  - into ritual and ceremony.
  - into organizations and programs.
  - into focusing upon some person or minister instead of Christ.

c) False ministers are disguised just like Satan—as ministers of light. Satan often appears as an angel or messenger of light, especially in industrialized societies. His position is always presented as the truth, as the path of intelligence, knowledge, and enlightenment. His way is always presented as the way to go, as the way that . . .

- progresses
- develops
- assures
- fulfills
- educates
- satisfies
- looks good
- tastes good
- feels good

Satan never presents himself as Satan; neither does he present sin as sin (Tasker. *The Second Epistle of Paul to the Corinthians*. "Tyndale Bible Commentaries," ed. by RVG Tasker. Grand Rapids, MI: Eerdmans, 1958, p.153). Satan always presents himself as the supreme intelligence who knows what is best for man and who will provide real pleasure, enjoyment, and fulfillment for man. When Satan presents his way to men, it attracts, appeals, and pulls man to desire the way of the world. Satan's way always seems to be the way of light, that is, of intelligence or of pleasure.

d) False ministers are of Satan: disguised as ministers of righteousness. Since Satan disguises himself into an angel or messenger of light, so do his ministers. They appear to be ministers of righteousness, and they preach and teach that a man is saved by righteousness, a righteousness of . . .

- morality
- goodness
- justice
- education
- development
- ministry
- giving
- serving
- helping

They stress the life and teachings of Jesus, all the good qualities of life—all the traits that should characterize people. They tell people to copy the life of Jesus and to focus their hearts upon these good qualities of life, and if they do, God will accept them. However, they make one fatal mistake: they ignore and deny . . .

- the righteousness of Jesus Christ which He had to secure for man by living the ideal, perfect, sinless life.
- the death of Jesus Christ which He had to die in order to bear the judgment, condemnation, and punishment of sin for man.
- the resurrection of Jesus Christ which He had to experience in order to conquer death and to provide a new life for man.

Scripture unmistakably teaches that God accepts no person apart from Jesus Christ—no matter how moral or good. Because Jesus Christ paid such a great price—the supreme price of dying for our sins—God loves Jesus Christ with a supreme love. Therefore, God will accept only the person who honors His Son. There is no other way to be acceptable to God. Not even the preaching of morality and goodness will stir God to accept a person. God wants men to live moral and good lives, but the first thing He wants is for man to love and worship

His Son, Jesus Christ. And to be acceptable to God, we must do first things first: we must love His Son Jesus Christ. Then we must go forth giving all we are and have to meet the needs of a desperate world that is dying without any relationship with God.

The point is this: the strategy of Satan is to turn men away from the truth, away from Christ. He leads ministers to preach what is true righteousness, but he has them to ignore the truth of *God's supreme love*, the death of Jesus Christ for the sins of men, and the absolute demand of God: that men must follow the example of Jesus Christ, give all they *are and have* to meet the desperate needs of men.

The ministers of Satan are ministers of righteousness, but they are not ministers of *the righteousness of God which is Jesus Christ Himself.* They are in the pulpits throughout the world, but they are the ministers of the world's way of righteousness. They are not the ministers of God's righteousness, which is the righteousness and death and resurrection of the Lord Jesus Christ.

> **"And this is his commandment, That we should believe on the name of his Son Jesus Christ, and love one another [serve, give all we are and have as Christ did], as he gave us commandment" (1 Jn.3:23).**

e) False ministers are to be judged according to their works.

> **"For I say unto you, That except your righteousness shall exceed the righteousness of the scribes and Pharisees, ye shall in no case enter into the kingdom of heaven" (Mt.5:20).**
>
> **"Many will say to me in that day, Lord, Lord, have we not prophesied in thy name? and in thy name have cast out devils? and in thy name done many wonderful works? And then will I profess unto them, I never knew you: depart from me, ye that work iniquity" (Mt.7:22-23).**
>
> **"[God] will render to every man according to his deeds. . . . for there is no respect of persons with God" (Ro.2:6, 11).**
>
> **"But though we, or an angel from heaven, preach any other gospel unto you than that which we have**

> preached unto you, let him be accursed. As we said before, so say I now again, If any man preach any other gospel unto you than that ye have received, let him be accursed" (Gal.1:8-9).

C. YOU AND FALSE DOCTRINE AND TEACHING

1. *You must not teach the traditions, ideas, and commandments of men as doctrine.*

   > "Thus have ye made the commandment of God of none effect by your tradition. Ye hypocrites, well did Esaias prophesy of you, saying, This people draweth nigh unto me with their mouth, and honoureth me with their lips; but their heart is far from me. But in vain they do worship me, teaching for doctrines the commandments of men" (Mt.15:6^b-9).

   > "Not giving heed to Jewish fables [false ideas], and commandments of men, that turn from the truth" (Tit.1:14).

Thought

As a minister of Christ, you must not teach the traditions, ideas, and commandments of men as doctrine. Christ covers some very *real* dangers that you as a minister must guard against.

a) You must not set aside God's Word for tradition. Religious traditions may be described as institutional or personal.

- Institutional traditions are such things as rituals, rules, regulations, schedules, forms, services, procedures, organizations—anything that gives order and security to the persons involved.

- Personal traditions are such things as church worship, rituals, prayers, habits, ceremonies, and objects which a person uses to keep himself religiously secure.

Christ was attacking the fact that some ministers put their traditions before God's Word. Some keep their traditions *while* neglecting and ignoring God's Word. You must guard yourself against this danger.

> "Making the word of God of none effect through your tradition, which ye have delivered: and many such like things do ye" (Mk.7:13).

b) You must not be hypocritical: you must not give lip service while keeping your heart far from God. Too many are *religiously deceived* (cp. the Pharisees and Scribes). They study, witness, show care, help the needy, and keep the rules. They struggle and would fight to maintain religious tradition, yet Christ says they are hypocrites. Why? Because their heart is not God's. They personally refuse to accept Jesus as the Son of God, as the Messiah and Savior of the world. They just do not know God personally, not in the depths of their heart (Jn.14:6).

As a minister, you must guard against this danger. You must maintain your personal walk with the Lord.

> "Wherefore the Lord said, Forasmuch as this people draw near me with their mouth, and with their lips do honor me, but have removed their heart far from me, and their fear toward me is taught by the precept of men" (Is.29:13).

c) You must guard against worshipping with an empty heart. Christ taught . . .

- that true worship must be "in spirit and in truth."

> "God is a Spirit: and they that worship him must worship him in spirit and in truth" (Jn.4:24).

- that a person who denies Christ or denies God's Word cannot truly worship God.

> "Jesus saith unto him, I am the way, the truth, and the life: no man cometh unto the Father, but by me" (Jn.14:6).
> "Sanctify them through thy truth: thy word is truth" (Jn.17:17).

- that a person can worship, but his worship may be empty, worthless, and unacceptable. The religionists of Christ's day were professing religion with their lips, but denying Christ, God's Son, in their heart (cp.v.17-20).

> "And this is his commandment, That we should believe on the name of his Son Jesus Christ, and love one another, as he gave us commandment" (1 Jn.3:23).

d) You must not teach tradition as God's commandment. Tradition is man's *idea* of what should be or what should not be done. Some traditions are good; some are bad. But even the good ones are not to be taught as though they were the commandments of God. As important as some traditions may be they are not as important as God's Word.

> "For this cause also thank we God without ceasing, because, when ye received the word of God which ye heard of us, ye received it not as the word of men, but as it is in truth, the word of God, which effectually worketh also in you that believe" (1 Th.2:13).
>
> "All scripture is given by inspiration of God, and is profitable for doctrine, for reproof, for correction, for instruction in righteousness" (2 Tim.3:16).

2. *You must not be carried away with different kinds of teachings. You must not preach or teach the fables, myths, speculations, ideas, and false doctrines of men.*

> "Be not carried about with divers [different kinds] and strange doctrines" (Heb.13:9).
>
> ". . . charge some that they teach no other doctrine. Neither give heed to fables and endless genealogies, which minister questions, rather than godly edifying which is in faith: so do" (1 Tim.1:3-4).
>
> "For the time will come when they will not endure sound doctrine; but after their own lusts shall they heap to themselves teachers, having itching ears; and they shall turn away their ears from the truth, and shall be turned unto fables" (2 Tim.4:3-4).
>
> "That we henceforth be no more children, tossed to and fro, and carried about with every

wind of doctrine, by the sleight of men, and cunning craftiness, whereby they lie in wait to deceive" (Eph.4:14).

Thought
As the minister of Christ, you must not be carried away with different kinds of teachings. You must not preach and teach the fables, myths, speculations, ideas, and false doctrines of men. You are to preach the Word of God and the Word of God alone.

Note 1 Tim.1:3-4 above. The word "charge" (parangello) is a strong word. It is a military word that means to pass commands down through the ranks. Scripture gives you, the minister of Christ, three negative charges, three negative orders. You have your orders: you must not do two things.

a) You must not teach any doctrine other than the doctrine of God's Word.

- You must not add to the doctrine of God's Word.
- You must not take away from the doctrine of God's Word.
- You must not formulate new doctrine for the church.

You must not begin to think there are defects in the Word of God that need correcting. You must not change or alter the Word of God to any degree whatsoever. In the clear words of this Scripture, you have your charge, your orders: you must "teach no other doctrine" (1 Tim.1:3).

b) You must not give attention to the fables (false teachings) and genealogies of men. Why? Because they arouse questions rather than godly edification.

The word "fables" (muthois) refers to *all forms* of false and fictional teaching or doctrine. It means the *false ideas* and speculations of men about God and Christ and about the teachings of God's Word. The doctrines of men are only speculations, fables, narratives, stories, fictions, and falsehoods (A.T. Robertson. *Word Pictures in the New Testament*, Vol.4, p.561).

> "But refuse profane and old wives' fables, and exercise thyself rather unto godliness" (1 Tim.4:7).
> "And they shall turn away their ears from the truth, and shall be turned unto fables" (2 Tim.4:4).

> "Not giving heed to Jewish fables, and commandments of men, that turn from the truth" (Tit.1:14).
>
> "For we have not followed cunningly devised fables, when we made known unto you the power and coming of our Lord Jesus Christ, but were eyewitnesses of his majesty" (2 Pt.1:16).

The word "genealogies" refers to those who take comfort in a godly heritage and tradition. The Jews were guilty of this. They took great pride in their godly forefathers, so much so they felt that the godliness of their forefathers rubbed off on them. The more godly forefathers they had in their roots, the more prestigious and acceptable they felt before God and men. They felt the stronger their roots, the more man and God would accept and esteem them. Note the reference to "endless genealogies." There were apparently those who were spending enormous amounts of time in structuring and discussing the godly heritage of the past. Apparently, the practice had seeped into the church. There were those . . .

- who were stressing heritage and tradition over Christ.
- who were depending upon a godly heritage for salvation instead of trusting Christ.
- who were spending more time in genealogies than in edifying and building up the godliness of the church.
- who were concentrating upon questions and theories rather than upon building godly behavior among believers.

Some persons take great comfort in their godly heritage. They actually feel that God would never reject them . . .

- because of their godly wives, husbands, children, parents.
- because they belong to a traditional church with a godly genealogy and reputation.
- because they have a godly pastor or friend with whom they are close.

> "Bring forth therefore fruits worthy of repentance, and begin not to say within yourselves, We have Abraham to our father: for I say unto you, That God is able of these stones to raise up children unto Abraham" (Lk.3:8).

> "Then they reviled him, and said, Thou art his disciple; but we are Moses' disciples" (Jn.9:28).

As the minister of Christ, you must not teach the fables and godly heritages of men. You must teach the Word of God and the Word of God alone.

3. *You must turn away from empty talk and the opposition of false science and false knowledge.*

> "O Timothy, keep that which is committed to thy trust, avoiding profane and vain babblings [talk], and oppositions of science falsely so called: which some professing have erred concerning the faith" (1 Tim.6:20-21).

Thought

This is the last charge—the final words—of Paul written to the minister Timothy. Being the last words, the charge is of critical importance.

You, the ministers of Christ, must turn away from empty talk and the opposition of false science and false knowledge. You are charged to do two things.

First, you must keep that which is committed to your trust. What is it that has been committed to you? What is the trust that has been placed into your hands?

The great trust committed to the minister of God is . . .

- the faith, the great Christian faith.
- the glorious truth of God, the truth which He has revealed to men in His Word and in the Lord Jesus Christ.
- the wonderful gospel of God, the gospel that is revealed in the sending of God's Son to earth in order to save men.

The picture of the word "trust" is this: it is a *deposit*, the picture of a faithful and diligent banker who looks after the money *deposited* into his care. You, the minister of God, are to guard, keep, look after, and care for the faith and truth of God—the faith and truth of His Son, His Word, His Revelation, and His gospel. You must never forget that God has deposited—actually laid—the truth of God into your hands. You have been entrusted with the gospel of God, the glorious message of His Son, the Lord Jesus Christ.

William Barclay's comments are worthy of quote:

"If in our day the Christian faith were to be twisted and distorted, it would not only be we who were the losers; those of generations still to come would be robbed of something infinitely precious. We are not only the possessors, we are also the trustees of the faith. That which we have received, we must also hand on" (*The Letters to Timothy, Titus, and Philemon*, p.161).

> **"But as we were allowed of God to be put in trust with the gospel, even so we speak; not as pleasing men, but God, which trieth our hearts" (1Th.2:4).**
>
> **"For this cause also thank we God without ceasing, because, when ye received the word of God which ye heard of us, ye received it not as the word of men, but as it is in truth, the word of God, which effectually worketh also in you that believe" (1 Th.2:13).**
>
> **"According to the glorious gospel of the blessed God, which was <u>committed to my trust</u>. And I thank Christ Jesus our Lord, who hath enabled me, for that he counted me faithful, putting me into the ministry" (1 Tim.1:11-12).**
>
> **"But [God] hath in due times manifested his word through preaching, which is committed unto me according to the commandment of God our Saviour" (Tit.1:3).**

Second, you must turn away from false teaching. The description of false teaching is graphic.

a) False teaching is described as profane and vain babblings.

- The word "profane" (bebelos) means common, irreverent, and godless talk.
- The word "vain" means empty and meaningless.
- The word "babbling" means "empty voices" (Kenneth Wuest. *The Pastoral Epistles*, Vol.2, p.103).

Therefore, the charge is to take all *empty talk* and turn away from it. Have absolutely nothing to do with common, irreverent, godless, and *empty voices*—no matter who is sounding forth the words. This would, of course, include:

- false claims to truth
- all forms of false teaching
- worldly philosophy
- novel ideas of religion
- cursing
- gossip
- criticism
- off-colored jokes
- suggestive talk

b) False teaching is described as "science," but as "science falsely called."

- The word "science" (gnoseos) means knowledge, the false knowledge of the world in all its humanistic search for truth.
- The word "oppositions" (antitheses) means antithesis, that is, to stand against some thesis, truth, or fact. What is being condemned is the false knowledge of men, the things that men teach that are contrary to God's glorious revelation in Christ and in the Word of God. The minister of God—in fact, any person—is a fool to stand against truth and fact, whether of God or of true science.

The charge is strong, very strong: turn away from men and their teachings when they stand against Christ and the teachings of God's Word. Have nothing to do with the false science or false knowledge of men. The men and their false teachings may concern philosophy, psychology, education, sociology, religion—any area of science or knowledge—but turn away from them if they are false. How do you tell if the teaching is false? By the Word of God, the revelation and record of Christ and of the truth of God. If the science or knowledge stands in opposition to the Word of God, turn away from it. It is false, and future investigation will prove it to be false if the investigation is performed *intelligently and honestly*.

Note that some persons had turned to false teaching. The seriousness of the situation is seen in this: these are the last words of this letter to Timothy. The very last thing that Paul says to Timothy is to turn away from false teaching. What a warning to you and to all the ministers of God!

> "They on the rock are they, which, when they hear, receive the word with joy; and these have no root, which for a while believe, and in time of temptation fall away" (Lk.8:13).
> "And Jesus said unto him, No man, having put his hand to the plough, and looking back, is fit for the kingdom of God" (Lk.9:62).
> "Nevertheless I have somewhat against thee, because thou hast left thy first love" (Rev.2:4).

4. *You must guard against the false teaching of religion and of the state.*

> "And he charged them, saying, Take heed, beware of the leaven of the Pharisees [the teaching of false religionists], and of the leaven of Herod [the teaching of the State]" (Mk.8:15).

Thought
What did Jesus mean by the leaven of the Pharisees and of Herod or world leaders? (Matthew refers to the Sadducees instead of Herod. Most Herodians, followers of Herod, were Sadducees. See Mt.22:16; Acts 23:8.)

a) The leaven of the Pharisees (religionists) was their doctrine or teaching (Mt.16:12) and their hypocrisy, deception, and play-acting (Lk.12:1). The Pharisees *fermented and soured everyone they touched*. The Pharisees believed in a personal God and in the Scripture as God's Word, but they added to God's Word. They added rules and regulations, rituals and ceremonies which put undue restrictions upon man's behavior. This led to three gross errors.

- It led people to think that their good behavior and their religious rituals and ceremonies made them acceptable to God. A religion of good works was being depended upon for righteousness.

- It led to a religion of social respectability, to an external religion. If a person was socially respectable and did all the right things, then he was judged acceptable to God.
- It led to an attitude and an air of self-righteousness. If a person kept the rules and regulations, he naturally felt righteous and sometimes demonstrated it. There was a dependence upon oneself, upon keeping the right rules and thereby being righteous.

b) The Sadducees or Herodians were the liberal-minded of their day. Their leaven or false teaching was twofold.

- They took away from God's Word, denying all Scripture except the Pentateuch, the first five books of the Old Testament.
- They were free thinkers and rationalists who were secular and materialistic-minded. Therefore, they were willing to collaborate with the Romans in doing away with Jewish culture and in instituting Roman and Greek culture. Because of this, Rome placed their leaders in the governing positions (the Sanhedrin) and gave them wealth. Their worldly-mindedness, secular philosophy, and liberal theology were always a threat to any man (see *The Preacher's Outline & Sermon Bible,*® note—Mt.16:1-12).

Note the double warning that Jesus gave: "Take heed, beware." This stressed the supreme importance of guarding against the leaven of both religionists and world leaders. The charge to you, the minister of Christ, is twofold.

a) You must take heed, guard against, the false teaching of religion and of the state. The words "take heed" mean to see, behold, discern, and acquaint yourself by closely observing and experiencing. Two things are needed for you to "take heed": active thought and a discerning mind. The thing to be heeded must be actively observed, thought through, and discerned. In the present passage, the charge is a *present imperative*. The disciple is to "take heed" of leaven beginning right now, and he is to continue taking heed, always observing and discerning false teaching.

b) You must beware of the false teaching of religion and of the state. The word "beware" means to see, perceive, grasp, and understand in order to watch out for something; to turn the mind upon an object and consider and keep a watchful eye upon it; to guard and protect against something. Again, the charge is a present imperative. You are to begin immediately to beware and to continue your watch, always looking out for the danger of false teaching within religion and the state.

5. *You must not preach man's empty ideas and discussions—questionable things—but love and faith and the need for a pure conscience.*

> "**Now the end of the commandment is charity [love] out of a pure heart, and of a good conscience, and of faith unfeigned: from which some having swerved have turned aside unto vain jangling [empty ideas and discussions]: desiring to be teachers of the law, understanding neither what they say, nor whereof they affirm**" (1 Tim.1:5-7).

Thought
As the minister of Christ, you must not preach the empty ideas and discussions of men—the questionable things—but love and faith and the need for a pure conscience. Note the Scripture above. Two significant things are being said to the minister of Christ.

a) You must not put empty ideas and discussions above love. The end of God's commandment is love (agape, God's kind of love). Therefore, you and all other ministers are to focus upon growing in love and in teaching love. The great call of believers is . . .

- to know the love of God and to love God.
- to love each other as brothers in the Lord.
- to love the lost of the world so much that we are driven to take the gospel to them.

But note where this kind of love comes from. Its source is not found in men; it does not just arise out of the heart of man. The love which we are to know and possess comes from three sources.

- Love comes from a pure heart: a heart forgiven by God and cleansed from all impurities; a heart that is not weighed down by selfishness, worldliness, envy, covetousness, and immorality.
- Love comes from a good conscience: a conscience that knows there is nothing between it and God, between it and men; a conscience that knows it has been true to God's Word and has taught no error.
- Love comes from unfeigned or sincere faith: a faith that is set upon God and His Word, that holds to God's Word and trusts and teaches God's Word and God's Word only.

The end of God's commandment—of all that God has ever said to man—is love. Therefore as a minister, you must commit your life to learn more and more about the love of God and to teach the love of God more and more. But to do this you must be totally committed...

- to having a pure heart before God.
- to having a good (clear) conscience before God.
- to following *the faith*, that is, the teachings and doctrine of God's Word.

However, this is not true with some—not true with false teachers. Note exactly what Scripture says: some have swerved and turned aside to empty discussions. The term "vain jangling" sounds just like what false teaching amounts to: *janglings*—vain, empty janglings. The term means empty arguments, discussions, and speculations—the speculative ideas of men about God, Christ, and the Word of God. Note that false teachers swerve and turn aside from the doctrines of God's Word to these vain janglings. But note: you, the true minister of God, are called by Christ to preach and teach the love of God demonstrated in the death of His Son and declared in His Word, even in the Holy Scriptures.

> "**Now the Spirit speaketh expressly, that in the latter times some shall depart from the faith, giving heed to seducing spirits, and doctrines of devils; speaking lies in hypocrisy; having their conscience seared with a hot iron**" (1 Tim.4:1-2).

> "For there are many unruly and vain talkers and deceivers, specially they of the circumcision [religionists]" (Tit.1:10).
>
> "The beginning of the words of his mouth is foolishness: and the end of his talk is mischievous madness" (Eccl.10:13).

b) You must not put your own ambition and personal ideas above the truth. The picture is that of a person who is ambitious...

- to be recognized as an original teacher or preacher.
- to be recognized as a creative person.
- to be recognized as the creator of a novel idea or doctrine.
- to be recognized as the author of a new concept or doctrine.
- to be recognized as the founder of a new movement.

The picture is that of a person who so desires to fit in with the latest fashion of teaching that he neglects or ignores the truth. He disregards the truth in order to fit in with his peers. The false teacher's ambition is allowed to cloud his understanding of the truth.

William Barclay points out that the false teacher who is ambitious often...

- demonstrates arrogance instead of humility.
- focuses upon teaching rather than learning.
- looks down upon simple-minded people.
- regards those who do not agree with his conclusions as ignorant fools. (*The Letters to Timothy, Titus, and Philemon*, p.37.)

As the minister of Christ, you must not put your personal ambition and ideas above the truth.

> "But in vain they do worship me, teaching for doctrines the commandments of men" (Mt.15:9).
>
> "Jesus answered and said unto them, Ye do err, not knowing the scriptures, nor the power of God" (Mt.22:29).

"If any man teach otherwise, and consent not to wholesome words, even the words of our Lord Jesus Christ, and to the doctrine which is according to godliness; he is proud, knowing nothing, but doting about questions and strifes of words, whereof cometh envy, strife, railings, evil surmisings, perverse disputings of men of corrupt minds, and destitute of the truth, supposing that gain is godliness: from such withdraw thyself" (1 Tim.6:3-5).

CHAPTER 8

What Your Daily Walk as a Minister Must Be

As a minister of Christ, you must walk in three things every day of your life: in Christ, in the Scriptures, and in prayer. These three things are absolute essentials as you live and minister for Christ in the midst of a broken and hurting world.

Contents

A. YOU AND CHRIST — 191

1. You must make sure—absolutely sure—that your belief in Christ is the right kind of belief. — 191

2. You must make sure—absolutely sure—that you are a new creation in Christ Jesus. — 192

3. You must constantly examine yourself—make sure you continue in the faith of Christ—lest you become disqualified, unfit, and rejected. — 194

4. You must always walk in Christ: you must always seek *first* the kingdom of God and His righteousness. — 194

5. You must live a crucified life in Christ, a life of self-denial and sacrifice. — 195

6. You must be inwardly renewed day by day, changed into the image of Christ. — 197

7. You must put on the whole armour of God and be strong in Christ. — 200

B. You and Scripture ... 202

1. You must study and obey the Scriptures daily: you must live by the Word of God and proclaim it. ... 202

2. You must memorize the Word of God; let it dwell in your heart and life all day every day. ... 205

3. You must be consistent in the Scriptures—studying and living as Scripture dictates. ... 207

C. You and Prayer ... 208

1. You must pray daily, pray as Christ taught you to pray in the Lord's prayer. ... 208

2. You must pray daily for the church and for believers. Paul's prayer for the church and for believers is a good pattern to use and to pray through. ... 210

3. You must pray daily for the whole world—for all people everywhere. ... 211

4. You must pray daily for more laborers. ... 213

5. You must pray always—moment by moment—striving to gain an unbroken consciousness of the Lord. ... 214

6. You must take some extended time for fervent prayer when very special needs exist. ... 218

Chapter 8
What Your Daily Walk as a Minister Must Be

A. YOU AND CHRIST

1. *You must make sure—absolutely sure—that your belief in Christ is the right kind of belief.*

> "For God so loved the world, that he gave his only begotten Son, that whosoever <u>believeth</u> in him should not perish, but have everlasting life" (Jn.3:16).
>
> "That if thou shalt <u>confess</u> with thy mouth the Lord Jesus, and shalt <u>believe in thine heart</u> that God hath raised him from the dead, thou shalt be saved. For with the heart man believeth unto righteousness; and with the mouth confession is made unto salvation" (Ro.10:9-10).
>
> "And being made perfect, he became the author of eternal salvation unto all them that <u>obey</u> him" (Heb.5:9).
>
> "But without faith it is impossible to please him:- for he that cometh to God must believe that he is, and that he is a rewarder of them that <u>diligently seek</u> him" (Heb.11:6).

Thought
As a minister of Christ, you must have the right kind of faith—a true saving faith—in Christ. You are saved by believing in Jesus Christ. But what does *believing* mean? How can you know that your belief is the *right kind of belief*, a true *saving faith*?

The right kind of faith, saving faith, is not this:
- Saving faith is not head knowledge, not just a mental conviction and intellectual assent.
- Saving faith is not just believing the fact that Jesus Christ is the Savior of the world.
- Saving faith is not just believing history, that Jesus Christ lived upon earth as the Savior just as George

Washington lived upon earth as the President of the United States.

- Saving faith is not just believing the words and claims of Jesus Christ in the same way that a person would believe the words of George Washington.

The right kind of faith, saving faith, is two things.

a) Saving faith is believing in Jesus Christ, who and what He is, that He is the Savior and Lord of life. You must believe in Jesus Christ with your heart, believe to such a degree that you *give your whole life* to Him. You must confess Jesus Christ as Savior and Lord and turn your life over—completely and totally—to live for Him (Ro.10:9-10).

b) Saving faith is commitment—the commitment of your total being and life to Jesus Christ. It is the commitment of all you *are and have* to Christ. Saving faith gives everything to Christ; therefore, it involves all of your affairs. You trust Christ to take care of your past (sins), your present (welfare), and your future (destiny). You entrust your whole life, being, and possessions into Christ's hands. You lay yourself upon Jesus' keeping, confiding in Him about your daily necessities and acknowledging Him in all the ways of life. You follow Christ in every area and in every detail of life, seeking His instructions and leaving your welfare up to Him. Saving faith is simply commitment of your whole being, all you *are and have* to Christ.

As a minister, you must make sure that what you profess is true. You must make sure—absolutely sure—that your belief in Christ is the right kind of belief, that you have a true saving faith. Your life and ministry will come up short—very short—if you do not know Christ yourself, know Him personally and intimately.

2. *You must make sure—absolutely sure—that you are a new creation in Christ Jesus.*

> **"Therefore if any man be in Christ, he is a new creature: old things are passed away; behold, all things are become new" (2 Cor.5:17).**

> "Put off concerning the former conversation [behavior] the old man, which is corrupt according to the deceitful lusts; and be renewed in the spirit of your mind; and ... put on the new man, which after God is created in righteousness and true holiness" (Eph.4:22-24).
>
> "Put off the old man with his deeds; and ... put on the new man, which is renewed in knowledge after the image of him that created him" (Col.3:9-10).

Thought

The message of the gospel is this: a person can become a new creation in Christ Jesus. A person can be changed, truly changed, and become a better person—just like a new man. As a minister, you preach and teach this gospel, the gospel that a person can be changed and start life all over again—by the power of Christ. You must, therefore, make sure you yourself are a changed person, that you are what you preach:

a) You must make sure you are a new creation in Christ (2 Cor.5:17) ...

- that old things have passed away.
- that all things are become new.

b) You must make sure you have put off the behavior of your old man and have put on the behavior of the new man (Eph.4:22-24; Col.3:9-10) ...

- that the spirit of your mind has been renewed.
- that you are living a life of righteousness and true holiness.
- that your knowledge (mind) is being renewed and conformed to the image of Christ more and more (Col.3:10).

As a minister, you must be a new creation, a new man, in Christ. You cannot be His representative nor adequately preach that a person can be changed by Christ, that he can start life all over again, not unless you have been changed. To preach one thing and live something else is hypocritical. You must, therefore, make sure you yourself are a new creation, a new man, before you can represent Christ and teach and preach to others.

3. *You must constantly examine yourself—make sure you continue in the faith of Christ—lest you become disqualified, unfit, and rejected.*

> "Examine yourselves, whether ye be in the faith; prove your own selves. Know ye not your own selves, how that Jesus Christ is in you, except ye be reprobates?" (2 Cor.13:5).

Thought

As a minister, you must make sure you are genuine—constantly make sure. Living in sin makes your faith suspect, especially since you are a professing minister of Christ. There is no place for sin in a minister's life, no excuse for a minister to *continue practicing* some sin. You must constantly examine yourself and make sure there is no known sin in your life. When you find sin, you must repent, turn away from it, and confess it to Christ, asking forgiveness. And He will forgive you. But note: if you find sin in your life and do not turn away from it, then you are what Scripture calls *"reprobate."* Reprobate means to be disqualified and unfit for the ministry. Reprobate means you are *disapproved* and rejected by God.

As a minister, you must constantly examine yourself and make sure you are genuine—make sure you continue in the faith, that you are living a righteous and godly life.

4. *You must always walk in Christ: you must always seek first the kingdom of God and His righteousness.*

> "But seek ye first the kingdom of God, and his righteousness; and all these things [the necessities of life] shall be added unto you" (Mt.6:33, cp. v.25-34).

Thought

As a minister, you are always to walk in Christ: you are to seek *first* the kingdom of God and His righteousness. You are not to be preoccupied with material possessions, not even with the necessities of life such as food, clothing, and housing. Your first duty and preoccupation is to seek God *first*. God gives you the greatest promise in all the world: your necessities—all of your needs—will be met if you *will* seek His kingdom and His righteousness *first*.

There are two ways you can go about taking care of yourself in this world.

    a) Working and seeking in your own strength: depending upon your own ability and energy alone, fighting and struggling to make it through life, and fretting and worrying about succeeding and about how to keep what you have secured.

    b) Working and seeking in both God's strength and your own strength: trusting and acknowledging God while doing all you can; putting your hand to the plow and plowing; working diligently and not looking back, and while working, trusting the results to God. God says He will see to it that such a trusting person will always have the necessities of life.

God is your heavenly Father, and He knows your needs. You are very, very special to Him. Just do one simple thing and He will take care of you and meet all your needs: walk in Christ, always seek first the kingdom of God and His righteousness.

5. *You must live a crucified life in Christ, a life of self denial and sacrifice.*

> "And he said to them all, If any man will come after me, let him deny himself, and take up his cross daily, and follow me" (Lk.9:23).
>
> "Knowing this, that your old man is crucified with him, that the body of sin might be destroyed, that henceforth we should not serve sin" (Ro.6:6).
>
> "Likewise reckon ye also yourselves to be dead indeed unto sin, but alive unto God through Jesus Christ our Lord" (Ro.6:11).
>
> "[We are] always bearing about in the body the dying of the Lord Jesus, that the life also of Jesus might be made manifest in our body. For we which live are alway delivered unto death for Jesus' sake, that the life also of Jesus might be made manifest in our mortal flesh" (2 Cor.4:10-11).

> "I am crucified with Christ: nevertheless I live; yet not I, but Christ liveth in me: and the life which I now live in the flesh I live by the faith of the Son of God, who loved me, and gave himself for me" (Gal.2:20).
>
> "And they that are Christ's have crucified the flesh with the affections and lusts" (Gal.5:24).

Thought

You must count yourself—consider yourself—crucified with Christ. What does this mean? It means this: when Christ died upon the cross, He denied Himself—sacrificed Himself totally—for us. To be crucified with Christ means just this:

- You sacrifice yourself—deny yourself, count yourself as dead—and live for Christ (Gal.2:20).
- You treat yourself as though you are dead to self, but alive to God (Ro.6:11).
- You sacrifice yourself—deny yourself completely and totally—to Christ and His cause: to follow Him (Lk.9:23).

Note Lk.9:23: the verse tells you what you must do to follow Christ.

> "And he said to them all, If any man will come after me, let him deny himself, and take up his cross daily, and follow me" (Lk.9:23).

a) You must deny yourself. Man's nature and tendency is to indulge himself, to do what he wants, to do his own thing. But you are not to indulge yourself: you are not to seek more and more of this world and its things and comforts. You are to deny yourself by discipline and control, by loving and caring for others, by sacrificing and giving to others, and by helping and ministering to others.

b) You must take up your cross. The cross does not mean merely bearing one's particular hardship in life, such as poor health, abuse, criticism, gossip, opposition, persecution, unemployment, invalid parents, spouse, a wayward child. The cross is always an instrument of death, not just an object to carry or bear. Therefore, to take up your cross means that you die to self daily—die mentally and actively. You let the mind of Christ, the mind of humbling yourself to the point of death, be in you and fill your thoughts every day (Ph.2:5-8; 2 Cor.10:3-5). You put your will, your desires, your wants, your ambitions to death. In their stead, you follow Christ and do His will all day long. Now, note a crucial fact: this is not negative, passive behavior. It takes positive, active behavior to *will*, to *deny self*, to *take up one's cross*, to *follow Christ*. You have to act, work, get to it, and be diligent, consistent, and enduring in order to die to self.

c) You must follow Jesus. Man's tendency, however, is to follow someone else and to give his first allegiance to something else. Within the world, there are many things available for you to serve and put first. There are . . .

- service organizations
- social acceptance
- humanitarian needs
- religion (institutional)
- fleshly stimulation
- self (fame, honor)
- recreation
- sports
- comfort
- education
- profession
- houses
- pleasure
- livelihood
- family
- appearance
- clubs
- hobby
- health
- clothing

As a minister, you must live a crucified life in Christ, a life of self-denial. You must walk day by day dying to yourself—your own desires and wishes—and live for Jesus Christ and His kingdom.

6. *You must be inwardly renewed day by day, changed into the image of Christ.*

> **"For which cause [the glory of God] we faint not; but though our outward man perish, yet the inward man is renewed day by day. For our light affliction, which is but for a moment, worketh for us a far more exceeding and eternal weight of glory; while**

we look not at the things which are seen, but at the things which are not seen: for the things which are seen are temporal; but the things which are not seen are eternal" (2 Cor.4:16-18).

"But we all, with open face beholding as in a glass the glory of the Lord, are changed into the same image from glory to glory, even as by the Spirit of the Lord" (2 Cor.3:18).

Thought

Your walk before the Lord is a day by day affair. You must struggle day by day to be inwardly renewed, to be changed more and more into the image of Christ. Note five significant points in 2 Cor.4:16-18 above.

a) You must not faint in your call and ministry. This means you must not give up or quit; you must not lose heart or become discouraged; you must not allow anything to defeat you: not people, circumstances, events, fatigue, exhaustion, or even persecution and severe opposition. Nothing, absolutely nothing, must be allowed to drive you from the ministry nor keep you from preaching the gospel of the Lord Jesus Christ.

b) Your outward man perishes every day.

- The "outward man" is the *earthen vessel* (2 Cor.4:7), the *human body* (2 Cor.4:10), the *mortal flesh* (2 Cor.4:11), and the *earthly house* (2 Cor.5:1).

- The word "perish" (diaphtheiretai) means to age, wear out, waste away, deteriorate, decay, corrupt, and die.

Your "outward man" or body is wearing out and wasting away every day. It is in the process of perishing and dying. As you age your body will become weaker and weaker, less able to go on: it will ache, slow down, need more rest, and most likely develop some serious problems or diseases. In addition to the normal wear and tear upon the body, people may put enormous demands and pressure upon you and even persecute you. But note the glorious truths of the next three points.

c) The minister's "inner man" is renewed day by day. The inner man is . . .

- your spirit that has been "born again" or created anew by the Spirit of God (Jn.3:3, 5-6).
- your spirit that was dead in trespasses and sins until it was quickened and made alive by Christ (Eph.2:2, 4-5).
- the "new creature" (2 Cor.5:17) and the "new man" (Eph.4:24; Col.3:10).
- the highest and deepest part of your being where the Holy Spirit dwells.
- the "hidden man of the heart" (1 Pt.3:4).

You are renewed day by day when you draw near God for strength and growth, for relief and deliverance. But remember: it is the presence and power of God within your body that renews you. You must seek His presence and power, His renewal, day by day. Seeking Him is your duty. When you fulfill your duty—seeking Him—then He renews and conforms you into the image of Christ day by day.

d) Your afflictions are light when compared to the glory you shall receive in heaven. Note the phrase "weight of glory." This picture should always be kept in mind by every minister. The picture is that of a set of scales sitting before the minister. You balance your afflictions on one end and the eternal glory you are to receive on the other end. The afflictions may be heavy and severe, but when you place the eternal glory you are to receive on the scales, the afflictions become light. It is as though they weigh nothing.

e) Your eyes must not be focused on the physical and temporal, but on the spiritual and eternal. The word "look" (scopeo) means to focus your eyes and attention on a set goal or end. The goal, of course, is spending eternity with God in the new heavens and earth. You must not look at the things which are seen (the physical and corruptible), but at the things which are not seen (the spiritual and incorruptible). The reason is strikingly clear: the things which are seen are temporal (brief, temporary, fading, passing, fleeting, and transient); but the things which are not seen are eternal (lasting, endless, forever, permanent, immortal, and glorious).

> "His lord said unto him, Well done, good and faithful servant; thou hast been faithful over a few things, I will make thee ruler over many things: enter thou into the joy of thy lord" (Mt.25:23).
>
> "Then shall the righteous shine forth as the sun in the kingdom of their Father. Who hath ears to hear, let him hear" (Mt.13:43).
>
> "And if children, then heirs; heirs of God, and joint-heirs with Christ; if so be that we suffer with him, that we may be also glorified together. For I reckon that the sufferings of this present time are not worthy to be compared with the glory which shall be revealed in us" (Ro.8:17-18).
>
> "Who shall change our vile body, that it may be fashioned like unto his glorious body, according to the working whereby he is able even to subdue all things unto himself" (Ph.3:21).
>
> "If we suffer, we shall also <u>reign</u> with him: if we deny him, he also will deny us" (2 Tim.2:12).
>
> "When Christ, who is our life, shall appear, then shall ye also appear with him in glory" (Col.3:4).

The point is this: if you will keep your eyes on the spiritual and eternal—on Christ and on the great glory He has planned for you as one of His dear servants—you will be inwardly renewed day by day, changed more and more into the image of Christ. May the Spirit of God help you to focus upon the spiritual and eternal as you serve our wonderful Lord day by day. Amen and Amen!

7. *You must put on the whole armour of God and be strong in Christ.*

> "Finally, my brethren, be strong in the Lord, and in the power of his might. Put on the whole armour of God, that ye may be able to stand against the wiles of the devil. For we wrestle not against flesh and blood, but against principalities, against powers, against the rulers of the darkness of this world, against spiritual wickedness in high places. Wherefore take unto you the whole armour of God, that ye may be able to withstand in the evil day, and having done all, to stand. Stand therefore . . .

- "having your loins girt about with truth . . .
- "having on the breastplate of righteousness . . .
- "[having] your feet shod with the preparation of the gospel of peace;
- "above all, taking the shield of faith, wherewith ye shall be able to quench all the fiery darts of the wicked.
- "And take the helmet of salvation,
- "and the sword of the Spirit, which is the word of God . . .
- "praying always with all prayer and supplication in the Spirit, and watching thereunto with all perseverance and supplication for all saints" (Eph.6:10-18).

Thought

As a minister, your calling is not to a life of enjoyment and ease but to a life of hard conflict. There are foes within and foes without. From the cradle to the grave, there is constant struggle against the corruptible lusts of the flesh and the imposing temptations offered by the world and Satan—a struggle against fleshly corruptions that inevitably lead to death. What can you do? Learn and know that your warfare is not human or physical, but spiritual. You are not struggling against flesh and blood—against another person—but against spiritual forces that possess unbelievable power. You must, therefore, protect yourself. How? By putting on the *armor of God*. There are seven pieces to the armor of God:

a) The belt of *truth*: you must put on the truth of Christ and of the Word of God.

b) The breastplate of *righteousness*: you must put on the righteousness of Christ and live righteously as you walk day by day.

c) The sandals of the *gospel of peace*: you must put on the gospel of peace—make sure you possess the gospel yourself—and share the gospel wherever your feet take you.

d) The shield of *faith*: above all you must put on faith—belief in God and His Word. Faith—believing God and His Word and promises—will quench all the fiery temptations and trials of the devil.

e) The helmet of *salvation*: put on salvation. Salvation means deliverance. Put on the salvation of Christ and work out your own salvation or deliverance (Ph.2:12). Do all you can in saving and delivering yourself and God will deliver you. The result will be a glorious salvation and deliverance from all the temptations, trials, and corruptions of this world.

f) The sword of the *Word of God*: take up the Word of God—study, learn, memorize, and use the Word. Live by the Word of God and you will be protected more and more from the onslaught of the temptations and trials of the enemy. Use the Word of God to fight and win battle after battle, day after day.

g) The supernatural provision, *prayer*: put on prayer—clothe yourself in prayer—a constant spirit of prayer. As you enter conflict after conflict throughout the day, pray and ask God to protect and deliver you from the temptations and trials of the enemy.

As a minister, you must put on the armor of God. You can never stand against the onslaught of Satan's temptations and trials unless you are clothed in God's armor.

A suggestion: pray for the armor of God—each piece of the armor—every morning as you begin the day. Ask God to clothe you with each piece of armor. (See *The Preacher's Outline & Sermon Bible,*® outline and notes—Eph.6:10-20 for more discussion.)

B. YOU AND SCRIPTURE

1. *You must study and obey the Scriptures daily: you must live by the Word of God and proclaim it.*

> "**Study to show thyself approved unto God, a workman that needeth not to be ashamed, rightly dividing the word of truth**" (2 Tim.2:15).
> "**All scripture is given by inspiration of God, and is profitable for doctrine, for reproof, for correction, for instruction in righteousness**"(2 Tim.3:16).

"Meditate upon these things [the teachings of God's Word]; give thyself wholly to them; that thy profiting may appear to all" (1 Tim.4:15).

"These were more noble than those in Thessalonica, in that they received the word with all readiness of mind, and searched the scriptures <u>daily</u>, whether those things were so" (Acts 17:11).

"And now, brethren, I commend you to God, and to the word of his grace, which is able to build you up, and to give you an inheritance among all them which are sanctified" (Acts 20:32).

"As newborn babes, desire the sincere milk of the word, that ye may grow thereby: if so be ye have tasted that the Lord is gracious" (1 Pt.2:2-3).

"This book of the law shall not depart out of thy mouth; but thou shalt meditate therein day and night, that thou mayest observe to do according to all that is written therein: for then thou shalt make thy way prosperous, and then thou shalt have good success" (Josh.1:8).

"But his delight is in the law of the LORD; and in his law doth he meditate <u>day and night</u>" (Ps.1:2).

"My hands also will I lift up unto thy commandments, which I have loved; and I will meditate in thy statutes" (Ps.119:48).

Thought

As a minister, you must study and obey the Scriptures *daily*. Two significant points need to be noted.

a) The Bible is God's Word: it is *inspired* by God (2 Tim.3:16). The Word "inspired" means *breathed by God*. God has given you the Bible so that you will know how to live upon the earth. You are to study the Bible...

- for *doctrine* or *teaching*
- for *reproof*
- for *correction*
- for *instruction in righteousness*

Note these four things: they cover the whole scope of life—everything we need to live a life that conquers and overflows with the fulness of life.

As a minister of God, you must always remember this: the Scripture alone will perfect or mature you and equip you to do every good work. You were made for God; therefore you must live by the Word of God. Your aim must be to study and learn exactly how God wants you to live and minister.

b) You must study and live by the Word of God. Note 2 Tim.2:15 above. The word "study" means to set your heart upon: be diligent, hurry, rush, and seek the *approval of God*. God's approval is to be your concern. A believer is a fool if he does not seek the approval of God. To be disapproved is to be displeasing and unacceptable to God. How then can you secure the approval of God?

- By being a workman. The idea is that of a diligent worker who toils and labors to the point of exhaustion.

But note: your work is pinpointed and identified. You are to be a workman by studying the Word of God and rightly dividing it. The words "rightly divide" (ortho-tomounta) mean to cut straight. You are to cut straight to the truth; you are not to take crooked paths and side tracks to the truth. You are to study the truth and rightly divide it. Once you have studied and learned the Word of God, you are to *accurately teach* the Word of God. You are not to teach . . .

- your own ideas
- the theories of other people
- what you think
- what other men think

You are not to mishandle the Word of God: twist it to fit what you think or want it to say; add to or take away from it; over-emphasize or under-emphasize its teachings. Any person who mishandles God's Word is not approved of God. This is the point of this verse: if you want God's approval—if you want to be acceptable to God—you must study; rush and seek to be a true teacher of God's Word. You must be a *workman* who studies God's Word, a workman who studies diligently: *who correctly analyzes and accurately divides—rightly handles and skillfully teaches the Word of Truth* (Amplified New Testament).

As a minister, if you study and obey the Scriptures daily, you will not be ashamed when you face the Lord Jesus Christ in the day of judgment.

2. *You must memorize the Word of God; let it dwell in your heart and life* all day, every day.

> "Let the word of Christ <u>dwell in you</u> richly in all wisdom; teaching and admonishing one another in psalms and hymns and spiritual songs" (Col.3:16).
>
> "Wherewithal shall a young man cleanse his way? by taking heed thereto according to thy word .... Thy word have I <u>hid in mine heart</u>, that I might not sin against thee" (Ps.119:9, 11).
>
> "Thy words were found, and I did eat them; and thy word was unto me the joy and rejoicing of mine heart: for I am called by thy name, O LORD God of hosts" (Jer.15:16).

Thought

As a minister, you must memorize the Word of God; you must let the Word of God dwell in you richly. You must have a heart rich with the Word of Christ. You are to let the Word of Christ dwell in your heart. Throughout Scripture this is the only time "the Word of God" is referred to as "the Word of Christ." The emphasis of Colossians is Christ; therefore, the Word of God becomes the *Word of Christ* in this great book. (Cp. 2 Cor.2:17; 4:2; 1 Th.1:8; 2:13; 4:15; 2 Th.3:1.)

Three significant points are made about the Word of Christ or the Word of God.

a) The choice is up to you: the Word of Christ does not naturally dwell within your heart. The word "dwell" (enoikeito) means to be at home or to make a home; to abide or dwell within. You must make room within your heart for the Word of Christ. You must let the Word of Christ enter your heart and make a home within your heart. You must let the Word of Christ dwell and abide in your heart. You must clean out all the old furnishings of your heart and let the Word of Christ settle down as the permanent resident within your heart.

Note the word "richly." It is important, for the Word of Christ must be allowed to dwell *richly* within your heart. You are not to be satisfied with just a meager visit by the Word of Christ. You are to let the Word of Christ *dwell richly* within you. The Word of Christ must be allowed to furnish your heart with all the wealth of its commandments and promises, instructions and warnings.

b) The reason why you are to let the Word of Christ dwell within you is clearly stated: you are to teach and admonish others in all wisdom. This is the believer's task, the very reason God has not yet taken us home to heaven: to teach and admonish one another. By teaching is meant the instruction of the Word and by admonition is meant the warning of Scripture. But how can we teach and admonish others if we . . .

- do not know the Word of Christ?
- do not let the Word of Christ dwell in us?

The answer is obvious: we can't. And note another fact: it is not enough to know the Word of Christ. You must be living the Word of Christ. Knowing the Word and not living it is hypocrisy. As a minister, your very life must be the home, the dwelling place for the Word of Christ. When people look at you, they must immediately see that your life is indwelt by the Word of Christ. Something else should be pointed out as well. You can teach and admonish others, but not *in wisdom*. You can teach the world's philosophy and ideas about reality and truth—God and the universe—but they are only the crude notions of men. The truth and wisdom of life are found in the *Word of Christ and in the Word of Christ alone*.

c) There is a way to tell whether or not the Word of Christ dwells in you: Are you teaching and admonishing others in psalms and hymns and spiritual songs, singing with grace in your heart *to the Lord*? As you walk throughout the day are you . . .

- talking about Christ?
- sharing the Word of Christ with others?

- teaching others about Christ?
- admonishing and encouraging and warning others in Christ?
- singing to yourself and with others about Christ?

What a contrasting picture of how so many of us live! The minister is to live and move and have his being in Christ, and he is to let Christ live and move and have His being in him. For you, *to live must be Christ.* You are to walk all day long talking about and sharing Christ, teaching and admonishing others in the Word of Christ, singing the psalms of Scripture, the hymns of the church, and the spiritual songs that arise out of a heart filled with the joy of the Lord and His Word.

3. *You must be consistent in the Scriptures—studying and living as Scripture dictates.*

> **"But continue thou in the things which thou hast learned and hast been assured of, knowing of whom thou hast learned them" (2 Tim.3:14).**

Thought
As a minister, you must continue on in the Scriptures—studying and living as Scripture dictates. Note the Scripture above. Timothy had been taught the Scriptures all of his life. When he was only a child, his mother Eunice and his grandmother Lois had rooted him in the Scriptures (2 Tim.1:5; 3:15). They were both strong believers in the Lord. Paul had also grounded Timothy in the Scriptures. But note a most critical point:

- it is not enough to have learned the Scripture.
- it is not enough to be assured that the teachings of Scripture are true.
- it is not enough to know that your teachers teach the truth.

Timothy knew all this. He had learned the Scriptures and he had found the Scriptures to be true. The claims and promises of Scripture had worked in his own life. Timothy also knew his teachers; their lives bore testimony to the truth of Scripture. But this was not enough.

Note the word "continue" (mene). It means to abide, dwell, remain, and stay in the Scripture. Simply stated, you must *live* in the Scripture—live, move, and have your being in the Scripture. And more, you must *live out* the Scripture—continue to walk in the truths of the Scripture.

As a minister, you must do what Scripture says. Note four significant points in this verse.

a) You must learn the Scripture.

b) You must be assured of the Scriptures, apply them to your life, and experience the truth and assurance of them.

c) You must know your teachers, those whom you sit under at conferences, revivals, school, and other places. You must *make sure* they teach the truth of the Scripture.

d) You must continue in the Scripture: abide and dwell, remain and stay in the Scripture. You must live and move and have your being in Scripture. You must live out the Scripture—walk day by day obeying and doing exactly what God says and commands in the Scripture.

C. You and Prayer

1. *You must pray daily, pray as Christ taught you to pray in the Lord's prayer.*

   > "After this manner therefore pray ye: . . .
   > - **Our Father**
   > - **Which art in heaven**
   > - **Hallowed be thy name**
   > - **Thy kingdom come**
   > - **Thy will be done in earth, as it is in heaven**
   > - **Give us this day our daily bread**
   > - **And forgive us our debts, as we forgive our debtors**
   > - **And lead us not into temptation, but deliver us from evil**
   > - **For thine is the kingdom, and the power, and the glory, for ever. Amen"** (Mt.6:9-13).

Thought

As a minister, you must pray daily the Lord's prayer: pray through the points of the prayer. What is the Lord's prayer? Is it a prayer to be recited as it so often is—just by memory, or just as a form prayer?

Note the words "After this manner . . . pray ye." Note also Luke's account where the disciples asked Jesus to teach them to pray (Lk.11:1-2). The prayer was given to show the disciples *how to pray*—how they should go about praying, not the *words* they should pray. The very context of what Christ had just taught shows this clearly (cp. Mt.6:5-8).

The Lord's prayer is a model prayer that is to be *prayed through*. It is "after this manner," *in this way, like this*, that you are to pray. Christ was teaching the disciples how to pray. He was giving words, phrases, thoughts that are to be the points of your prayer. You are to develop the points as you pray. An example would be something like this:

- "Our Father . . .": "Thank you, Father, that you are our Father—that you have adopted me as a child of God, a son of yours. Thank you for the believers of the world who make up the family of God. Thank you for the church, the body of Christ that gives us the family of God. Thank you for loving me that much." And on and on you are to pray.

- ". . .which art in heaven": "Thank you for heaven—that you are in heaven—that you have chosen me to be with you in heaven. Thank you for the hope and anticipation of heaven." And on and on you are to pray.

Christ taught His disciples to pray "after this manner." When you pray through the Lord's prayer, you find you have covered the scope of what God wants you to pray.

How much pain the Lord's heart must bear because of the way man has abused and misused His prayer! How desperately believers need to pray through the Lord's prayer! How desperately the *prophets and teachers* of the Word need to pray as Christ taught! How much you and all of the ministers of God need to preach and teach that the Lord's prayer is to be *prayed through* and not just recited. (See *The Preacher's Outline &*

Sermon Bible,® outline and notes—Mt.6:9-13 for more discussion.)

2. *You must pray daily for the church and for believers. Paul's prayer for the church and for believers is a good pattern to use and to pray through.*

> "For this cause I bow my knees unto the Father of our Lord Jesus Christ, of whom the whole family in heaven and earth is named, that he would grant you, according to the riches of his glory...
>
> - to be strengthened with might by his Spirit in the inner man
> - that Christ may dwell in your hearts by faith
> - that ye, being [may be] rooted and grounded in love
> - [that ye] may be able to comprehend with all saints what is the breadth, and length, and depth, and height
> - and to know the love of Christ, which passeth knowledge
> - that ye might be filled with all the fulness of God" (Eph.3:14-19).
>
> "Praying always with all prayer and supplication in the Spirit, and watching thereunto with all perseverance and supplication for all saints" (Eph.6:18).

Thought

As a minister, you must pray daily for the church and for believers. Paul's prayer is a good pattern to use and to pray through. This is probably the second most important prayer in all the Bible, ranking second only to the Lord's model prayer (Mt.6:9-13). Because of its importance, we are wise to use it as a daily guide in praying for the church and believers. Certainly, this is the reason God has included it in the Holy Scripture. Note the points and detail as it is read and studied. Its focus is a mature believer in Christ. A suggestion: begin to pray daily for the church and believers by following the points of the prayer. For example, ask God to strengthen His church and people by His Spirit—strengthen and make them stronger and stronger.

And then pray through the other requests of the prayer. What a difference there would be in the church and among God's people if we would bathe each other in the points of this prayer! As a minister of God, begin now. Pray through the Lord's prayer and Paul's prayer for the church and believers every day.

3. *You must pray daily for the whole world—for all people everywhere.*

> "I exhort therefore, that, first of all, supplications, prayers, intercessions, and giving of thanks, be made for <u>all men</u>; for kings, and for all that are in authority; that we may lead a quiet and peaceable life in all godliness and honesty. For this is good and acceptable in the sight of God our Saviour; who will have all men to be saved, and to come unto the knowledge of the truth" (1 Tim.2:1-4).

Thought
As a minister, you must pray daily for the whole world—for all people everywhere. Not a single person is to be omitted or left out of your prayers. You are to pray for all persons:

- the high and the low
- the educated and the uneducated
- the important and the unimportant
- the rich and the poor
- the leader and the followers
- the old and the young
- the friend and the enemy

Pray for all men. Do not neglect, ignore, or bypass any person. Every person needs prayer; every person needs God: His salvation, care, direction, approval, and acceptance. Therefore, pray for all men.

Note: this is an *exhortation* (parakaleo) to pray, which means that it is both an encouragement and a charge. You are both *encouraged and charged* to pray. You are given the encouragement and charge to pray just as a soldier is encouraged and charged to fight.

"First of all" stresses just how important prayer is. "First of all"—above all else, of supreme importance—put prayer first. "First of all"—before all else—pray for all men.

Note that four kinds of prayer are mentioned. This also stresses the importance of praying for all men.

a) There is "supplication" (deeseis). This refers to the prayers that focus upon special needs—deep and intense needs. When you see special needs in the lives of people—all people—you are to supplicate for them. That is, you are to be carrying the need before God with a great sense of urgency: you are to plead and beg for the person or persons. The idea is that of intense and deep brokenness before God in behalf of others, that God would help and save the person.

Just think what a different world this would be, what a different community we would have, if we really took the names and needs of people before God and pleaded for them in an intense brokenness and tears. Just think . . .

- how many more loved ones would be saved and helped.
- how many more within our community, state, country, and world would be saved and helped.
- how fewer problems would exist within society.

Scripture emphatically declares: "Ye have not, because ye ask not" (Jas.4:2).

b) There are "prayers" (proseuchas). This refers to the special times of prayer throughout the day that you set aside for devotion and worship. You are to have set times for prayer, times that you set aside to worship God and when you pray for all men.

c) There are "intercessions" (enteuxeis). This refers to bold praying; to standing before God in behalf of another person. Christ is your Intercessor, the One who stands between God and you in your behalf. But you are also to intercede for men, to carry their names and lives before God. You are to boldly approach God and pray for them, expecting God to hear and answer—all in the name of Christ. You are to intercede for all men—to stand in the gap between them and God—boldly praying and asking God to be merciful and gracious in salvation and in deliverance.

d) There is "thanksgiving" (eucharistias). This means that you thank God for hearing and answering—thank Him for what He has done and is going to do for all men.

> "Ask, and it shall be given you; seek, and ye shall find; knock, and it shall be opened unto you" (Mt.7:7).
> "The effectual fervent prayer of a righteous man availeth much. Elias was a man subject to like passions as we are... he prayed earnestly that it might not rain: and it rained not on the earth by the space of three years and six months. And he prayed again, and the heaven gave rain, and the earth brought forth her fruit" (Jas.5:16-18).

4. *You must pray daily for more laborers.*

> "Therefore said he unto them, The harvest truly is great, but the labourers are few: pray ye therefore the Lord of the harvest, that he would send forth labourers into his harvest" (Lk.10:2.) (See *The Preacher's Outline & Sermon Bible,*® note—Mt.9:36-38 for more discussion.)

Thought

As a minister, you must constantly—all day long—keep this fact before your mind: there are not enough laborers, and the need is overwhelming. You must, therefore, pray diligently for more laborers. You must make this your constant prayer as you walk throughout the day: you must increasingly be asking God to raise up more and more laborers. Jesus gives four reasons why in the verse above.

a) There is a great harvest of precious souls to be reached with the gospel. The number is staggering, and the vast majority are without Jesus, reeling to and fro under the weight of the problems of a sinful and dying world. All men everywhere are fainting, weary, bewildered, scattered, and are as sheep without a shepherd. Laborers are needed, desperately needed, to reach the harvest of souls throughout the fields of the world.

> "Say not ye, There are yet four months, and then cometh harvest? Behold, I say unto you, Lift up your eyes, and look on the fields; for they are white already to harvest. And he that reapeth receiveth wages, and gathereth fruit unto life eternal: that both he that soweth and he that reapeth may rejoice together" (Jn.4:35-36).

> "And let us not be weary in well doing: for in due season we shall reap, if we faint not" (Gal.6:9).

b) The laborers are few, very few.

> "How then shall they call on him in whom they have not believed? and how shall they believe in him of whom they have not heard? and how shall they hear without a preacher? and how shall they preach, except they be sent? as it is written, How beautiful are the feet of them that preach the gospel of peace, and bring glad tidings of good things!" (Ro.10:14-15).

c) The need is urgent: the crop of souls is ripe, ready for *harvest*. Some want the *gospel*, the answer to life. They are actually ready to be reaped, wanting purpose, meaning, and significance in their lives. They might not know what is causing the longing, emptiness, and unfulfillment within their hearts; they might not know how to identify it, but they are ready to listen and grab hold of the answer. And Jesus is the answer. You must, therefore, pray for more laborers to take the glorious gospel to them.

d) God is the One who has to send forth laborers. He is the Source of laborers, and prayer is the method He uses to send them forth. Pray, therefore; diligently pray and keep on praying for laborers.

5. *You must pray always—moment by moment—striving to gain an unbroken consciousness of the Lord.*

> "Continue in prayer, and watch in the same with thanksgiving; withal praying also for us, that God would open unto us a door of utterance, to speak the mystery of Christ, for which I am also in bonds: that I may make it manifest, as I ought to speak" (Col.4:2-4).
>
> "Pray without ceasing" (1 Th.5:17).
>
> "And he spake a parable unto them to this end, that men ought always to pray, and not to faint" (Lk.18:1).
>
> "Watch and pray, that ye enter not into temptation: the spirit indeed is willing, but the flesh is weak" (Mt.26:41).
>
> "Seek the LORD and his strength, seek his face continually" (1 Chron.16:11).
>
> "And ye shall seek me, and find me, when ye shall search for me with all your heart" (Jer.29:13).

Thought

As a minister, you must pray always—moment by moment—striving to gain an unbroken consciousness of the Lord. Prayer is the first duty of the believer. Therefore, prayer is bound to be your first duty, the first duty of the minister. Note Col.4:2-4 above. Four important instructions are given, instructions that desperately need to be heeded.

a) First, *continue steadfastly in prayer*. The word "continue" (proskartereite) means to be constant, persevering, and unwearied in prayer. It means to be in constant and unbroken prayer, to be in constant and unbroken fellowship and communion with God. It means to walk and breathe prayer, to live and move and have your being in prayer. It means to never face a moment when you are not in prayer.

How is this possible? When you have so many duties and affairs that demand your attention, how can you continue and walk in unbroken prayer? What Scripture means is that you . . .

- develop an *attitude of prayer*.
- walk in a *spirit of prayer*.
- take a mental break from your work and spend a moment *in prayer*—all throughout the day.

- *pray always* when your mind is not upon some duty.

- *arise early* and pray before daily activities begin. Spend a worship time with God in prayer. Make this a continued practice.

- *pray before going to bed.* Spend an extended time in prayer before going to bed. Make this a continued practice.

In all honesty, the vast majority of us waste minute after minute every hour in useless daydreaming and wandering thoughts—wasting precious time that could be spent in prayer. If we would learn to capture these minutes for prayer, we would discover what it is to walk and live in prayer. Note a critical fact: this is your duty. It is not something God can do for you. You are the one who has to discipline yourself to pray. If you do not pray, then prayer never gets done.

Scripture is clear: you are to "continue in prayer."

> "**Casting down imaginations, and every high thing that exalteth itself against the knowledge of God, and bringing into captivity every thought to the obedience of Christ**" (2 Cor.10:5).
>
> "Be careful for nothing; but **in everything** by prayer and supplication with thanksgiving let your requests be made known unto God" (Ph.4:6).
>
> "Seek the lord and his strength, seek his face **continually**" (1 Chron.16:11).

b) Second, *watch in prayer*. The word "watch" (gregorountes) means to stay awake, be alert, be sleepless, be active, concentrate. It means to fight against distractions, drowsiness, sluggishness, wandering thoughts, and useless daydreaming. It means to discipline your mind and control your thoughts in prayer. Being very honest, this is a problem that afflicts every believer sometime. Overwork, tiredness, pressure, strain—an innumerable list of things can make it very difficult to concentrate in prayer. This is the very reason Paul stresses the need to *watch in prayer*. But note: vigilance in prayer is your duty. Again, it is not something that God does for you. You are responsible for watching and concentrating.

You are the one who is to discipline your mind and control your thoughts. For this reason, you must never give up in prayer. You must...

- always struggle against drowsiness and wandering thoughts.
- learn to concentrate—to discipline your mind and control your thoughts.
- teach yourself to watch in prayer.

> "And he cometh unto the disciples, and findeth them asleep, and saith unto Peter, What, could ye not watch with me one hour? Watch and pray, that ye enter not into temptation: the spirit indeed is willing, but the flesh is weak" (Mt.26:40-41).

c) Third, pray with thanksgiving. When someone does something for you, you thank that person. The One Person who has done more for you than anyone else is God. Therefore, you are to thank Him. In fact, God continues to bless and help you; His hand is constantly upon your life, looking after and caring for you; therefore, you should continually thank Him. Your praise should be lifted up to Him all through the day as you go about your daily affairs. An hour should never pass when you have not praised and thanked God several times. You should never forget His Son—that He actually took your sins upon Himself and bore the judgment and punishment of them. This alone should continually fill your heart with thanksgiving and praise.

> "Giving thanks <u>always</u> for all things unto God and the Father in the name of our Lord Jesus Christ" (Eph.5:20).
>
> "In every thing give thanks: for this is the will of God in Christ Jesus concerning you" (1 Th.5:18).

d) Fourth, pray for others, in particular for their ministry. Be an intercessor for the other ministers of God. Remember: Paul was in prison, but note that for which he requested prayer. Paul did not ask the church to pray for his release. He requested prayer for his ministry. He wanted the believers praying that God would give him...

- opportunity for witnessing—for sharing the mystery or salvation of Christ.
- boldness in witnessing (Col.4:4).

You must always remember that prayer is one of the laws of the universe. Granted, it is a law that is denied by most and ignored by others. Even those who understand it to be one of God's laws often neglect it. Nevertheless, God has established the spiritual law that He works in response to prayer. Whether we believe it or not, God clearly says that prayer is a law of the universe (cp. Jas.4:2). Prayer is the law by which He works and moves in behalf of men and their world. Therefore, if you want the blessings of God upon your life and ministry—if you want the work of God going forth in power and bearing fruit—you must pray for the ministers of the gospel. You must learn to intercede in prayer both for yourself and for the other ministers of God scattered all over the world.

6. *You must take some extended time for fervent prayer when very special needs exist.*

> "**And in the morning, rising up a great while before day, he [Jesus] went out, and departed into a solitary place, and there prayed**" (Mk.1:35).
>
> "**And when he [Jesus] had sent them away, he departed into a mountain to pray. And when even was come, the ship was in the midst of the sea, and he alone on the land**" (Mk.6:46-47).
>
> "**And it came to pass in those days, that he [Jesus] went out into a mountain to pray, and continued all night in prayer to God**" (Lk.6:12).
>
> "**And he [Jesus] was withdrawn from them about a stone's cast, and kneeled down, and prayed. Saying, Father, if thou be willing, remove this cup [the cross] from me: nevertheless not my will, but thine, be done**" (Lk.22:41-42).

Thought

As a minister, you must take some extended time for fervent prayer when very special needs exist. This was the constant practice of your Lord. The above Scriptures clearly show this.

a) Jesus arose in the morning, a great while before day, and prayed (Mk.1:35). Why? Because He was exhausted from the pressure of constant ministry. Just the day before He had ministered all day and on into the late hours of the evening. He needed a very special time with the Father, a time when the Father could renew and strengthen Him.

b) Jesus sent the crowd away and went up into a mountain to pray (Mk.6:46-47). Why? Because He was about to need extraordinary strength to perform a spectacular miracle, a miracle that was to prove His deity, that He was truly the Son of God. He was to calm the storm and save the lives of the apostles. Christ needed a very special time with the Father right before confronting the need to demonstrate His power over nature.

c) Jesus went up into a mountain to pray all night to God (Lk.6:12). Why? To seek the leadership of the Father. The very next morning was to be one of the great days of His life: the day that He was to choose His apostles.

d) Jesus withdrew from the apostles—got all alone—knelt down, and prayed (Lk.22:41-42). Why? Because He was about to face the crisis of His life, death upon the cross. Christ needed the very special strength and assurance of the Father.

The point is this: if Christ Himself needed extended times for fervent prayer, how much more do you as a minister of God? You—and all other ministers of God—must begin to take more and more time for prayer. You must begin to seek God more and more for the desperate needs of your people, ministry, community, country, and world.

CHAPTER 9

What Your Personal Life and Behavior as a Minister Must Be

How you take care of you body and mind, how you behave and conduct yourself, and how you handle financial matters are of critical importance to God. He cares deeply about how you live and behave among both the godly and ungodly of the world.

Contents

A. You and Your Body and Mind	223
1. You must present your body as a living sacrifice to God.	223
2. You must know that your body is the temple of the Holy Spirit.	224
3. You must struggle to control your mind—even every thought—and think only positive thoughts.	225
4. You must discipline and subject your body to Christ lest you become a castaway.	227
5. You must exercise your body both spiritually and physically.	228
B. You and Your Conduct	229
1. You must live a life of godly character.	229
2. You must live a life of separation, a life separate from the world.	231
3. You must be a man of God.	233

4. You must be faithful through temptations and trials, faithful no matter how severe the temptations and trials may be.	235
5. You must flee youthful lusts.	236
6. You must shun godless and empty talk and avoid questionable teachings and arguments.	237
7. You must know that perilous times are coming and turn away from selfish and ungodly men.	240

C. You and Your Financial Support — 242

1. You must receive financial support without being embarrassed or feeling guilty, but you must not seek luxury.	242
2. You must not covet worldly wealth.	243
3. You must work at secular employment if needed in order to preach the gospel.	244
4. You must trust God to meet your financial needs.	245

Chapter 9
What Your Personal Life and Behavior as a Minister Must Be

A. **You and Your Body and Mind**

1. *You must present your body as a living sacrifice to God.*

    "I beseech you therefore, brethren, by the mercies of God, that ye present your bodies a living sacrifice, holy, acceptable unto God, which is your reasonable service" (Ro.12:1-2)

    Thought
    God demands your body. God is not interested only in your spirit; He is vitally interested in your body. Your body is to be God's—to be presented as a living sacrifice to God. What does a living sacrifice mean?

    a) A living sacrifice means a *constant, continuous sacrifice*, not just an occasional dedication of your body. You do not sacrifice your body to God today, and then take your body back into your own hands and do your own thing tomorrow. A *living sacrifice* means that you dedicate your body *to live for God and to keep on living for God.*

    b) A living sacrifice means a *sacrifice of your body wherever you are*. A particular place is not needed. The sacrifice of your body is a living sacrifice; it is to be made while your body is living right where it is. And the offering of a living sacrifice is to be made today—*right now* while your body is living.

    c) A living sacrifice means that your body *sacrifices its own desires and it lives for God*. Your body lives a holy, righteous, pure, clean, and moral life for God. Your body does not pollute, dirty, nor contaminate itself with the sins and corruptions of the world. Your body is sacrificed for God and dedicated to live as He commands.

d) A living sacrifice means that your body *lives for God by serving God*. It means that your body sacrifices and gives up its own ambitions and desires, and it serves God while upon this earth. Your body gives itself to the work of proclaiming the love of God and of ministering to a world reeling in desperate needs. Your body sacrifices itself to serve God and Him alone. Your body is dedicated to God as a living sacrifice.

As a minister, you are to dedicate your body to God. Your body is to be a *living sacrifice* for God in the home, church, school, office, plant, restaurant, club, park, car, and plane. No matter where your body is, your body is to be sacrificed to God.

2. *You must know that your body is the temple of the Holy Spirit.*

> "What? know ye not that your body is the temple of the Holy Ghost which is in you, which ye have of God, and ye are not your own? For ye are bought with a price: therefore glorify God in your body, and in your spirit, which are God's" (1 Cor.6:19-20; cp. Acts 2:38; Ro.8:9).
>
> "Know ye not that ye are the temple of God, and that the Spirit of God dwelleth in you? If any man defile the temple of God, him shall God destroy; for the temple of God is holy, which temple ye are" (1 Cor.3:16-17).
>
> "And I will pray the Father, and he shall give you another Comforter, that he may abide with you for ever; even the Spirit of truth; whom the world cannot receive, because it seeth him not, neither knoweth him: but ye know him; for <u>he dwelleth with you, and shall be in you</u>" (Jn.14:16-17).
>
> "And what agreement hath the temple of God with idols? for ye are the temple of the living God; as God hath said, I will dwell in them, and walk in them; and I will be their God, and they shall be my people" (2 Cor.6:16).

Thought

As a minister, your body and spirit belong to God (1 Cor.6:19-20). Before you accepted Jesus Christ, you did what you wanted with your body: gave it over to such things as immorality, drunkenness, overeating, greed, and to a host of other things. But now, since you have accepted Jesus Christ and committed your life to Him, He owns your body and spirit. He bought and purchased your body upon the cross when He died for you. Therefore, you owe your body to God. Your body is now the temple for God's presence, for the indwelling of God's precious Holy Spirit. God's Spirit actually lives within your body. You must, therefore, glorify God in your body and in your spirit. (Also see p. 4,43,51,146.)

3. *You must struggle to control your mind—even every thought—and think only positive thoughts.*

> "Casting down <u>imaginations</u>, and every high thing that exalteth itself against the knowledge of God, and bringing into captivity <u>every thought</u> to the obedience of Christ" (2 Cor.10:5).
>
> "Finally, brethren, whatsoever things are <u>true</u>, whatsoever things are <u>honest</u>, whatsoever things are <u>just</u>, whatsoever things are <u>pure</u>, whatsoever things are <u>lovely</u>, whatsoever things are of <u>good report</u>; if there be any virtue, and if there be any praise, <u>think on these things</u>" (Ph.4:8).
>
> "For they that are after the flesh do mind [keep their minds on] the things of the flesh; but they that are after the Spirit the things of the Spirit" (Ro.8:5).
>
> "We have the <u>mind</u> of Christ" (1 Cor.2:16).
>
> "Thou wilt keep him in perfect peace, whose mind is stayed [kept] on thee: because he trusteth in thee" (Is.26:3).

Thought
As a minister, you are to focus your thoughts upon the good things of life and upon God. You are to give your mind to *positive thinking*. In fact, you are to think only positive thoughts. You are never to keep an immoral, fleshly, worldly, selfish, sinful, or evil thought in your mind. You cannot help wrong thoughts flashing across your mind, but you must not harbor them, allow them to roost in your mind. Sinful and negative thoughts disrupt and destroy peace. For this reason, you are to struggle to conquer your mind and thoughts. You are to exert

every cell of energy possible to captivate and control every thought. What we think is so important that God tells us what we are to think.

a) You are to captivate every thought and make it obedient to Christ (2 Cor.10:5):

- Cast down *every imagination*: thoughts that flash across your mind, that are uncontrolled, wild, evil, lustful, immoral, selfish, unjust, wrong, untrue, devilish, and set against God.

- Cast down *every high thing* that exalts itself against the knowledge of God: false ideas about God, false doctrine, false teaching, false reasoning; the human pride and arrogance, self-sufficiency and self-righteousness that set themselves up against God.

- Struggle to captivate *every thought* and make it obedient to Christ: a *phenomenal statement*—every thought controlled and subjected to Christ! This is the spiritual objective of the true Christian believer. God created man for fellowship and communion, and the believer knows it; therefore, the believer wars—struggles and fights—to captivate every thought and focus it upon God and His righteousness. As a minister, you must seek to walk in an unbroken fellowship and communion with God.

b) You are to think on these things (Ph.4:8):

- "Whatsoever things are *true*": real and genuine. Many things in the world seem to be true, but they are not; they are false and deceptive, an illusion and a counterfeit. You are to keep your mind upon things that are true.

- "Whatsoever things are *honest*": honorable, worthy, revered, highly respected, and noble.

- "Whatsoever things are *just*": right and righteous behavior. It has to do with right behavior toward man and God. You are to keep your thoughts upon your duty toward men and God—upon doing what is right toward both.

- "Whatsoever things are *pure*": morally clean, spotless, stainless, chaste, undefiled, free from moral pollution, filth, dirt, and impurities. Your mind and thoughts are to be pure—every thought.

- "Whatsoever things are *lovely*": pleasing, winsome, kind, gracious; things that stir love and kindness. Your thoughts are not to be thoughts of unkindness and meanness, grumbling and murmuring, criticism and reaction. Your thoughts are to be focused upon things that are lovely—that build people up, not tear them down.

- "Whatsoever things are of *good report*": reputable, high-toned, worthy things; things of the highest quality. You are to think only upon worthy things, not to fill your mind with junk; you are not to listen to *bad reports*, no matter how *juicy* they may seem. Neither are you to fill your mind with junk, whether through rumor, radio, television, music, off-colored jokes, or some other source. Your thoughts are to be focused only upon worthy things—only upon that which is of *good report*.

- "If there be any virtue [excellence] and if there be any praise [in any thought], think on these things." Positive thinking is your answer to peace as a Christian minister.

4. *You must discipline and subject your body to Christ lest you become a castaway.*

> **"But I keep under my body, and bring it into subjection: lest that by any means, when I have preached to others, I myself should be a castaway" (1 Cor.9:27).**

Thought
As a minister, you must control your body; you must not let your body control you. How? By simply not giving in to it—by denying the body whatever it craves. It is tough at first, but you can do it by simply not giving in even if beads of sweat pop out (Heb.12:4). You can control your body by refusing to give in no matter the pain—by doing exactly what the disciplined athlete does. And in a few days or weeks the most glorious thing happens: the body is conquered, brought under control. The athletes and consistent exercisers of the world know this.

Therefore, you will never be excused for not disciplining your body.

You master your own body. The phrase "keep under" means to bruise, to beat back. You literally beat back your body and its cravings in order to bring it into subjection. The word *subjection* means to enslave, to lead about as a slave.

Note why you must discipline and subject your body: lest you be a "castaway." The Greek word means reprobate, rejected, disqualified, unfit, and failing to stand the test. As a minister, you must not live a carnal, fleshly life. A carnal, fleshly life demonstrates and proves that you are not genuine. And Scripture says this: if your life is not genuine, you will be disqualified, put on the shelf, and cast away. You must, therefore, keep your body under control: discipline and subject it to Christ and His righteousness.

5. *You must exercise your body both spiritually and physically.*

> "**Bodily exercise profiteth [a] little: but godliness is profitable unto all things, having promise of the life that now is, and of that which is to come**" (1 Tim.4:8).

Thought

As a minister of Christ, you must exercise your body both spiritually and physically. You are compared to an athlete.

a) You are to exercise (gumnasia) yourself in godliness as much as an Olympic athlete exercises his body. How much energy, effort, time, and dedication does an Olympic athlete put into his training? His sport is his life—unequivocally so. So it is with you: godliness is to be your life. All of your energy, effort, time, and dedication are to be given over to godliness. You are to know no *exercise* but the exercise of godliness.

b) Bodily exercise is profitable, but godliness is more profitable, far more profitable. You should exercise your body regularly; you should keep yourself physically fit. But the focus of your life is to be godliness. The reason is clear: godliness bears fruit—great fruit—both in this life and in the life to come. God promises to bless the godly person now while he walks upon this earth, and eternally when he receives the life to come. But know this: you must have a healthy and strong body—a body as healthy and strong as it can be—in order to be able to work long hours, in order to endure, last, and complete your day to day tasks. How much more work would get done for Christ if ministers would exercise their bodies? The truth is this: we could exercise our spirits to godliness much more if we exercised our bodies on a regular and consistent basis. A suggestion: begin an exercise program today if you are not physically fit—begin today and be consistent, pleasing the Lord.

B. YOU AND YOUR CONDUCT

1. *You must live a life of godly character.*

"This is a true saying, If a man desire the office of a bishop [minister], he desireth a good work. A bishop then must be blameless, the husband of one wife, vigilant, sober, of good behaviour, given to hospitality, apt to teach; not given to wine, no striker, not greedy of filthy lucre; but patient, not a brawler, not covetous; one that ruleth well his own house, having his children in subjection with all gravity; (for if a man know not how to rule his own house, how shall he take care of the church of God?) Not a novice, lest being lifted up with pride he fall into the condemnation of the devil. Moreover he must have a good report [testimony, witness] of them which are without [the church; unbelievers]; lest he fall into reproach and the snare of the devil" (1 Tim.3:1-7).

"If any be blameless, the husband of one wife, having faithful children not accused of riot or unruly. For a bishop must be blameless, as the steward of God; not self willed, not soon angry, not given to wine, no striker, not given to filthy lucre; but a lover of hospitality, a lover of good men, sober, just, holy, temperate; holding fast the faithful word as he hath been taught, that he may be able by sound doctrine both to exhort and to convince the gainsayers [those who oppose the minister]" (Tit.1:6-9).

Thought

The office of *bishop* is probably the same office as elder or presbyter or minister in the New Testament. All three words refer to the same person, to the minister of the gospel and of the church. What are the qualifications of the minister? Who should be preaching the gospel and filling the pulpits of the Lord's church? Who should be considering the ministry? What kind of person? The importance of these passages cannot be over stressed when it comes to the building and protection of God's church and people.

a) As a minister, you must meet some personal qualifications:

• Blameless: without reproach	1 Tim.3:2; Tit.1:6
• Husband of only one wife	1 Tim.3:2; Tit.1:6
• Vigilant: watchful, guarding oneself and one's people	1 Tim.3:2; Tit.1:7
• Sober	1 Tim.3:2; Tit.1:8
• Good behavior	1 Tim.3:2
• Given to hospitality	1 Tim.3:2; Tit.1:8
• Able to teach	1 Tim.3:2; Tit.1:9
• Not given to drunkenness of any sort	1 Tim.3:3; Tit.1:7
• Not a striker: not violent but gentle	1 Tim.3:3; Tit.1:7
• Not greedy of money or possessions	1 Tim.3:3; Tit.1:7
• Patient: kind, enduring, persevering	1 Tim.3:3
• Not a brawler: not a fighter but a peacemaker	1 Tim.3:3
• Not covetous: not seeking worldly pleasures, possessions, power, or recognition	1 Tim.3:3

- Not self-willed: not stubborn,
  arrogant, or overbearing — Tit.1:7
- Not angry: not quick-tempered
  or hotheaded — Tit.1:7
- Loves good men
  (the Greek means good
  things as well as good people) — Tit.1:8
- Just: honest, upright, and fair — Tit.1:8
- Holy: pure, clean, and moral — Tit.1:8
- Temperate: self-controlled — Tit.1:8
- Holds fast to the faithful
  Word of God — Tit.1:9

b) As a minister, you must meet some family qualifications:
- Manage your own family well — 1 Tim.3:4-5; Tit.1:6
- Teach and lead your children to obey — 1 Tim.3:4-5; Tit.1:6
- Be the husband of one wife. — 1 Tim.3:2; Tit.1:6

c) As a minister, you must meet a spiritual qualification:
- Not be a new convert, but be spiritually mature — 1 Tim.3:7

d) As a minister, you must meet a community qualification:
- Be a good testimony and witness — 1 Tim.3:7

2. *You must live a life of separation, a life separate from the world.*

> **"And be not conformed to this world: but be ye transformed by the renewing of your mind, that ye may prove what is that good, and acceptable, and perfect, will of God" (Ro.12:2).**
>
> **"Wherefore come out from among them, and be ye separate, saith the Lord, and touch not the unclean thing; and I will receive you, and will be a Father unto you, and ye shall be my**

sons and daughters, saith the Lord Almighty" (2 Cor.6:17-18, cp. v.14-16).

"Thou therefore endure hardness, as a good soldier of Jesus Christ. No man that warreth entangleth himself with the affairs of this life; that he may please him who hath chosen him to be a soldier" (2 Tim.2:3-4).

"Love not the world, neither the things that are in the world. If any man love the world, the love of the Father is not in him. For all that is in the world, the lust of the flesh, and the lust of the eyes, and the pride of life, is not of the Father, but is of the world" (1 Jn.2:15-16).

Thought

As a minister, you are to come out from among unbelievers and be separate (2 Cor.6:14-18). What does this mean? Of course, it does *not* mean that you are to leave the cities, communities, and workplaces of the world. You are not to isolate yourself from unbelievers. It does not mean that you have nothing to do with unbelievers—never talking, sharing, or associating with them. Both believers and unbelievers are in the world, and they have to share the world together.

What God means is at least two things.

a) God means that you differ from unbelievers, differ radically. Therefore . . .

- you are not to be "unequally yoked" with unbelievers. You are not to be *yoked*, not to be intimately involved, in a relationship with unbelievers (2 Cor.6:14).

- you are not to be in "fellowship" with unbelievers. You are not to share and participate in the worldly life and functions and events of unbelievers (2 Cor.6:14).

- you are not to be in "communion" with unbelievers. You are not to be closely bound in partnership with unbelievers. You are not to be so united with unbelievers that there has to be open and mutual sharing of person and possessions (2 Cor.6:14).

- you are not to be attached nor in covenant with unbelievers. You must not follow the worthless leader of the unbelievers, Satan (2 Cor.6:15).
- you are not to move about in the sphere, the realm, the life and position of the infidel, the person who has rejected Jesus Christ (2 Cor.6:15).
- you are not to worship with unbelievers (2 Cor.6:16).

b) God means that you are not to touch the unclean thing (2 Cor.6:17-18). You are no longer to live as the sinners of the world live. You are not to participate in the sins of unbelievers.

3. *You must be a man of God.*

> "But thou, O man of God, flee these things [the love of money and of possessions]: and follow after
> - righteousness
> - godliness
> - faith
> - love
> - patience
> - meekness.
>
> Fight the good fight of faith, lay hold on eternal life, whereunto thou art also called, and hast professed a good profession before many witnesses" (1 Tim.6:11-12).

Thought

As a minister, you must be a *man of God*. This means three things:

a) You, the man of God, must flee the passion for wealth. You are to flee the love of money—run away from it. Note a shocking fact, shocking because so many people love money and the things it can buy:

- The man who loves money is not a *man of God*. The man of God is the person who flees the love of money. The man of God does not love the world nor seek after the things of the world. He flees from the love and passions of this world.

b) You, the man of God, must follow after the things of God. The word "follow" is strong. It means to run after; to run swiftly after; to hotly pursue; to seek eagerly and earnestly. It has the idea of aiming at and pursuing until something is gained; of never giving up until you have reached your goal. There are six things you, the man of God, are to pursue.

- *Righteousness:* to be right with God and to do right.
- *Godliness:* to seek to be like God; to walk as God would walk if He were on earth; to seek after the character of God.
- *Faith:* both to believe God and to be faithful to God.
- *Love:* to have a sacrificial and selfless love—a love so great that it loves the unworthy, undeserving, ungodly, sinners, and even enemies of this world.
- *Patience:* to endure, persevere, and be steadfast.
- *Meekness:* to be gentle, tender, humble, mild, and considerate, but strongly so.

c) You, the man of God, must fight the good fight of faith and lay hold on eternal life. This is the picture of an athletic contest. The word "fight" means to agonize, struggle, battle, contend, and fight for the prize. It is the idea of a *desperate effort and struggle*. Note: the believer is in a desperate struggle for eternal life. Laying hold of the prize of eternal life is the struggle. Eternal life is the goal for which you, the man of God, are fighting.

Note an extremely significant point: what your profession as a minister is. When you commit your life to the ministry, you are professing . . .

- that you believe in eternal life—that eternal life is a reality.
- that you and all others who trust Christ shall live forever. You profess the reality of eternal life before "many witnesses"—all who know you and come in contact with you. The point is this: you, the man of God, must live up to your profession. You must do exactly what you profess: fight the good fight of faith and lay hold of eternal life.

4. *You must be faithful through temptations and trials, faithful no matter how severe the temptations and trials may be.*

"Are they ministers of Christ? (I speak as a fool) I am more;
- in labours more abundant
- in stripes above measure
- in prisons more frequent
- in deaths oft.
- Of the Jews five times received I forty stripes save one.
- Thrice was I beaten with rods
- once was I stoned
- thrice I suffered shipwreck, a night and a day I have been in the deep
- in journeyings often
- in perils of waters
- in perils of robbers
- in perils by mine own countrymen
- in perils by the heathen
- in perils in the city
- in perils in the wilderness
- in perils in the sea
- in perils among false brethren
- in weariness and painfulness
- in watchings often
- in hunger and thirst
- in fastings often
- in cold and nakedness.

Beside those things that are without, that which cometh upon me daily, the care of all the churches. Who is weak, and I am not weak? who is offended, and I burn not? If I must needs glory, I will glory of the things which concern mine infirmities" (2 Cor.11:23-30).

Thought

As a minister, you must be more than a minister. You must go well beyond most believers in ministering, laboring, and suffering. Paul was able to say that he was more of a minister of Christ than the false leaders and teachers. He was able to make such a claim because he went well beyond in laboring and sacrificing for Christ.

As a minister of Christ, you must go well beyond most in laboring and sacrificing for Christ.

- Diligent labor and sacrifice are the strongest answers to critics.

- Diligent labor and sacrifice are the only conceivable ways the world and its desperate needs will be reached and met for Christ. You must heed the commission of the Lord—you who have been called to be His ministers.

5. *You must flee youthful lusts.*

> **"Flee also youthful lusts: but follow righteousness, faith, charity, peace, with them that call on the Lord out of a pure heart. But foolish and unlearned questions avoid, knowing that they do gender strifes" (2 Tim.2:22-23).**

Thought

As a minister—especially a young minister—you must flee youthful lusts and follow after the things of God. Passionate desires and cravings are normal and natural. God made us to desire and crave. It is when we use our passions to hurt and damage that they become evil.

a) What are the lusts and cravings of youth—of young (or older) ministers?

- *The desires of the eye*: youth have a normal desire to have and possess, but the desire can become lust after persons and possessions.

- *The desires of the flesh*: youth desire companionship, but the desire can become lust for illicit sex.

- *The desire for acceptance*: youth desire friendship, recognition, and place or position. They want to fit in; but the desire can lead to self-seeking, pride, arrogance, or to a sense of inferiority or low self-esteem.

- *The desire to act and act now*: youth desire to see things now because they burst with enthusiasm and energy.

But the desire can lead to impatience and mistreatment of people.
- *The desire to be original and creative*: youth want the new and fresh idea, the better thought, and the better way to do things. But this can lead to a critical and argumentative spirit, or to cheating in order to be recognized.

b) What are the things of God that you as a young (or older) minister must follow?
- *Righteousness*: to be right with God and to do right.
- *Faith*: both to believe God and to be faithful to God.
- *Love*: to have a sacrificial and selfless love—a love so great that it loves the unworthy, undeserving, ungodly, sinners, and even enemies.
- *Peace*: to be bound, joined, and woven together with God and others; to keep and maintain good relationships with God and others.

6. *You must shun godless and empty talk and avoid questionable teachings and arguments.*

"But shun profane and vain babblings [discussions, talk]: for they will increase unto more ungodliness. And their word will eat as doth a canker: of whom is Hymenaeus and Philetus; who concerning the truth have erred, saying that the resurrection is past already; and overthrow the faith of some" (2 Tim.2:16-18, cp. 1 Tim.6:20-21).

"But avoid foolish questions, and genealogies, and contentions, and strivings about the law [the Word of God]; for they are unprofitable and vain" (Tit.3:9).

"Therefore said he unto them, The harvest truly is great, but the labourers are few: pray ye therefore the Lord of the harvest, that he would send forth labourers into his harvest. Go your ways: behold, I send you forth as lambs among wolves.... <u>salute no man by the way</u>" (Lk.10:2-4).

Thought

As a minister, you must keep away from three very damaging things.

a) You must keep away from godless chatter and discussion (2 Tim.2:16-18). This is descriptive language: it pictures so much talk that goes on among people, even among ministers.

- So much talk is "profane" (bebelos): common, irreverent, and godless talk.
- So much talk is vain: empty and meaningless.
- So much talk is *babbling*: nothing more than empty voices chattering away in empty and godless discussions.

The charge is direct and forceful: avoid, shun, keep away from godless and empty talk. What are some examples of talk that is godless and empty? There is such talk as . . .

- false teaching
- off-colored conversation
- worldly philosophy
- indecent insinuations
- cursing or foul language
- criticism
- theological theories
- gossip
- immoral suggestions
- suggestive enticements

Note the Scripture: such talk is not only ungodly and empty, it leads to more and more ungodliness. Such talk actually increases ungodliness in the heart and life of a person. In fact, the picture could be no more descriptive: ungodly talk eats away at a person just like a cancerous growth.

This is often ignored and neglected by most people, for most people want to go about doing their own thing. However, if we took this charge seriously, just think how it would affect the control of . . .

- television
- films
- decisions
- differences
- discussions
- opinions
- music
- arguments
- positions (theological, social, political)

This charge affects every form of communication and relationship imaginable. Imagine—no communication and no talk is ever to take place that is ungodly and empty. Why? Because ungodly and empty talk eats like a cancer. It leads you into more and more ungodliness and emptiness.

b) You must turn away from questionable teachings and arguments. Note: three things are pictured in Tit.3:9.

- There were some ministers and teachers who were spending their time sitting and discussing foolish (moros), useless, and stupid questions—discussions that accomplished nothing for the cause of Christ nor for the welfare of humanity.

- There were some ministers and teachers who were wasting time on genealogies, that is, on their roots and heritage. They felt they were acceptable to God because they had good parents and forefathers. They even felt the more outstanding they could show their roots to be, the more outstanding they would be in the eyes of society and God.

- There were ministers and teachers who were arguing and striving over the law, that is, over the Old Testament Scriptures. The false teachers of Paul's day were just like the false teachers of today and down through the centuries: they professed Christ but felt Christ was not enough to save them. They felt it took both the law and Christ to save them. To be saved a person had to believe in Christ, yes; but he also had to undergo the basic ritual of the law (circumcision, baptism, church membership, confirmation) and commit his life to keeping the law of God, including the thousands and thousands of rules surrounding the law.

Paul is saying that you, the true minister, should not become embroiled in the controversies of Scripture. They are "unprofitable and vain," useless and empty—of no value whatsoever. Christ is all that is needed. He and His Word are to be proclaimed and controversies turned away from. The proclamation of Christ and His Word must be the occupation of the minister, the very purpose for the minister's existence.

c) You must not waste time in empty conversation. Note Luke 10:2-4 above. The hour is urgent: the fields are ripe and the harvest of souls is waiting. You must not waste time by stopping along the way and carrying on needless conversation. Such time is to be spent in ministry and prayer. Your mission is to be focused upon another world that lasts forever, a world into which every man is to eventually enter. Many are to enter the next world lost and doomed to be separated from God forever. Man desperately needs to sense the urgency and commitment necessary to enter the Kingdom of God. This world and its needless affairs are not to be engaged in by the Christian minister. (Note: all affairs are not needless, but so many are.) You must not waste time in needless conversation. You must always be sharing the glorious hope and salvation that is in Christ Jesus our Lord.

7. *You must know that perilous times are coming and turn away from selfish and ungodly men.*

"**This know also, that in the last days perilous times shall come. For men shall be . . .**
- **lovers of their own selves**
- **covetous**
- **boasters**
- **proud**
- **blasphemers**
- **disobedient to parents**
- **unthankful**
- **unholy**
- **without natural affection**
- **trucebreakers**
- **false accusers**
- **incontinent**
- **fierce**

- **despisers of those that are good**
- **traitors**
- **heady**
- **highminded**
- **lovers of pleasures more than lovers of God**
- **having a form of godliness, but denying the power thereof: from such turn away" (2 Tim.3:1-5).**

Thought

As a minister, you must know the ungodly marks of the last days and turn away from ungodly men. In the last days, men shall be:

- *Lovers of their own selves*: selfish and self-centered.
- *Covetous*: lovers of money and possessions.
- *Boasters*: braggarts, pretenders.
- *Proud*: conceited, arrogant, putting oneself above others.
- *Blasphemers*: slanderers, insulters, cursers of God and man.
- *Disobedient to parents*.
- *Unthankful*: having no gratitude or appreciation.
- *Without natural affection*: having abnormal affection, being homosexual; without love and care.
- *Trucebreakers*: breakers of agreements and promises; being untrustworthy and treacherous.
- *False accusers*: slanderers.
- *Incontinent*: undisciplined and uncontrolled; given over to pleasure and indulgence, passion and sexual cravings, lust and lewdness.
- *Fierce*: savage and untamed.
- *Despisers of the good*: hating both good people and good things.
- *Traitors*: betrayers of country, friends, family, team; having little, if any, attachment or loyalty.

- *Heady*: headstrong and reckless, rash and hasty, giving little thought to the consequences.
- *Highminded*: puffed up and conceited; feeling more important than others.
- *Lovers of pleasure more than lovers of God*.
- *Religious, but belonging to a powerless religion*: having a form of godliness, but denying the power of God to save from sin, death, and judgment to come.

C. You and Your Financial Support

1. *You must receive financial support without being embarrassed or feeling guilty, but you must not seek luxury.*

   "And in the same house remain, eating and drinking such things as they give: for the labourer is worthy of his hire. Go not from house to house" (Lk.10:7).

Thought
As a minister, Christ stresses three significant things that are to govern you and your financial support.

a) "The laborer is worthy of his hire"; therefore, you should be given compensation and taken care of (1 Tim.5:18). Scripture even says that ministers are worth double compensation and double appreciation and that double appreciation and honor should be expressed to you (1 Tim.5:17).

The point is this: you are never to be taken advantage of. You are to be looked after by seeing that you have housing, food, and drink—all the necessities of life.

"Even so hath the Lord ordained that they which preach the gospel should live of the gospel" (1 Cor.9:14).

"Let him that is taught in the word communicate [give, support] unto him that teacheth in all good things" (Gal.6:6).

"For the scripture saith, Thou shalt not muzzle the ox that treadeth out the corn. And, The labourer is worthy of his reward" (1 Tim.5:18).

b) The laborer is to accept compensation. You are not to be self-conscious or embarrassed in receiving payment for your labor.
c) *However*, you are not to seek luxury, going from house to house and person to person seeking more and more of the better things of life. *You are to live in simplicity, giving all that you have beyond your own needs to meet the needs of others.* You are to seek to meet the needs of men, not to secure the things of this world. What a contrast of value: things vs. people. How mixed up so many ministers allow their values to become. You must accept compensation but never seek luxury.

> **"If ye then be risen with Christ, seek those things which are above, where Christ sitteth on the right hand of God. Set your affection on things above, not on things on the earth" (Col.3:1-2).**
>
> **"Jesus said unto him, If thou wilt be perfect, go and sell that thou hast, and give to the poor, and thou shalt have treasure in heaven: and come and follow me" (Mt.19:21).**
>
> **"Let him . . .labour, working with his hands the thing which is good, that he may have to give to him that needeth" (Eph.4:28).**

2. *You must not covet worldly wealth.*

> **"I have coveted no man's silver, or gold, or apparel" (Acts 20:33).**

Thought
As a minister, you must not accumulate estates through the ministry. You must not covet silver or gold or clothing. In the ancient world, rich clothing was a sign of wealth. Today many persons in the church are as many were in the day of Paul, they have plenty, and some are even rich. They have . . .

- money
- stylish clothes
- property
- transportation
- stocks
- bonds

But note: Paul did not covet what the people of his day had, and you are not to covet what the people of your day have. Your mind and thoughts are not to be focused upon worldly things. Money, property, clothing, and the latest in transportation must hold no appeal for you. Your craving must be for something far more important:

- the Kingdom of God and His righteousness.
- meeting the desperate needs of the world.
- delivering men out of the slavery of sin and death.
- sharing the gospel of everlasting life.

As a minister of the gospel, you must be totally committed to sharing the gospel. And total commitment involves not only verbal preaching and teaching, but the spread of the gospel through the financial support of others. You must give all *you are and have* to send the gospel around the world.

3. *You must work at secular employment if needed in order to preach the gospel.*

> **"And because he [Paul] was of the same craft, he abode with them, and wrought: for by their occupation they were tentmakers" (Acts 18:3).**
>
> **"Yea, ye yourselves know, that these hands have ministered unto my necessities, and to them that were with me. I [Paul] have showed you all things, how that so labouring ye ought to support the weak, and to remember the words of the Lord Jesus, how he said, It is more blessed to give than to receive" (Acts 20:34-35.** See *The Preacher's Outline & Sermon Bible,*® note, pt.2—Acts 20:33-35 for more discussion.)

Thought

As a minister, you must labor at secular employment when required. Paul was usually supported in his ministry and did not have to work at secular work. In fact, he was soon to receive financial support from the Philippian church when Silas and Timothy arrived, and the support would free him to preach the gospel and minister full time (Acts 18:5; cp. 1 Th.3:6; 2 Cor.11:9; Ph.4:15). But note this verse. Paul did not hesitate to work with his hands in order to get the gospel out to people. He would do whatever was necessary to reach people and meet their desperate need for Christ and the glorious life of joy and eternity that Christ gives. You, too, must be willing to work at secular employment if needed in order to get the gospel out. (Cp. Acts 20:34; 1 Th.2:9; 2 Th.3:8; 1 Cor.4:11-12; 9:12-15; 2 Cor.11:7-9; 12:14.)

> "**I must work the works of him that sent me, while it is day: the night cometh, when no man can work**" (Jn.9:4).
>
> "**For we cannot but speak the things which we have seen and heard**" (Acts 4:20).
>
> "**For though I preach the gospel, I have nothing to glory of: for necessity is laid upon me; yea, woe is unto me, if I preach not the gospel!**" (1 Cor.9:16).

4. *You must trust God to meet your financial needs.*

> "**Carry neither purse, nor scrip, nor shoes**" (Lk.10:4).

Thought
Christ sent forth His ministers with strict financial instructions: they were not to carry a money-bag (purse, ballantion) nor a traveller's bag (pera) nor two pair of sandals. They were to trust God for provisions, not worrying about money for food, housing, or clothing (Mt.6:24-34). Worrying about such things would be cumbersome, taking away precious time that should be spent in ministering. Also, they were preaching a message of faith and trust in God. They needed to live what they were preaching and become a living picture of the dependency that God wants from every minister.

As a minister of Christ, you must trust God to meet your every need, and you must set a dynamic example of what it means to trust and depend upon God.

> "**Therefore take no thought, saying, What shall we eat? or, What shall we drink? or, Wherewithal shall we be clothed? (For after all these things do the Gentiles [unbelievers] seek:) for your heavenly Father knoweth that ye have need of all these**

things. But seek ye first the kingdom of God, and his righteousness; and all these shall be added unto you" (Mt.6:31-33).

"Not that I speak in respect of want: for I have learned, in whatsoever state I am, therewith to be content. I know both how to be abased, and I know how to abound: every where and in all things I am instructed both to be full and to be hungry, both to abound and to suffer need. I can do all things through Christ which strengtheneth me" (Ph.4:11-13).

"Trust in the LORD, and do good; so shalt thou dwell in the land, and verily thou shalt be fed" (Ps.37:3).

"Commit thy way unto the LORD; trust also in him; and he shall bring it to pass" (Ps.37:5).

CHAPTER 10

What Your Relationship With Others as a Minister Must Be

Relationships are very sensitive within any society or body of people, no matter how small or large. The relationship you are to have with your family and with other ministers, and even with those who oppose and criticize you, are clearly spelled out by Scripture.

Contents

A. YOU AND YOUR FAMILY	249
1. You must walk in a spirit of submission and love with your wife.	249
2. You must be the husband of one wife.	254
3. You must manage your own family well.	256
B. YOU AND OTHER MINISTERS	258
1. You must understand that you are one with all other ministers and that you are equal in God's eyes, that all ministers are coworkers together with God.	258
2. You must leave judging other ministers up to God.	260
3. You must receive and support travelling ministers: evangelists, Bible teachers, missionaries, and other preachers.	262

4. You must not ordain other ministers too quickly, and you must restore fallen ministers.	264
5. You must make sure—absolutely sure—that accusations against another minister are true before correcting the other minister.	266

C. YOU AND THOSE WHO OPPOSE, CRITICIZE, AND PERSECUTE YOU 268

1. You must go forth and preach the gospel, but know that you go into an antagonistic world.	268
2. You must know that the world will persecute you.	269
3. You must trust God when you are criticized, judged, slandered, censored, and attacked.	272
4. You must love your enemies, love all who curse, hate, persecute, and despitefully use you.	276

D. YOU AND OTHER BELIEVERS 280

E. YOU AND UNBELIEVERS 280

CHAPTER 10
What Your Relationship With Others Must Be

A. YOU AND YOUR FAMILY

1. *You must walk in a spirit of submission and love with your wife.*

    "Wives, submit yourselves unto your own husbands, as unto the Lord. For the husband is the head of the wife, even as Christ is the head of the church: and he is the saviour of the body. . . . Husbands, love your wives, even as Christ also loved the church, and gave himself for it; that he might sanctify and cleanse it with the washing of water by the word, that he might present it to himself a glorious church, not having spot, or wrinkle, or any such thing; but that it should be holy and without blemish" (Eph.5:22-23, 25-27).

    Thought
    As a minister, you above all others must walk in a spirit of submission and love with your wife.

    First, your wife must walk in a spirit of submission. There are two reasons why the wife is to be submissive to her husband.

    a) To submit is God's will. In fact, it is a commandment of God. There is to be no equivocation, no argument, not even a question about it: "Wives submit yourselves unto your own husbands."

    God is God, and as God, He has the right to demand anything of us. But note the words "as to the Lord." When we as believers do anything, we are to do it *as to the Lord*. Why? Because we love Him. The Lord has loved and given Himself for us, given Himself that He might save us. He loved us; therefore, we love Him. This is always the first reason we obey Him. We love Him; therefore, when He says to do something, we do it *as to Him*—to please Him.

    Now, let us ask ourselves: What kind of spirit is the Christian wife to have as she obeys God?

- A spirit of slavery or love?
- A spirit of grudgery or love?
- A spirit of resentment or love?
- A spirit of reaction or love?

The answer is obvious: she acts out of love. She loves the Lord; therefore, to please Him she submits herself to the Lord. The point is this: God instructs wives to walk in a spirit of submission to their husbands. Therefore, Christian wives do not obey the Lord out of resentment and reaction because of the commandment. They obey the Lord out of love because they love both the Lord and their husbands. Therefore, your wife must focus and set her life upon pleasing both the Lord and you, her husband. If the Lord says do it, then she does it because she loves the Lord and wants to please Him above all else.

b) To submit is God's order for the family (Eph.5:22). There is to be a *partnership* and *order* within the family. This is basic for the family and society to exist. In fact, no organization, no matter what it is, can survive and exist without a spirit of partnership and order. Note three important facts.

- The husband is the head of the wife. The word "head" in Scripture refers to authority *not being*. Neither man nor woman is superior to the other in being. Men and women are equal in God's eyes. There is an *essential partnership* between men and women. Neither is independent of the other. Both are from the other, and the relationship that exists between them has come from God.

    "Nevertheless neither is the man without the woman, neither the woman without the man, in the Lord. For as the woman is of the man, even so is the man also by the woman [born of her]; but all things of God" (1 Cor.11:11-12).

    There is neither male nor female in God's eyes. He sees both men and women as one, each as significant as the other.

    "There is neither Jew nor Greek, there is neither bond nor free, there is neither male

nor female: for ye are all one in Christ Jesus" (Gal.3:28).

When God talks about man being the head of the woman, He is not talking about ability or worth, competence or value, brilliance or advantage. God is talking about *function and order* within an organization. Every organization has to have a head for it to be operated in an efficient and orderly manner. There are no greater organizations than God's universe, His church, and His Christian family. Within God's order of things there is a partnership, but every partnership must have a head, and God has ordained that man is the head of the partnership.

- The great pattern for the wife to follow is Christ and the church. Christ is the head of the church. This simply means that Christ has authority over the church. So long as the church lives by this rule, the church experiences love and joy and peace—orderliness—and it is able to carry out its function and mission on earth to the fullest. So it is with the husband; he is the head of the family, the ultimate authority in the family. The wife is to be submissive to that authority just as the church is to be submissive to Christ. So long as she and the rest of the family live by this rule, the family experiences love, joy, and peace—orderliness—and it fulfills its function and purpose on earth. This, of course, assumes that the husband is fulfilling his part in the family. As in any organization, each member must do his part for the organization to be orderly and accomplish its purpose.

- The husband is the savior of the body just as Christ is the Savior of the church. Christ is the great Protector and Comforter of the church. So the husband is to be the protector and comforter of the wife. By nature, that is, by the constitution and build of the body, the husband is stronger than the wife. Therefore, in God's order of things, he is to be the main protector and comforter of the wife. These two functions are two of the great benefits which the wife receives from a loving husband who is faithful to the Lord.

Second, you must love your wife. The love which you, the husband, are to have for your wife is the very love of God Himself (agape love). *Agape* love is a selfless and unselfish love, a giving and sacrificial love. It is the love of the mind and will as well as of the heart. It is not only a love of affection and feelings, it is a love of the *will and commitment*. It is a love that wills and commits itself to love a person. It is the love that works for the highest good of the person loved . . .

- that loves even if the person *does not deserve to be loved*.
- that loves even if the person is *utterly unworthy of being loved*.

Just imagine! What would happen in most marriages if the husband so loved his wife, loved her . . .

- with a *selfless and unselfish love*?
- with a *giving and sacrificial love*?
- with a *love of the will as well as of the heart*?
- with a *love of commitment as well as of affection*?

One thing that would happen in most marriages would be this: the wife would melt in the husband's arms and willingly accept his authority as the head of the family.

Note that the standard of the husband's love is the love of Christ for the church. The love of Christ for the church can be described in one simple statement: Christ *gave Himself* for the church. Christ loved the church so much that He gave Himself—*sacrificed Himself totally*—gave all He was and had for it. This is the love the husband is to have for his wife.

The sacrificial love of the husband involves three things. Note that the very things said about Christ and the church are to be true of the husband and wife.

a) The husband's love involves being *set apart and cleansed*. The word *sanctify* means to be set apart. When a young man asks a young lady to be his wife, he sets himself apart for her and for her alone. His word, his act, his promise of marriage also causes her to set herself apart. When he speaks the word and makes the promise of marriage, he and she both are thereafter set apart and cleansed for each other.

A dirty bride or groom—a dirty, defiled marriage—is unthinkable. The one thing above all else that will keep the marriage sanctified and cleansed is the husband's sacrificial love. If the husband will love his wife to the point that he gives himself sacrificially, his love will not only protect him, but it will go a long way in protecting the sanctity and purity of his wife.

b) The husband's love involves having no spot or wrinkle or any such thing. Spots would mean the mistakes that tarnish one's life and marriage, mistakes so serious that they are very difficult to wash off one's body and out of one's mind. They would include such things as . . .

- mistreatment and abuse.
- loose and immoral behavior.
- withdrawal and avoidance.

Wrinkles would mean things that cause friction and rattle the nerves and that need to be ironed out. They would include such things as . . .

- temper and reaction.
- broken promises and serious neglect.
- severe selfishness and rejection.

c) The husband's love involves being holy and without blemish. The word "holy" (hagia) means to be separate and untouched by evil. The husband's love—if it is a real love—will stir him to be holy and unblemished and go a long way in stirring his wife to be holy and without blemish.

This point is striking—a real eye-opener. It shows just how dependent the marriage is upon the love of the husband—how much effect the husband's love has upon the marriage. Few wives could reject such love; few wives would refuse to walk hand in hand with their husbands if they truly loved them with the love that is unselfish and sacrificial.

> "Husbands, love your wives, even as Christ also loved the church, and gave himself for it" (Eph.5:25).
>
> "Likewise, ye husbands, dwell with them according to knowledge, giving honour unto the wife, as unto the weaker vessel, and as being heirs together of the grace of life; that your prayers be not hindered" (1 Pt.3:7).

2. *You must be the husband of one wife.*

> "A bishop then must be blameless, the husband of one wife" (1 Tim.3:2; cp. Tit.2:6.) (See *The Preacher's Outline & Sermon Bible,*® notes—Mt.5:31-32; 19:1-12 for what Christ had to say about marriage and divorce.)

Thought

As a minister, you must be "the husband of one wife." From the earliest times of church history, this qualification has been interpreted differently. Some have held . . .

- that the minister must have a wife; he must be married to be a minister.

- that the minister must never have more than one wife; he must never marry again, even if his wife died. This position holds that second marriages are completely forbidden.

- that the minister must not have more than one wife at a time. (Remember: polygamy was the common practice of society when the church was first born.)

- that a minister must live a life of strict morality; he "must be a loyal husband, preserving marriage in all its purity" (William Barclay, *The Letters to Timothy, Titus, and Philemon,* p.87).

As a minister, you must go before the Lord and seek the meaning of this qualification for yourself. But you must be honest and open to hear the Lord and then beg of Him the courage and discipline to do what He says. This is an absolute essential for all who are believers, for nothing is any more traumatic than the loss of a spouse through death or separation and divorce.

And if there is ever a time that we must reach out and minister to our brothers and sisters, it is when they lose their spouses.

The point is this: should you be allowed to serve as a minister if you have had more than one wife, either through death or divorce? The Pulpit Commentary has an excellent comment on this point:

> "If we consider the general laxity in regard to marriage, and the facility of divorce, which prevailed among Jews and Romans at this time, it must have been a common thing for a man to have more than one woman living who had been his wife. And this [was] a distinct breach of the primeval law (Gen.ii.24), [and] would properly be a bar to any one being called to the 'office of a bishop'. . . . It is utterly unsupported by any single passage in Scripture that a second marriage should disqualify a man for the sacred ministry. As regards the opinion of the early Church, it was not at all uniform, and amongst those who held that this passage absolutely prohibits second marriages in the case of a [bishop], it was merely a part of the asceticism of the day" (Vol.21, p.51).

A.T. Robertson very simply says, "Of one wife [mias gunaikos]. One at a time, clearly" (*Word Pictures in the New Testament*, Vol.4, p.572).

William Barclay says, "In its context here we can be quite certain that this means that the Christian leader must be a loyal husband, preserving marriage in all its purity" (*The Letters to Timothy, Titus, and Philemon*, p.87).

Thompson Chain Reference Bible, in listing its subjects, simply says "Polygamy Forbidden."

Scripture and the Lord Jesus Christ Himself say:

> **"And he answered and said unto them, Have ye not read, that he which made them at the beginning made them male and female, and said, For this cause shall a man leave father and mother, and shall cleave to his wife: and they twain shall be one flesh? Wherefore they are no more twain, but one flesh. What therefore God hath joined together, let not man put asunder" (Mt.19:4-6).**
>
> **"And I say unto you, Whosoever shall put away his wife, except it be for fornication, and shall marry**

another, committeth adultery: and whoso marrieth her which is put away doth commit adultery" (Mt.19:9).

"A bishop then must be blameless, the husband of one wife, vigilant, sober, of good behavior, given to hospitality, apt to teach" (1 Tim.3:2).

"If any be blameless, the husband of one wife" (Tit.1:6).

"Neither shall he multiply wives to himself, that his heart turn not away" (Dt.17:17).

3. *You must manage your own family well.*

"One that ruleth well his own house, having his children in subjection with all gravity; (for if a man know not how to rule his own house, how shall he take care of the church of God?)" (1 Tim.3:4-5).

"If any be blameless, the husband of one wife, having faithful children not accused of riot [wild living] or unruly" (Tit.1:6).

"And, ye fathers, provoke not your children to wrath: but bring them up in the nurture and admonition of the Lord" (Eph.6:4).

Thought

As a minister, you must meet one significant family qualification: you must rule your own household and rule it well. The home is a miniature of the church; the home is the proving ground for leadership in the church. The husband is the head of the home. This does not mean that he is the dictator, tyrant, or bully of the home. It means that he is the leader of the wife and children. He leads them all . . .

- in the building of a loving, joyful, and peaceful home.
- in the fulfillment of their life's calling and task upon earth.

It means that you are not bossed about or dominated by your wife; that you do not allow your children to disobey, rebel, or talk back to you or their mother; that you take the lead in controlling your home for Christ and His kingdom.

Note the word "gravity" (semnotes). It means dignity. The minister must rule his home with dignity, respect, and love.

As the Amplified New Testament says: "With true dignity, commanding their respect in every way and keeping them respectful."

As Scripture says, "For if a man know not how to rule his own house, how shall he take care of the church of God?" (1 Tim.3:5).

Note Titus 1:6 above. As a minister, you must have faithful children. By faithful is meant believing in the Lord Jesus Christ and remaining faithful to Him. Your children are to be above reproach; they are not to be "loose in morals and conduct or unruly and disorderly" (Amplified New Testament).

Note Eph.6:4 above. As a minister, you (and your wife) must not provoke your children to wrath. Four things will provoke a child.

- a) Failing to accept the fact that things do change will provoke a child. Time and generations do change. This does not mean that a child should be allowed to do everything that his generation does. But it does mean that parents need to be alert to the changes between generations. Allow the child to be a part of his own generation instead of trying to conform the child to the parent's generation. The parent's childhood generation does not exist any longer nor will it ever exist again.

- b) Over-controlling a child will also provoke a child to wrath. Over-control ranges all the way from stern restriction and discipline to child abuse. Disciplining and restricting a child *too much* will either stifle the growth of the child or stir him to react and rebel, causing the child to flee from the parent.

- c) Under-controlling a child can provoke a child. It should be noted that this is the most prevalent problem in an industrialized society. There is a tendency for those with plenty or with wealth to pamper, indulge, and give a child everything imaginable—well beyond what a child needs and what is really best for him. When you fail to train a child, he feels neglected and unwanted, and when he gets older, he is often angered.

d) Living an inconsistent life before a child can provoke a child. A parent who tells a child one thing and then turns around and does the opposite thing himself is full of hypocrisy and false profession. Yet, how common! How many children are doing things because their parents do them. Seeing an inconsistent life in a parent can provoke children.

Note the exhortation of Scripture: you are to bring up your child in the ways of the Lord, in the nurture and admonition of the Lord.

- The word "nurture" (paideia) means "the whole training and education of children which [involves] . . . the cultivation of mind and morals . . . commands and admonitions . . . reproof and punishment . . . correcting mistakes and curbing the passions . . . the increase of virtue" (*Thayers Greek-English Lexicon*).
- The word "admonition" (nouthesia) means counsel, exhortation, correction.

Note: the parent is not to rear the child after his own notions of what is best for the child, but after the nurture and admonition *of the Lord*. The Lord's Word is to be the guide for Christian parents in rearing their children.

B. YOU AND OTHER MINISTERS

1. *You must understand that you are one with all other ministers and that you are equal in God's eyes, that all ministers are coworkers together with God.*

    "Now he that planteth and he that watereth are one: and every man shall receive his own reward according to his own labour. For we are labourers together with God: ye are God's husbandry, ye are God's building" (1 Cor.3:8-9. See *The Preacher's Outline & Sermon Bible,*® note—1 Cor.3:5-9 for more discussion.)

Thought

As a minister, you and all other ministers are *as one*—as *equals*—in the eyes of God. The church and its believers are to see you as one, as equals before God.

a) Both the sower and the edifier, both he who plants and he who waters, are e*mphatically said to be one*. All ministers are called . . .

- by the same Lord.
- to the same office: the office of minister.
- to the same work: to serve God's church.
- to stand accountable before God and before God alone.

There is a *spiritual unity* between ministers. The work of the one who plants cannot be done without the work of the one who waters. Both are absolutely essential. You are not rivals, working against each other. You are planters and waterers, planting and watering lives for God. It is God who calls and places you in the ministry, and He uses you as He wills. If the church and its believers exalt or pitch you against other ministers, they are going against God's purpose for His gospel and the church.

b) You are personally responsible to God. You are to be rewarded for what you do, not for what another minister does. You must use your own gifts; you must not try to use someone else's gifts nor to be like someone else. God gave you special gifts for specific purposes, to accomplish specific tasks while you are upon earth. You must, therefore, diligently labor to use your gifts as God desires. In fact, you are to be rewarded for how well you use your gifts. Your task is not to try to be like another minister or to do as another minister does. Your task is to be who God called you to be and to do as God gifts you.

Note: you shall be judged for your labor, not for what men may term success.

"He also that had received two talents came and said, Lord, thou deliveredst unto me two talents: behold, I have gained two other talents beside them.

> His lord said unto him, Well done, good and faithful servant; thou hast been faithful over a few things, I will make thee ruler over many things: enter thou into the joy of thy lord" (Mt.25:22-23).
>
> "If any man speak, let him speak as the oracles of God; if any man minister, let him do it as of the ability which God giveth: that God in all things may be glorified through Jesus Christ, to whom be praise and dominion for ever and ever" (1 Pt.4:11).

c) Ministers are coworkers, and you all work together with God. You work with God, carrying out His will and doing what He wants done. Your concern is not what men think and want. Your mission is to serve right along by the side of God Himself.

> "Then saith he unto his disciples, The harvest truly is plenteous, but the labourers are few; pray ye therefore the Lord of the harvest, that he will send forth labourers into his harvest" (Mt.9:37-38).
>
> "Lift up your eyes, and look on the fields; for they are white already to harvest. And he that reapeth receiveth wages, and gathereth fruit unto life eternal: that both he that soweth and he that reapeth may rejoice together" (Jn.4:35-36).
>
> "But none of these things move me, neither count I my life dear unto myself, so that I might finish my course with joy, and the ministry, which I have received of the Lord Jesus, to testify the gospel of the grace of God" (Acts 20:24).
>
> "We then, as workers together with him, beseech you also that ye receive not the grace of God in vain" (2 Cor.6:1).

2. *You must leave judging other ministers up to God.*

> "Some men's sins are open beforehand, going before to judgment; and some men they follow after. Likewise also the good works of some are manifest beforehand; and they that are otherwise cannot be hid" (1 Tim.5:24-25).
>
> "Who are thou that judgest another man's servant? to his own master he standeth or falleth. Yea,

he shall be holden up: for God is able to make him stand" (Ro.14:4).

Thought
As a minister, your task is to deal with people and their sins. In fact, you are always involved with people, dealing with their weaknesses and strengths, their sins and virtues. Because of this you are sometimes tempted to pass judgment upon people; you are tempted to look upon some as being weak and noncommital and others as being strong and decisive. This is particularly true if you see or hear about weaknesses in other ministers. But this Scripture is an eyeopener. Judgment is to be left up to God, for only God knows the whole truth about a person. Only God knows . . .

- the genes, heritage, and childhood of a person that affect a person so much.
- every minute, hour, day, month, and year and every experience the person has lived.
- every trial and temptation the person has undergone.
- every thought, longing, and hope the person has had.

Only God knows all this and all the multitudes of ramifications of each of these. Therefore, only God can judge. But as stated, you are tempted to judge when you see one person commit open sin and another person do good works, in particular if the person is a minister. But you must not judge, for only God sees and knows everything about a person. Note how clearly Scripture states this fact.

- We do not clearly see the sins of people—not always. The sins of some people are clearly seen, and they make no attempt to hide them. These people shall suffer judgment; their sins definitely point to judgment. But some people are secret sinners; they hide their sins in their hearts and minds, and behind closed doors and in the dark. Their sins and judgment will be exposed later—in the terrible day of judgment.
- Likewise, the good works of some people are clearly seen, but the good works of others are not seen.

The point is this: you have no way to tell what is in a person's heart and life, what he is doing and thinking every moment of every day. You cannot even know your spouse or children or parents that well—not well enough to judge them. Judgment has to be left up to God, not to men—not even to you as a minister. The charge is clear and straightforward: leave the judgment up to God.

Note how strong the exhortation of Romans 14:4 is:

> **"Who art thou that judgest another man's servant? to his own master he standeth or falleth. Yea, he shall be holden up: for God is able to make him stand" (Ro.14:4).**

- You nor any other believer—minister or layman—has the right to judge the Lord's servant. The Lord alone has the right to judge His servant. You are not to play God by judging His servants. The servant belongs to Christ. Christ and Christ alone determines whether or not the servant stands or falls, is accepted or rejected.

- In fact, God shall hold His dear servant up. There is no question about the matter: the servant may slip and fall, but God will raise Him up. How do we know this? Because God says He will and God is able; God is able to make His servant stand.

  > **"Being confident of this very thing, that he which hath begun a good work in you will perform it until the day of Jesus Christ" (Ph.1:6).**

  > **"Who are kept by the power of God through faith unto salvation ready to be revealed in the last time" (1 Pt.1:5).**

  > **"Now unto him that is able to keep you [all other ministers and believers] from falling, and to present you faultless before the presence of his glory with exceeding joy, to the only wise God our Saviour, be glory and majesty, dominion and power, both now and ever. Amen" (Jude 24-25).**

3. *You must receive and support travelling ministers: evangelists, Bible teachers, missionaries, and other preachers.*

> "Whom [travelling ministers] if thou bring forward on their journey after a godly sort, thou shalt do well: because that for his [Christ's] name's sake they went forth, taking nothing of the Gentiles. We therefore ought to receive such, that we might be fellowhelpers to the truth" (3 Jn.6-8).

Thought
As a minister, you are to open your home and support travelling ministers. You are to have a strong testimony in the ministry of hospitality. You are to continue to receive and support travelling ministers. Note: it is said that this is exactly what God Himself would do. This is the godly way, the godly thing to do. That is, it is exactly what God would do; therefore, it is what you are to do. There are two strong reasons why.

a) Travelling ministers should be received and supported because they go forth for Christ. They have dedicated their lives to serving Christ by reaching the lost and growing believers, and the church needs their ministry. In addition, in many cases they have made the commitment to travel abroad for Christ by faith, without receiving a regular income.

b) Travelling ministers should be received and supported because you need to be a fellow-worker in the truth. There is no question: they are workers in the truth. Travelling evangelists, missionaries, prophets, and teachers alike are carrying the gospel of truth across the world. The only question is: Are you, the minister of the local church, going to be fellow-workers with them? John says that it is the very thing that God Himself would do. Therefore, you in the local church must labor with all those who walk in the truth of Jesus Christ and the Word of God. You must labor with all those chosen by God to carry forth the Word of truth, the Word of His dear Son, the Lord Jesus Christ.

> "A bishop [minister] then must be blameless, the husband of one wife, vigilant, sober, of good behaviour, given to <u>hospitality</u>, apt to teach" (1 Tim.3:2).
>
> "Use hospitality one to another without grudging" (1 Pt.4:9).

4. *You must not ordain other ministers too quickly, and you must restore fallen ministers.*

> **"Lay hands suddenly on no man, neither be partaker of other men's sins: keep thyself pure" (1 Tim.5:22).**

Thought

As a minister, you must guard ordination and guard yourself. In this particular passage, the laying on of hands can refer to ordaining men to the ministry of the Lord Jesus Christ or to restoring ministers who have fallen into sin and have been disciplined (cp. pt.5 below, 1 Tim.5:19-20). Ordaining men to the ministry of Christ is of critical importance.

a) Note the word "suddenly." You must not rush to ordain men. The reason is clearly understood.

> "Undue haste in Christian appointments has . . . led to unworthy men bringing havoc to the cause of Christ." (Donald Guthrie. *The Pastoral Epistles.* "Tyndale New Testament Commentaries," p.107).
>
> "Paul is warning Timothy not to ordain deacons, elders, or young preachers suddenly, without due consideration. Let them first prove themselves. Do not hurriedly appoint them to an office in the assembly, and then possibly within a few months or a year find them falling back into sin and bringing reproach upon the church" (Oliver Greene. *The Epistles of Paul the Apostle to Timothy and Titus.* Greenville, SC: The Gospel Hour, 1964, p.205).

b) The minister who has fallen into sin can take great heart from this passage (1 Tim.5:19-22). It teaches that the fallen minister *can* be restored to the ministry—just as effectively as he was before, perhaps even more because of the praise to Christ that results through God's mercy. It is God's eternal mercy and eternal grace that reaches out and saves the fallen minister; therefore, when the minister is reached, God's mercy and grace are seen to be ever so wonderful and glorious, beyond imagination. God is praised—gloriously praised. But note the Scripture:

> **"Lay hands suddenly on no man."**

The fallen minister is not to be reordained or replaced in the pulpit immediately after his repentance. You and other ministers are to wait until he has proven . . .

- that his repentance is genuine.
- that his rededication and recommitment to follow Christ sticks.
- that he is consistently being conformed and molded into the image of Jesus Christ on a daily basis.
- that he is committed to serving Christ and His church and is actively involved in reaching people for Christ and in ministering to the needs of the needy.

But note a critical point: this does not mean that you do not embrace the dear brother, that you withdraw fellowship from him, that you look upon him with distrust and suspicion. Contrariwise, you reach out and embrace him, love and care for him, nourish and nurture him. In fact, you do this immediately upon hearing about his fall. You go after him immediately, for he is too precious to lose to the world.

> **"Brethren, if a man be overtaken in a fault, ye which are spiritual, restore such an one in the spirit of meekness; considering thyself, lest thou also be tempted" (Gal.6:1).**
>
> **"Let him know, that he which converteth the sinner from the error of his way shall save a soul from death, and shall hide a multitude of sins" (Jas.5:20).**
>
> **"And above all things have fervent charity among yourselves: for charity shall cover the multitude of sins" (1 Pt.4:8).**
>
> **"For I will restore health unto thee, and I will heal thee of thy wounds, saith the lord; because they called thee an Outcast, saying, This is Zion, whom no man seeketh after" (Jer.30:17).**

c) Note that you as a minister are held responsible for those you ordain. The minister who lays hands on an unworthy man for ordination bears equal responsibility for his sins. In God's eyes you yourself become guilty of the man's sins—just as guilty as the man himself. This is the meaning of the exhortation: when ordaining men do not "be partaker of other men's sins: keep thyself pure."

You must, therefore, guard ordination and guard yourself.

5. *You must make sure—absolutely sure—that accusations against another minister are true before correcting the other minister.*

> "Against an elder [ministers] receive not an accusation, but before two or three witnesses. Them that sin rebuke before all, that others also may fear" (1 Tim.5:19-20).
>
> "Moreover if thy brother shall trespass against thee, go and tell him his fault between thee and him alone: if he shall hear thee, thou hast gained thy brother. But if he will not hear thee, then take with thee one or two more, that in the mouth of two or three witnesses every word may be established. And if he shall neglect to hear them, tell it unto the church: but if he neglect to hear the church, let him be unto thee as an heathen man and a publican" (Mt.18:15-17).

Thought

You must always follow the instructions laid out in the Bible when dealing with accusations against other ministers.

First, there must be two, preferably three, witnesses—credible witnesses—who saw the minister sin (1 Tim.5:19-20). The idea is that they must all appear before you and put their accusation in writing, or else be willing to appear face to face with the accused.

Second, as the minister of Christ, you must go to the minister and tell him the accusation (Mt.18:15-17). If he hears and repents, then he is restored. If he denies the accusation or does not hear and repent, then you are to take one or two others with you and again face him with the charges. If he still denies guilt or does not repent, then a third step is to be taken.

Third, he is to be brought "before all" and faced with the charges. The words "before all" most likely mean before all the elders or ministers rather than before the whole church (A.T. Robertson, *Word Pictures in the New Testament*, Vol.4, p.589). To go before the whole church would only add fuel to the flame of the immature and carnal believers within the church. It would make a public spectacle before the outside world. Such would naturally damage the church's testimony—even if an attempt was made to balance the damaged image by claiming disciplinary action. Note that the point of the discipline is the correction of the sinning minister and the prevention of other ministers from sinning: that they may fear exposure and embarrassment.

William Barclay has an excellent exposition of this verse that merits being read by all ministers:

> "Those who persist in sin are to be publicly rebuked. That public rebuke had a double value. It sobered the sinner into a consideration of his ways, and wakened him into a sense of shame; and it made others have a care that they did not involve themselves in a like humiliation. The threat of publicity is no bad thing, if it keeps a man in the right way, even from fear. A wise leader will know when there is a time to keep things quiet, and a time for public rebuke. But whatever happens, the Church must never give the world the impression that it is condoning sin" (*The Letters to Timothy, Titus, and Philemon*, p.135).

A very practical and warm exposition is also given by Oliver Greene:

> "It is possible for even a godly, separated, God-appointed elder to commit sin . . . . It is possible even for those who live very near to the heart of God to be caught off guard and commit sin that will bring shame and disgrace upon the church. But we are not to accuse an elder unless there are two or more witnesses to testify that the accusation is an accomplished fact. We should never repeat anything we hear about a minister, deacon, steward, elder, Sunday school teacher or any leader in the church. If we hear reports of evil, we should investigate in the right way, through the right people—and certainly we should not discuss the situation with unbelievers. It is very clear in verse 19 that an elder must not be accused unless there are at least two or three witnesses who can prove the truth of the accusation" (*The Epistles of Paul the Apostle to Timothy and Titus*, p.202).

C. YOU AND THOSE WHO OPPOSE, CRITICIZE, AND PERSECUTE YOU

1. *You must go forth and preach the gospel, but know that you go into an antagonistic world.*

   "Go your ways: behold, I send you forth as lambs among wolves" (Lk.10:3).

   Thought
   As a minister, you are sent forth as a sheep into the midst of wolves. This is the statement of Christ, so you must listen and stay alert. Within the world, some people will be as wolves.

   "For I know this, that after my departing shall grievous wolves enter in among you, not sparing the flock. Also of your own selves shall men arise, speaking perverse things, to draw away disciples after them. Therefore watch, and remember" (Acts 20:29-31).

   "Remember the word that I said unto you, The servant is not greater than his lord. If they have persecuted me, they will also persecute you; if they have kept my saying, they will keep yours also" (Jn.15:20).

   "For unto you it is given in the behalf of Christ, not only to believe on him, but also to suffer for his sake" (Ph.1:29).

   "That no man should be moved by these afflictions: for yourselves know that we are appointed thereunto" (1 Th.3:3).

   "Yea, and all that will live godly in Christ Jesus shall suffer persecution" (2 Tim. 3:12).

   What is to be your attitude and spirit toward those who oppose and persecute you? You are to do three things.
   a) You are to be as a sheep in the midst of wolves. A sheep is meek, harmless, and non-combative. As a minister of the Lord, you are to be harmless and noncombative.
   b) You are to protect yourself by turning and walking away from the rejection and persecution if possible.

> "And if the house be worthy, let your peace come upon it: but if it be not worthy, let your peace return to you. And whosoever shall not receive you, nor hear your words, when ye depart out of that house or city, shake off the dust of your feet. Verily I say unto you, It shall be more tolerable for the land of Sodom and Gomorrha in the day of judgment, than for that city" (Mt.10:13-15).

There will be some persons, houses, and cities that will reject the minister of Christ. When this happens, Christ tells you what to do: protect yourself as much as you can. Turn and walk away from the rejection and persecution, if possible.

c) You must do exactly what Christ and Scripture tell you to do in the next three points:
- You must know that the world will persecute you.
- You must trust God when you are criticized, judged, slandered, censored, and attacked.
- You must love your enemies, all who curse, hate, persecute, and despitefully use you.

2. *You must know that the world will persecute you.*

> "If the world hate you, ye know that it hated me before it hated you. If ye were of the world, the world would love his own: but because ye are not of the world, but I have chosen you out of the world, therefore the world hateth you. Remember the word that I said unto you, The servant is not greater than his lord. If they have persecuted me, they will also persecute you; if they have kept my saying, they will keep yours also. But all these things will they do unto you for my name's sake, because they know not him that sent me. If I had not come and spoken unto them, they had not had sin: but now they have no cloak for their sin. He that hateth me hateth my Father also. If I had not done among them the works which none other man did, they had not had sin: but now have they both seen and hated both me and my Father. But this cometh to

pass, that the word might be fulfilled that is written in their law, They hated me without a cause" **(Jn.15:18-25).**

Thought
As a minister, you must realize the chilling reality that the world will hate you.

a) The "world" refers to the unbelievers: the unredeemed, the lost, those who have never trusted Jesus Christ as Lord and Savior. The "world" stands for every person whose thoughts and lives are centered upon . . .

- the lust of the flesh: food, clothes, money, immorality. (Cp. Gal.5:16-21.)
- the lust of the eyes: evil and immoral thoughts, coveting, seeing and desiring people and things.
- the pride of life: position, honor, fame, self-centeredness, boasting, highmindedness. (Cp. 2 Tim.3:1-5.)

You are to "know" this: the world hated Christ *first*. Therefore, you are not to think some strange thing is happening to you when you are persecuted. You are not to become discouraged. You are to take heart, for Christ was victorious over the hatred of the world. He was triumphant even over the bitterness of death. He arose and ascended to the Father. You, too, will be victorious over opposition, victorious through His presence and power.

b) There are four unjustified reasons why the world hates you.

First, the world hates you because you are not of the world: you are a new creature (Jn.15:19). You are *called out* from the world: you are *in* the world, but you are not *of* the world. You are separated from the world, from its . . .

- spirit
- thoughts
- conversation
- pleasures
- passions
- covetousness
- friends
- comfort
- religion
- prejudices
- hoarding
- carnality

Because of your separation, the world does not love you; it rejects and hates you.

> "**They are not of the world, even as I am not of the world**" (Jn.17:16).
>
> "**Wherefore come out from among them, and be ye separate, saith the Lord, and touch not the unclean thing; and I will receive you, and will be a Father unto you, and ye shall be my sons and daughters, saith the Lord Almighty**" (2 Cor.6:17-18).

Second, the world hates you because you are identified with Christ (Jn.15:20). The servant is not above persecution: no servant is above his Lord. The Lord suffered persecution; therefore, you will suffer persecution. It is to be expected.

It is impossible for a true disciple to be above his Master or for a servant to be above his Lord. If our Master and Lord suffered persecution, so will we. Why? He is our Master and Lord; that is, we are His. What He stands for is what we stand for. Whatever there was about Him that caused men to persecute Him, the same is *in us*. They will persecute us for *the same thing* and for *the same reason*. The genuine believer sacrifices himself, *all he is and has*, to the Lord. He strives to conform his life to the Lord's; therefore, persecution is inevitable for the true believer.

Third, the world hates you because it does not really know God (Jn.15:21). The world is deceived in its concept and belief of God. The world conceives God to be the One who fulfills their earthly desires and lusts (Jn.6:2, 26). Man's idea of God is that of a *Supreme Grandfather* who protects and provides and gives no matter what a person's behavior is, just so the behavior is not too far out. The world believes that God (the Supreme Grandfather) will accept and work all things out in the final analysis. However, as a true minister of Christ, you teach against this, proclaiming that God is both loving and just. God does love us, but He demands righteousness of us. The world, of course, rebels against this concept of God.

Fourth, the world hates you because it is convicted of sin (Jn.15:22-24). Jesus said that two things convict the world.

- The message of the gospel convicts the world: it strips away the world's *cloke of sin*. You preach and teach the righteousness of the gospel; therefore, your message exposes the sins of people.
- Your life and the works of Christ convict the world of sin. Note the words, "they had not had sin." This does not mean that men would not be guilty of sin if Jesus had not come. What it means is that since He has come, men have seen exactly who God is. God has been revealed to men; therefore, they stand guilty of the most terrible sin of all: rejecting God and His Son. If He had not come, they would not be guilty of *this sin*.

  Note the claim of Jesus to be the revelation of God—to be equal with God. To hate Jesus is to hate the Father also.

c) The world is guilty; the world is without excuse. There is no sense for its hatred of Jesus. The world's hatred is a paradox; it is not understandable. Think about it. The world hates and opposes the One person . . .
  - who lived and spoke for righteousness more than anyone else ever has.
  - who cared and ministered more than anyone else ever has.
  - who worked for true love and justice and the salvation of the world more than anyone else ever has.

(How deceived the world and its humanity! To rush onward in madness for nothing but to return to dust and ashes. To seek life for only some seventy years, if that long.)

The world's hatred for Jesus Christ reveals that the true nature of the world is *evil*. The world is without excuse in its persecution of Christ and His ministers.

3. *You must trust God when you are criticized, judged, slandered, censored, and attacked.*

> **"But with me it is a very small thing that I should be judged of you, or of man's judgment: yea, I judge not mine own self. For I know nothing by myself; yet am I not hereby justified: but he that judgeth me is the Lord. Therefore judge noth-**

ing before the time, until the Lord come, who both will bring to light the hidden things of darkness, and will make manifest the counsels of the hearts: and then shall every man have praise of God" (1 Cor.4:3-5).

Thought

One of the serious problems in the Corinthian church concerned former ministers. Some of the church members were esteeming one minister above the other ministers. They were judging the gifts, ministry, and effectiveness of their former ministers; and the inevitable happened:

- Some of the people had been helped and blessed by Apollos, so they spoke up for Apollos.
- Others had been helped and blessed by Cephas, so they spoke up for Cephas.
- Still others had been helped and blessed more by Paul, so they defended Paul.

The matter became critical, for the people began to judge the ministers' preaching style, ability, eloquence, charisma, intelligence, gifts, call, and success—the whole scope of their ministry. Little groups were buzzing about talking up the merits of their favorite minister. Deep feelings settled in, and the fellowship of the church was threatened.

When you are criticized or attacked, what are you to do? These verses tell you. First, realize this: the judgment or approval of men matters little. Second, know that the judgment of Christ is all that matters. Note five points.

First, the Lord alone justifies a man and his ministry. This is a significant statement by Paul. He knows of no place where he is coming up short in the ministry. To his knowledge he is faithful in the ministry and pleasing to the Lord. But he is not justified and approved by his judgment. The Lord Jesus alone can put the stamp of approval upon his ministry. No man is able or competent in judging the fruitfulness, dedication, and success of a ministry. Only Christ can judge a man and the faithfulness of his life and ministry.

Second, believers are to judge nothing. They have no right or prerogative to judge.

- No believer can know the hidden things of darkness within a man. Only Jesus Christ can bring the secret, hidden things to light.
- No man knows the real motives within a man. Only Christ can reveal the motives and counsels of the human heart.

> "For there is nothing covered, that shall not be revealed; neither hid, that shall not be known" (Lk.12:2).
>
> "Therefore judge nothing before the time, until the Lord come, who both will bring to light the hidden things of darkness, and will make manifest the counsels of the hearts: and then shall every man have praise of God" (1 Cor.4:5).
>
> "If I sin, then thou markest me, and thou wilt not acquit me from mine iniquity" (Job 10:14).
>
> "Who can understand his errors? cleanse thou me from secret faults" (Ps.19:12).
>
> "Thou hast set our iniquities before thee, our secret sins in the light of thy countenance" (Ps.90:8).
>
> "For mine eyes are upon all their ways: they are not hid from my face, neither is their iniquity hid from mine eyes" (Jer.16:17).
>
> "And they consider not in their hearts that I remember all their wickedness: now their own doings have beset them about; they are before my face" (Hos.7:2).

Third, there is to be no judgment of ministers nor of anyone else until the Lord returns. He and He alone has the right and is capable of judging ministers and believers. Both ministers and believers will have the praise of God when Christ returns and judges their work, not before. No matter how successful men may judge one another to be—no matter how much praise men may heap upon one another—no person will have the praise of God until Christ returns and judges the secret things of a man's heart and life. This is the reason men are not to judge the ministers and servants of God.

> "Who art thou that judgest another man's servant? to his own master he standeth or falleth. Yea, he shall be holden up: for God is able to make him stand" (Ro.14:4).
>
> "There is one lawgiver, who is able to save and to destroy: who art thou that judgest another?" (Jas.4:12).
>
> "The heart is deceitful above all things, and desperately wicked: who can know it? I the LORD search the heart, I try the reins, even to give every man according to his ways, and according to the fruit of his doings" (Jer.17:9-10).

Fourth, criticism and disapproval hurt and cut the heart, but they do not matter at all in the judgment of God. Man's judgment of you, God's dear minister, has no bearing whatsoever upon what God will do with you. The congregation or some clique in the church may cut you to shreds, and they may break your heart, but they have absolutely nothing to do with the judgment of your faithfulness and unfaithfulness.

Men may put you on trial. You may be "judged" (anakrino), that is scrutinized, investigated, questioned, and cross-examined either to your face or behind your back. You may be judged as to your eloquence, intelligence, ability, or whatever else some may or may not like. But none of it matters to God—not one word, not even one critical or negative thought.

Fifth, note another significant fact: Paul does not even judge himself. Paul knew precisely what every honest and thinking person knows.

- No minister can honestly judge his own ministry: its true success, his motives for every single thing he has done, how much fruit he has really borne in people's lives and how much should have been borne.
- A person who begins to judge his own works either begins to think too highly of himself or too lowly. To varying degrees he becomes prideful or discouraged.

Paul, of course, is not talking about a minister evaluating his ministry for the purpose of strengthening it. He is talking about passing judgment upon his ministry in comparison to other ministries, as to its fruitfulness. Is his ministry as good as someone else's? Is it as fruitful? Are his motives as pure as they should be in the work which he does? Is Christ as pleased with his ministry as He is with the ministry of others?

This is the kind of thing Paul does not judge and believers are not to judge. No man has the right to judge such things.

> "**Judge not, that ye be not judged**" **(Mt.7:1).**
>
> "**Therefore thou art inexcusable, O man, whosoever thou art that judgest: for wherein thou judgest another, thou condemnest thyself; for thou that judgest doest the same things**" **(Ro.2:1.** See *The Preacher's Outline & Sermon Bible,*® outline and notes—Ro.2:17-29).
>
> "**Let us not therefore judge one another any more: but judge this rather, that no man put a stumblingblock or an occasion to fall in his brother's way**" **(Ro.14:13).**

4. *You must love your enemies, love all who curse, hate, persecute, and despitefully use you.*

> "**But I say unto you, Love your enemies, bless them that curse you, do good to them that hate you, and pray for them which despitefully use you, and persecute you**" **(Mt.5:44).**
>
> "**Therefore if thine enemy hunger, feed him; if he thirst, give him drink: for in so doing thou shalt heap coals of fire on his head**" **(Ro.12:20).**
>
> "**And the Lord make you to increase and abound in love one toward another, and toward all men, even as we do toward you**" **(1 Th.3:12).**
>
> "**Beloved, let us love one another: for love is of God; and every one that loveth is born of God, and knoweth God**" **(1 Jn.4:7).**

Thought

As a minister of Christ, you—above all others—must love all people, even your enemies. You must set the example of love, of what the love of Christ really is. You must demonstrate how men are to live upon earth, that men are to live in love and peace upon earth. How is it possible to love your enemies, those who curse, hate, persecute, and despitefully use you?

The Greek word "love" here is *agape* love. This is the love that wishes well and does well, even to your enemies. It is a love that demonstrates kindness, benevolence, and esteem. It is the love of the mind, reason, and choice. It is a sacrificial love, that is, a love that cares, gives, and works for another person's good—no matter how the person may respond or treat you (see notes—Jn.21:15-17).

The word Christ uses in saying "Love your enemies" is *agape*: the love that must be willed. You must use your mind and reason and deliberately choose to love your enemy.

Note four things:

- Your love for an enemy is different from the love you hold for your family. It would be impossible to love an enemy with affection. Christ knew this.

- You sacrifice yourself, bear all, in order to work for your enemy's good. You deliberately choose to love a world of antagonistic men for their own good (their salvation and hope of eternity).

- Your love (agape love) is not complacent acceptance of open wickedness and license. It is not sitting back and allowing a person to do as he pleases. It is not allowing selfishness and deception and a wallowing around in license. Agape love is putting a stop to sin and license as much as possible. It is restraint, control, discipline, and even punishment when it protects the offender from himself and protects those whom he hurts. Very simply pictured, it is a parent controlling a child for his own good and for the good of those who love him.

- Agape love is God's love. You can have agape love only as you allow God to love through you. You deliberately will to love as God loves, and God empowers you to do so (Ro.5:5).

The real meaning of love involves five very practical acts (Mt.5:44).

a) Love: "Love your enemies." You are to *love all men, even enemies*. You are to respect and honor all men (1 Pt.2:17). Every human being has something that is commendable, even if it is nothing but the fact that he is a fellow human being with a soul to be reached for God. Note two facts.

First, loving your enemies is against human nature. The behavior of human nature is to react: to hate, strike back, and wish hurt. At best human nature treats enemies with coldness and distance. The root of human reaction against enemies is self and bitterness.

Second, the one thing that you can have for enemies is *mercy and compassion*. Those who are enemies may choose to remain antagonistic, but you can still forgive in mercy and compassion. In fact, if you do not have compassion for those who hate you, you have gained nothing of the spirit of Christ.

b) Do good: "Do good to them which hate you." Imagine the impact of these words to the world of Jesus' day. They were an enslaved people conquered and hated by the Romans, yet Jesus was saying, "Do good to them."

Note that *doing good* goes beyond words; it actually does things for the person who hates. It reaches out to him through his family and friends, employment and business. It searches for ways to do good to him, realizing that he needs to be reached for Christ. If no immediate way is found, then you are to continue to bless him, ever waiting for the day when the hater will face one of the crises that comes to every human being. And then you go and do good, ministering as Christ Himself ministered.

> "Therefore if thine enemy hunger, feed him; if he thirst, give him drink: for in so doing thou shalt heap coals of fire on his head" (Ro.12:20).
>
> "See that none render evil for evil unto any man; but ever follow that which is good, both among yourselves, and to all men" (1 Th.5:15).
>
> "If thou see the ass [donkey] of him that hateth thee lying under his burden, and wouldest forbear to help him, thou shalt surely help with him" (Ex.23:5).
>
> "If thine enemy be hungry, give him bread to eat; and if he be thirsty, give him water to drink" (Pr.25:21).

c) Bless people: "Bless them that curse you." People do curse, and sometimes they curse other people. When someone curses you, you are to bless your curser, not rail back. You are to speak softly, to use kind and reconciling words.

> "Bless them which persecute you: bless, and curse not" (Ro.12:14).
>
> "Not rendering evil for evil, or railing for railing: but contrariwise blessing; knowing that ye are thereunto called, that ye should inherit a blessing" (1 Pt.3:9).
>
> "A soft answer turneth away wrath: but grievous words stir up anger" (Pr.15:1).

d) Pray for others: "Pray for them which despitefully use you." Note, this refers not only to those who speak despitefully but to those who *use you despitefully*. It is an attempt to shame and to hurt both your name and body. Someone tries to shame, dishonor, disgrace and reproach you. And they go even farther; they misuse, mistreat, abuse, attack, and persecute you. What are you to do? Christ says, "Pray for them. When they despitefully use you, pray for them." (1) Pray for God to forgive the persecutor. (2) Pray for peace between yourself and the persecutor. (3) Pray for the persecutor's salvation and correction.

> "Then said Jesus [upon the cross], Father, forgive them; for they know not what they do. And they parted his raiment, and cast lots" (Lk.23:34).
>
> "And he [Stephen] kneeled down, and cried with a loud voice, Lord, lay not this sin to their charge. And when he had said this, he fell asleep [died]" (Acts 7:60).

Prayer for the persecutor will greatly benefit you. It will keep you from becoming bitter, hostile, and reactionary.

e) Offer the other cheek: "Unto him that smiteth thee on the one cheek offer also the other." The word for cheek (siagon) really means the jaw or jawbone. It is a strong blow, a punch, and not just a slap of contempt. Of course, there is contempt and bitterness, but there is also physical injury. Christ is saying that you are not to strike back, not to retaliate against . . .

- bitter insults or contempt
- bodily threats or injury

When suffering *for the gospel's sake*, for your personal testimony for Christ, you are to respond to physical abuse just as your Lord did. You are to demonstrate *moral strength through a quiet and meek spirit*, trusting God to touch the heart of your persecutors.

> "And they spit upon him, and took the reed, and smote him on the head" (Mt.27:30).

> "And when he had thus spoken, one of the officers which stood by struck Jesus with the palm of his hand, saying, Answerest thou the high priest so?" (Jn.18:22).

> "Recompense to no man evil for evil. Provide things honest in the sight of all men" (Ro.12:17).

> "Thou shalt not avenge, nor bear any grudge against the children of thy people, but thou shalt love thy neighbor as thyself: I am the LORD" (Lev.19:18).

D. YOU AND OTHER BELIEVERS

(See the points that apply in Chapter V, "What Your Commission and Work Are," p.63-108; Chapter IX, Point B, "You and Your Conduct," p.278-294. Also see *Subject Index*, Duty - Work, Toward Others, p.395.)

E. YOU AND UNBELIEVERS

(See the points that apply in Chapter V, "What Your Commission and Work Are," p.63-108; Chapter IX, Point B, "You and Your Conduct," p.278-294. Also see *Subject Index*, Duty - Work, Toward Others, p.395.)

CHAPTER 11

What Your Attitude Toward Suffering Must Be

Suffering is a universal experience: we all suffer and suffer much throughout life. As a minister of God—as a leader within society—you must help to ease the suffering of everyone. To do this, you must have both a healthy and a Biblical attitude toward suffering.

Contents

1. You must trust God to deliver you through whatever suffering afflicts you, no matter its severity.   283

2. You must conquer your sufferings—your thorn in the flesh—for Christ's sake.   293

3. You must triumph over all suffering—all the trials and temptations—that attack you.   297

CHAPTER 11
What Your Attitude Toward Suffering Must Be

1. *You must trust God to deliver you through whatever suffering afflicts you, no matter its severity.*

   "Blessed be God, even the Father of our Lord Jesus Christ, the Father of mercies, and the God of all comfort; who comforteth us in all our tribulation, that we may be able to comfort them which are in any trouble, by the comfort wherewith we ourselves are comforted of God. For as the sufferings of Christ abound in us, so our consolation also aboundeth by Christ. And whether we be afflicted, it is for your consolation and salvation, which is effectual in the enduring of the same sufferings which we also suffer: or whether we be comforted, it is for your consolation and salvation. And our hope of you is stedfast, knowing, that as ye are partakers of the sufferings, so shall ye be also of the consolation. For we would not, brethren, have you ignorant of our trouble which came to us in Asia, that we were pressed out of measure, above strength, insomuch that we despaired even of life: but we had the sentence of death in ourselves, that we should not trust in ourselves, but in God which raiseth the dead: who delivered us from so great a death, and doth deliver: in whom we trust that he will yet deliver us; ye also helping together by prayer for us, that for the gift bestowed upon us by the means of many persons thanks may be given by many on our behalf" (2 Cor.1:3-11)

Thought

Suffering has always posed a problem for man. It may be disease, accident, trial, temptation, abuse, or death. But no matter what the suffering is, every person who suffers has wondered, "Why me? Why do I haveto suffer this affliction?" Suffering is the great discussion of this passage. Note seven points.

First, God is the Father of mercies and the God of all comfort (2 Cor.1:3).

a) The word "mercies" (oiktirmon) means compassion, pity, and mercy. It means looking upon people in need and having compassion and mercy upon them.

- Note that God is not the God of mercies but the *Father* of mercies. His very nature and behavior toward you is that of a Father, not of a God. He is your Father, a Father who is merciful and compassionate, and who showers His mercies and compassions upon you.

- Note that the word *mercies* is plural. God does not show mercy just once nor just here and there. God showers His mercies upon you continuously (cp. Ro.12:1; Ph.2:1; Col.3:12; Heb. 10:28).

b) The word "comfort" (parakleseos) means to be by the side of another; to relieve and support; to give solace, consolation, and encouragement. But there is always an underlying meaning to the word. There is the idea of strength, of enablement, of confidence. It consoles and relieves a person, but it strengthens him at the same time. It charges a person to go out and face the world. The word is used ten times in 2 Cor.1:3-7.

- Note that the word *comfort* (parakleseos) is the same word that is used for the Holy Spirit (paraklete). The Holy Spirit is given the title *The Comforter* by Christ.

    "If ye love me, keep my commandments. And I will pray the Father, and he shall give you another Comforter, that he may abide with you for ever; even the Spirit of truth; whom the world cannot receive, because it seeth him not, neither knoweth him: but ye know him; for he dwelleth with you, and shall be in you. I will not leave you comfortless: I will come to you" (Jn.14:15-18).

c) How do we know God is like this? How do we know that God is "the Father of mercies" and the "God of all comfort"? *Because of Jesus Christ.* God is "the Father of our Lord Jesus Christ." It was God . . .

- who "so loved the world, that he gave his only begotten Son, that whosoever believeth in him should not perish, but have everlasting life" (Jn.3:16).
- who demonstrated "his love toward us, in that, while we were yet sinners, Christ died for us" (Ro.5:8).

A father could show no greater mercy than to give the life of his son to save others. This is exactly what God did: He gave Christ to die for His enemies, for those who were in rebellion against Him. God has had mercy upon you, and He continues to have mercy upon you. He continues to pour out His mercy and comfort upon men. Why? Because of His nature: His very nature is that of a Father—a Father of mercies and a God of all comfort.

> **"But God, who is rich in mercy, for his great love wherewith he loved us, even when we were dead in sins, hath quickened us together with Christ, (by grace ye are saved;) and hath raised us up together, and made us sit together in heavenly places in Christ Jesus: that in the ages to come he might show the exceeding riches of his grace in his kindness toward us through Christ Jesus" (Eph.2:4-7).**
>
> **"But the mercy of the Lord is from everlasting to everlasting upon them that fear him, and his righteousness unto children's children" (Ps.103:17).**
>
> **"For thy mercy is great above the heavens: and thy truth reacheth unto the clouds" (Ps.108:4).**
>
> **"It is of the Lord's mercies that we are not consumed, because his compassions fail not"(Lam.3:22).**

Second, God comforts you so that you might be a testimony to other sufferers (2 Cor.1:4).

a) The word "tribulation" (thlipsei) means to be weighed down exceedingly; to be pressed and crushed. It is the picture of a beast of burden being crushed beneath a load that is just too heavy. It is the picture of a person having a heavy weight placed on his breast and being pressed and crushed to the point that he feels he is going to die. Note the word is used four times in 2 Cor.1:3-7.

b) Note the words "us" and "all tribulation." Paul is *not only talking* about his own trials and sufferings but about yours as well. God comforts all believers. He does not have favorites; His mercies and comfort are for everyone, including you. And note: He comforts you in "*all*," not in just a few of your trials and sufferings. You do not have to bear a single trial or moment of suffering by yourself. Your Father—the Sovereign Majesty of the universe who controls all—is not off in the distance someplace far removed from you. His Spirit, the precious Holy Spirit, is right here with you to comfort you in all your suffering.

c) God's purpose in comforting you is to make you a testimony to others.

- God comforts you so that you can comfort others who are suffering.
- God carries you through trials so that you can carry others through trials.
- God strengthens you so that you can strengthen others.
- God helps you so that you can help others.
- God encourages you so that you can encourage others.

> "Comfort ye, comfort ye my people, saith your God" (Is. 40:1).
> "Now we exhort you, brethren, warn them that are unruly, comfort the feebleminded, support the weak, be patient toward all men" (1 Th.5:14).

Third, God matches your comfort to equal the sufferings (2 Cor.1:5). Note that the sufferings being stressed are "the sufferings of Christ," that is, the very kind of sufferings which Christ Himself bore. What kind of sufferings did Christ bear? Very simply, Christ bore every kind of suffering imaginable, even the suffering of death. He had to experience every situation, condition, and trial of man in order to become the *Perfect Sympathizer or Savior*. For this reason, He experienced the most humiliating experiences possible. He experienced . . .

- being born to an unwed mother (Mt.1:18-19).
- being born in a stable, the worst of conditions (Lk.2:7).
- being born to poor parents (Lk.2:24).

- having his life threatened as a baby (Mt.2:13f).
- being the cause of unimaginable sorrow (Mt.2:16f).
- having to be moved and shifted as a baby (Mt.2:13f).
- being reared in a despicable place, Nazareth (Lk.2:39).
- having His father die during His youth (Mt.13:53-58).
- having to support His mother and brothers and sisters (Mt.13:53-58).
- having no home, not even a place to lay His head (Mt.8:20; Lk.9:58).
- being hated and opposed by religionists (Mk.14:1-2).
- being charged with insanity (Mk.3:21).
- being charged with demon-possession (Mk.3:22).
- being opposed by His own family (Mk.3:31-32).
- being rejected, hated, and opposed by listeners (Mt.13:53-58; Lk.4:28-29).
- being betrayed by a close friend (Mk.14:10-11, 18).
- being left alone, rejected, and forsaken by all of His friends (Mk.14:50).
- being tried before the high court of the land on the charge of treason (Jn.18:33).
- being executed by crucifixion, the worst possible death (Jn.19:16f).

Note that each of these experiences reaches the depth of humiliation. Christ stooped to the lowest point of human experience in every condition in order to become the *Perfect Sympathizer* (Savior). He can now identify with and feel for any person's circumstances, young or old.

> **"For verily he took not on him the nature of angels; but he took on him the seed of Abraham. Wherefore in all things it behooved him to be made like unto his brethren, that he might be a merciful and faithful high priest in things pertaining to God, to make reconciliation for the sins of the people. For in that he himself hath suffered being tempted, he is able to succour them that are tempted"** (Heb.2:16-18).

> "For we have not an high priest which cannot be touched with the feeling of our infirmities; but was in all points tempted likeas we are, yet without sin. Let us therefore come boldly unto the throne of grace, that we may obtain mercy, and find grace to help in time of need" (Heb.4:15-16).

The point is this: no matter what your suffering is nor how terrible it may be, God showers you with the comfort of His Son Jesus Christ. He does not just give you some strength and comfort to bear the suffering; He gives you *all the strength and comfort* necessary to handle all the suffering. There are no trials too great, no pressures too heavy, that God cannot *match them* with the comfort of the Lord Jesus Christ. Christ has borne every trial and suffering for you.

> "And when the Lord saw her, he had compassion on her, and said unto her, Weep not" (Lk.7:13).
>
> "I will not leave you comfortless: I will come to you" (Jn.14:18).
>
> "These things I have spoken unto you, that in me ye might have peace. In the world ye shall have tribulation: but be of good cheer; I have overcome the world" (Jn.16:33).

Fourth, God uses your suffering to stir up other believers (2 Cor.1:6-7). A person who suffers often becomes self-centered and begins to feel sorry for himself. He sometimes begins to feel self-pity and apathy and to want special attention. He may even become bitter. You must never let this happen to you. This is what these two verses are all about. Note that both the *affliction* and the *comfort* are for the same purposes. God uses both suffering and comfort in a believer to stir four things in other believers.

a) God uses suffering to stir consolation or comfort in others who suffer (see first point above, 2 Cor.1:3).

b) God uses suffering to stir salvation. A person cannot trust God today and not trust Him tomorrow. You cannot bless God when things are going well and curse God when things go bad. You have given your life to God; therefore, you must trust Him no matter the circumstance. You must continue with God throughout life . . .

- through the good times as well as the bad,
- through suffering as well as health,
- through rejection as well as acceptance,
- through persecution as well as honor.

The point is this: when other believers see you being comforted through some suffering, they are stirred to continue in the faith. They are stirred to continue on in the way of salvation no matter what suffering confronts them in the future.

"But he that shall endure unto the end, the same shall be saved" (Mt.24:13).
"If so be that we suffer with him, that we may be also glorified together" (Ro.8:17).

c) God uses suffering to stir endurance. Very simply, when you suffer and allow God to comfort you, others are encouraged to endure through their sufferings.

d) God uses suffering to stir sharing among believers. Believers who suffer are not to become self-centered, bitter, discouraged, apathetic, nor are they to begin complaining. They are to allow God to comfort them. This should be the hope and expectation of you and of every other believer. God expects you to suffer with the right attitude, to allow Him to share His comfort with you. Then you are to share the comfort of God with other believers.

Note this: as a minister, other believers should be able to expect you to bear up under suffering. They should be able to expect you to know the comfort of God so that you can share His comfort.

The point is this: How can you share the comfort of God unless you have suffered and experienced the comfort of God?

- God expects you to bear suffering and to receive His comfort.
- Other believers expect you to bear suffering and to receive God's comfort.

Why? Because you and other believers are to be comforting and ministering and helping each other. But how can you comfort each other unless you have experienced the comfort of God through suffering?

God uses your suffering to stir sharing with others. You and all other believers are to be busy in sharing God's comfort with each other. This is to be the hope and expectation that you are to have in each other.

> "If there be therefore any <u>consolation</u> in Christ, if any comfort of love, if any fellowship of the Spirit, if any bowels and mercies, fulfil ye my joy, that ye be likeminded, having the same love, being of one accord, of one mind" (Ph.2:1-2).

> "For our light affliction, which is but for a moment, worketh for us a far more exceeding and eternal weight of glory; while we look not at the things which are seen, but at the things which are not seen: for the things which are seen are temporal; but the things which are not seen are eternal" (2 Cor.4:17-18).

Fifth, God uses suffering to teach you to trust Him more and more (2 Cor.1:8-10). God allows great suffering. He allowed Paul, probably the greatest missionary of all time, to experience terrible suffering time and again. (See *The Preacher's Outline & Sermon Bible*®—2 Cor.1:8-10 for more discussion.) What was the suffering that is referred to in these three verses? We do not know. There is no record of it anyplace in Scripture. At first reading, it seems to be referring to the mob violence in Ephesus (Acts 19:23-41). However, this is unlikely, for Paul apparently escaped the particular trouble mentioned in the account of Acts.

The point to see is that God allowed Paul to suffer some terrible trouble. And note the intensity of the trouble: "we were pressed [weighed down, crushed by a very heavy weight]" . . .

- out of measure.
- above strength.
- we despaired even for our life.
- we had the sentence of death in ourselves (sensed he was going to die).

Why does God allow His dear servant to go through such suffering, especially when he is such a great servant, a servant who labors so faithfully for God? There are two primary reasons.

a) Note that God is called the "God which raises the dead." The one thing that man must learn is that he cannot save himself; he cannot raise himself up from the dead. Only God can save man and raise him up and give him eternal life. Suffering teaches a man that he is helpless to save himself. If he wishes to be saved, he must trust God. Therefore, suffering teaches you that you are not self-sufficient. You must have the presence and help of God if you wish to conquer the sufferings of this world—the sufferings that eventually end in the suffering of death.

b) God allows suffering to teach a daily trust for deliverance. Note: Paul says that God continued to deliver him through the trials of life and that he continued to trust God to deliver him. The point is this: you must trust God daily, trust Him to deliver you from daily sufferings.

> **"There hath no temptation taken you but such as is common to man: but God is faithful, who will not suffer you to be tempted above that ye are able; but will with the temptation also make a way to escape, that ye may be able to bear it" (1Cor.10:13).**
>
> **"Who delivered us from so great a death, and <u>doth deliver</u>: in whom we trust that he <u>will yet deliver</u> us" (2 Cor.1:10).**
>
> **"And the Lord shall deliver me from every evil work, and will preserve me unto his heavenly kingdom: to whom be glory for ever and ever" (2 Tim.4:18).**
>
> **"And deliver them, who through fear of death were all their lifetime subject to bondage" (Heb.2:15).**
>
> **"The Lord knoweth how to deliver the godly out of temptation, and to reserve the unjust unto the day of judgment to be punished" (2 Pt.2:9).**
>
> **"Be not afraid of their faces: for I am with thee to deliver thee, saith the Lord" (Jer.1:8).**

Sixth, Paul suffered greatly (2 Cor.1:8-10).

a) Paul's life was threatened by a huge, angry mob led by Demetrius, the silversmith (Acts 19:23-40).

b) Paul knew the trouble that awaited him in Asia. "Trials which befell me by the lying in wait of the Jews . . . in every city . . . bonds and afflictions await me" (Acts 20:18-27).

c) Paul says Priscilla and Aquila . . . risked their lives for him (Ro.16:3-4).

d) Paul says Andronicus and Junia . . . were his fellow prisoners (Ro.16:7).

e) Paul expresses the great victory experienced through terrifying trials (1 Cor.4:9-13).

f) Paul fought with beasts at Ephesus (1 Cor.15:32).

g) Paul says he was crushed by some fearful burden which made him despair of life itself. He told himself it was the sentence of death (2 Cor.1:8-10).

h) Paul expresses an extremely anxious mood while the memory of his days at Ephesus was still vivid (2 Cor.4:8-12; 6:4-11; cp. Acts 20:18-19).

i) Paul lists his terrifying trials. Clement of Rome says that Paul "was seven times in bonds," which seems to agree with Paul's description (2 Cor.11:23-27).

j) Paul, at some point while a prisoner in Rome, experienced some sorrow so great that it threatened to crush him into a frightening despair: he had feared lest "sorrow upon sorrow" befall him (Ph.2:27).

Seventh, God uses suffering to teach prayer and thanksgiving (2 Cor.1:11). This is a great lesson on suffering and prayer: the prayers of believers *"help"* us. Paul clearly says that the prayers of others helped him. Prayer causes God to move in your behalf and to deliver you through your suffering. And when you are strengthened and delivered, everyone praises God. Intercessory prayer, prayer for others, works.God hears and answers prayer, and He hears and answers your prayers for others. This is the reason Scripture stresses intercessory prayer.

"Now I beseech you, brethren, for the Lord Jesus Christ's sake, and for the love of the Spirit, that ye strive together with me in your prayers to God for me; that I may be delivered from them that do not believe in Judaea; and that my service which I have for Jerusalem may be accepted of the saints" (Ro.15:30-31).

"Praying always with all prayer and supplication in the Spirit, and watching thereunto with all perseverance and supplication for all saints" (Eph.6:18).

"For I know that this shall turn to my salvation [deliverance from trials and suffering] through your prayer, and the supply of the Spirit of Jesus Christ" (Ph.1:19).

"Confess your faults one to another, and <u>pray one for another</u>, that ye may be healed. The effectual fervent prayer of a righteous man availeth much" (Jas.5:16).

2. *You must conquer your sufferings—your thorn in the flesh—for Christ's sake.*

"And lest I should be exalted above measure through the abundance of the revelations, there was given to me a thorn in the flesh, the messenger of Satan to buffet me, lest I should be exalted above measure. For this thing I besought the Lord thrice, that it might depart from me. And he said unto me, My grace is sufficient for thee: for my strength is made perfect in weakness. Most gladly therefore will I rather glory in my infirmities, that the power of Christ may rest upon me. Therefore take pleasure in infirmities, in reproaches, in necessities, in persecutions, in distresses for Christ's sake: for when I am weak, then am I strong" (2 Cor.12:7-10).

Thought
You are God's messenger, very dear to Him, and you are His minister, chosen by Him to proclaim the unsearchable riches of His Son, the Lord Jesus Christ. Why then are you afflicted with a thorn—some permanent infirmity—in your body? Perhaps

Paul's experience will help you in answering the questions that arise in your mind.

Paul had experienced the spiritual power of Christ. God had given Paul deep and intimate spiritual experiences. There was the danger that he might begin to think too highly of himself; therefore, God gave Paul a "thorn in the flesh." Note three significant points.

First, Paul needed a "thorn" to keep him ever mindful that he was no better than other men (2 Cor.12:7). He was totally dependent upon God despite the indescribable spiritual experiences. What was his "thorn in the flesh"?

There are many guesses as to what the "thorn" was:

- some spiritual suffering such as constant attacks by Satan or opposition by men, or occasional evangelistic failure in order to keep Paul humble and on his face before God seeking supernatural strength.

- some physical suffering such as a recurring fever (for example, malaria), or epilepsy, or poor eyesight.

Just what the thorn was is not known. The best guess seems to be some physical ailment, for suffering is what this passage is all about (cp. 2 Cor.11:16-12:10). The words flesh, strength, weakness, and infirmities are used; and, although these same words could be used to describe spiritual sufferings, the context does not weigh toward spiritual suffering (cp. also 2 Cor.10:10).

The clearest description of the thorn is probably eye trouble (cp. 2 Cor.10:10; Gal.4:13-15; 6:11). Paul had been stricken blind for three days at his conversion, and he had been badly beaten and stoned several times (2 Cor.11:24-27). A serious injury to his eyes, or for that matter to any other part of his body, could have occurred at any of these tragedies.

Second, Paul wanted deliverance and relief; he wanted God to remove the thorn (2 Cor.12:8). Why?
Because...

- it pricked and bothered him.
- it distracted him from his labor.
- it made him appear personally weak and sickly.

Note that Paul prayed three times for God to remove the thorn. Jesus Christ had also prayed three times for the suffering of the cross to be removed (cp. Mt.26:36-46).

Third, there were three reasons why God refused to remove the thorn from Paul's flesh (2 Cor.12:9). Note these carefully and apply them to your own life and suffering.

a) God wanted to guard against Paul's being puffed up (see the first point of this note).

b) God wanted to reveal His power in Paul. The weaker the vessel, the more God is glorified when the vessel really serves Christ.

Note God's answer to Paul:

- "My grace is sufficient for thee": the presence, love, favor, and blessings of God are sufficient to help you walk through any suffering. The word "sufficient" (arkei) means the power or strength to withstand any danger. God's grace within you can carry you through anything. In Paul's case, it was physical suffering. In your case it may be either physical or spiritual attacks; but no matter: God's grace is sufficient to see you through whatever the thorn is.

- "My strength is made perfect in weakness": the weaker the believer, the more God can demonstrate His strength. If you are self-sufficient, you do not need God; but if you are weak, you need God: the help, provision, and sufficiency of God.

- "Most gladly therefore will I rather glory in my infirmities that the power of Christ may rest upon me." Note the point of this statement: infirmities or weaknesses are purposeful. You suffer for a reason: that the power of Christ may be demonstrated and clearly seen in your life. The word "rest" (episkenosei) means to fix a tent upon. The idea is that the power of Christ rests upon the suffering believer just as the Shekinah glory dwelt in the holy place of the tabernacle. What a glorious thought! The strength of Christ fixes itself upon you and dwells within you—filling you with the Shekinah glory of God—when you suffer.

c) God wanted to teach Paul to live "for Christ's sake." When Paul suffered some infirmity or weakness, it gave Christ the chance to infuse power into Paul and to overcome the weakness for Paul. The point is this: your infirmity gives Christ an opportunity to prove Himself. Therefore, you are to do what Paul did: take pleasure . . .

- "in infirmities": a general term meaning all kinds of sufferings and weaknesses, whether moral or physical. The power of Christ can overcome any weakness or temptation for you.
- "in reproaches": whether ridicule, insult, slander, rumor, or whatever.
- "in necessities": hardships, needs, deprivations, hunger, thirst, lack of shelter or clothing, or any other necessity.
- "in persecutions": verbal or physical attack, abuse, or injury.
- "in distresses": tight situations, perplexities, disturbances, anxious moments, inescapable problems and difficulties.

When you are weak, you are strongest. How? By the power of Christ. And the power of Christ is much stronger than all the combined forces of mankind.

As the minister of Christ, your great need is to acknowledge your weakness before the Lord. When you do, the Lord will pour His strength into your mind and heart. The Lord will empower you to overcome and conquer all infirmities and weaknesses. (Cp. pages 20, 325-340, 341-361.)

> "But Jesus beheld them, and said unto them, With men this is impossible; but with God all things are possible" (Mt.19:26).
>
> "For with God nothing shall be impossible" (Lk.1:37).
>
> "That he would grant you, according to the riches of his glory, to be strengthened with might by his Spirit in the inner man" (Eph.3:16).
>
> "Now unto him that is able to do exceeding abundantly above all that we ask or think, according to the power that worketh in us" (Eph.3:20).
>
> "But they that wait upon the Lord shall renew their strength; they shall mount up with wings as

eagles; they shall run, and not be weary; and they shall walk, and not faint" (Is.40:31).

"Fear thou not; for I am with thee: be not dismayed; for I am thy God: I will strengthen thee; yea, I will help thee; yea, I will uphold thee with the right hand of my righteousness" (Is.41:10).

"Fear not: for I have redeemed thee, I have called thee by thy name; thou art mine. When thou passest through the waters, I will be with thee; and through the rivers, they shall not overflow thee: when thou walkest through the fire, thou shalt not be burned; neither shall the flame kindle upon thee" (Is.43:1-2).

3. *You must triumph over all suffering—all the trials and temptations—that attack you.*

(See Chapter IV, points 1-4, "What Your Resources As A Minister Are," p.49-56 for discussion.)

CHAPTER 12

What Your Death and Reward as a Minister Will Be

The terrible and devastating grip of death confronts us all. Your loved ones die and eventually you, too, will face death. As a minister of Christ, what will your death be like? And what reward will you receive as a minister?

Contents

1. You will be carried immediately into heaven, transferred quicker than the blink of an eye into God's heavenly kingdom. — 301
2. You will receive eternal life. — 301
3. You will receive a new body, a transformed body, a glorious incorruptible body. — 304
4. You will receive the crown of righteousness. — 306
5. You will receive the crown of life. — 308
6. You will receive the crown of incorruption. — 309
7. You will receive the crown of rejoicing or soul-winning. — 309
8. You will receive the crown of glory. — 311
9. You will receive the perfection of all things. — 311
10. You will receive an eternal inheritance, be made an heir of God and a joint-heir with Christ. — 314

CHAPTER 12
What Your Death and Reward as a Minister Will Be

1. *You will be carried safely into heaven, into God's heavenly kingdom.*

    "**And the Lord shall deliver me from every evil work, and will preserve me [transfer, take me] unto his heavenly kingdom: to whom be glory for ever and ever**" **(2 Tim.4:18).**

    Thought
    When you or your loved one face death, God will transfer you from this world into the next world. It is a picture of time—of unbroken time. God will *immediately transfer* you from time and place you into eternity. In one moment of time you will be living in this world, conscious and aware, but within the same moment—in a split second—you will be transported into God's heavenly kingdom. That one moment of time will happen quicker than the blinking of an eye (11/100 of a second).

    Just imagine! There will be no loss of consciousness, no experience or awareness of death. One moment you will be a citizen of this world, and within the same split moment you will stand before the Lord as a citizen of heaven itself (2 Cor.5:6-8). It is the beautiful picture of the believer never having to taste or experience death. (See *The Preacher's Outline & Sermon Bible,*® notes—Col.3:1-4; Heb.2:9; cp. 2 Cor.5:5-8.)

2. *You will receive eternal life.*

    "**For God so loved the world, that he gave his only begotten Son, that whosoever believeth in him should not perish, but have everlasting life**" **(Jn.3:16).**

    "**And this is the record, that God hath given to us eternal life, and this life is in his Son. He that hath the Son hath life; and he that hath not the Son of God hath not life**" **(1 Jn.5:11-12).**

Thought

God has given you eternal life in His Son, the Lord Jesus Christ. As a minister of God, the one thing you want is to live, to live both abundantly and eternally. You want a full life while you are upon this earth, and you do not want to die. But note: to live forever in a corruptible world such as ours would not necessarily be a good thing. This is a world of evil, corruption, and death. Therefore, what you have now is not *real life*, not the fullest and best of lives. It is not what life was meant to be. The life that God gives is the fullest and the best life possible. God's life is perfect, perfect in both quality and eternity. God's life is eternal life, a life that overflows with abundance and continues on and on, never ending. This is the life for which man craves: this is the life you were meant to live.

Now, what is life? "Life" is one of the great words of Scripture. The word "life" (zoe) and the verb "to live" or "to have life" (zen) have a depth of meaning.

First, life is the energy, the force, the power of being and of existing. But what is the source of life? What is the energy and power to be and to exist? The source is God and His Son, the Lord Jesus Christ. The energy and power of life exists within God. There is no life apart from God. The basic source of all life is found in God and in God alone. Note exactly what Scripture says:

> "**Jesus saith unto him, I am . . . the life: no man cometh unto the Father, but by me**" (Jn.14:6).
>
> "**And this is life eternal, that they might know thee the only true God, and Jesus Christ, whom thou hast sent**" (Jn.17:3).
>
> "**For as the Father hath life in himself; so hath he given to the Son to have life in himself**" (Jn.5:26).

Second, life is the opposite of perishing. It is deliverance from condemnation and death. It is the stopping or cessation of deterioration, decay, and corruption.

> "**For God so loved the world, that he gave his only begotten Son, that whosoever believeth in him should not perish, but have everlasting life**" (Jn.3:16).

> "Verily, verily, I say unto you, He that heareth my word, and believeth on him that sent me, hath everlasting life, and shall not come into condemnation; but is passed from death unto life" (Jn.5:24).
>
> "And I give unto them eternal life; and they shall never perish, neither shall any man pluck them out of my hand" (Jn.10:28).

Third, life is eternal (aionios). It is forever. It is the very life of God Himself (Jn.17:3). However, eternal life does not refer just to duration. Living forever would be a curse for some persons. The idea of eternal life is also quality, a certain kind of life, a life that consistently knows the fullness of life, a life that overflows with love, joy, peace, power, purpose, meaning, significance, and responsibility.

> "I am come that they might have life, and that they might have it more abundantly" (Jn.10:10).

Fourth, life is satisfaction.

> "And Jesus said unto them, I am the bread of life: he that cometh to me shall never hunger; and he that believeth on me shall never thirst" (Jn.6:35).

Fifth, life is found only in God. This is mentioned in the first point above. God is the source and author of life, and it is God who has appointed Jesus Christ to bring life to man. Jesus Christ gives the very life of God Himself to believers.

> "For as the Father hath life in himself; so hath he given to the Son to have life in himself" (Jn.5:26).
>
> "Labour not for the meat which perisheth, but for that meat which endureth unto everlasting life, which the Son of man shall give unto you: for him hath God the Father sealed.... And this is the will of him that sent me, that every one which seeth the Son, and believeth on him, may have everlasting life: and I will raise him up at the last day" (Jn.6:27, 40).
>
> "And I give unto them eternal life; and they shall never perish, neither shall any man pluck them out of my hand" (Jn.10:28).

Sixth, life has now been revealed. It has been unveiled and is clearly seen in Jesus Christ. Jesus Christ shows man what life is.

> "In him was life; and the life was the light of men. And the light shineth in darkness; and the darkness comprehended it not" (Jn.1:4-5).
> "For as the Father hath life in himself; so hath he given to the Son to have life in himself" (Jn.5:26).
> "(For the life was manifested, and we have seen it, and bear witness, and show unto you that eternal life, which was with the Father, and was manifested unto us)" (1 Jn.1:2).

Note that God gives us life through His Son, the Lord Jesus Christ. Life only comes to a man by believing in Jesus Christ. A man outside Jesus Christ only exists. He merely has an animalistic existence. Real life is found only in God. This is to be expected and it is logically true, for God is the Creator of life. As the Creator of life, He alone knows what life really is and what it is supposed to be (Jn.3:36; 5:24; 6:47). This is the reason He sent His Son, the Lord Jesus Christ into the world: to show you what life is. When you look at Jesus Christ you see exactly what life is, exactly what it involves: existence, yes, but an existence of . . . (cp. Gal.5:22-23):

- love
- joy
- peace
- long suffering
- gentleness
- goodness
- faith
- meekness
- temperance or control

(Just think through each of the above for a moment to gain the full impact of the life that Christ gives.)

3. *You will receive a new body, a transformed body, a glorious incorruptible body.*

> "For our conversation [citizenship] is in heaven; from whence also we look for the Saviour, the Lord Jesus Christ: who shall change our vile body, that it may be fashioned like unto his glorious body,

according to the working hereby he is able even to subdue all things unto himself" (Ph.3:20-21).

"[This is] the resurrection of the dead. It is sown in corruption; it is raised in incorruption: it is sown in dishonour; it is raised in glory: it is sown in weakness; it is raised in power: it is sown a natural body; it is raised a spiritual body. There is a natural body, and there is a spiritual body" (1 Cor.15:42-44).

Thought

As a minister, you are to be focused upon the return of Christ. You are to be looking for the Lord's return—constantly looking—looking every day of your life. The word "look" (apekdechometha) means to yearn, to eagerly look and wait for the coming of the Lord Jesus to take you to heaven.

You are also to focus upon the glorious body you are to receive when Christ returns. Right now your body is vile, that is, lowly and humiliating. The human body is lowly and humiliating...

- because it has its origin out of the earth: it is nothing more than earthly chemicals or human flesh.
- because it is subject to sin, corruption, selfishness, evil, and destruction.
- because it is so weak: it is sickly and subject to disease, injury and maiming. It ages and deteriorates.
- because it is corruptible and dying, aging and mortal, offering no hope of ever lasting beyond a few short years—no hope whatsoever.

However, note the wonderful declaration: the Lord Jesus Christ will change your body and fashion it just like His glorious body. The word "fashion" (summorphon) points out a most wonderful thing. The word means the permanent, constant, and unchangeable being of a person. Your body shall be fashioned just like the glorious body of Christ. Imagine! To have a body that is permanent, constant, and unchanging. You will receive a spiritual body.

> "There is a natural body [somapsuchikon] and there is a spiritual body [soma pneumatikon]" (1 Cor.15:44).
>
> "Who shall change our vile body, that it may be fashioned like unto his glorious body, according to the working whereby he is able even to subdue all things unto himself" (Ph.3:21).
>
> We shall be "conformed to the image of His Son" (Ro.8:29).
>
> "We shall be like Him; for we shall see Him as He is" (1 Jn.3:2).

How is this possible? By the power of God, the very power which is able to subdue all things to Christ. The power of God that created the world . . .

- is sovereign over the world.
- is able to control the world.
- is able to subdue the world.
- is able to recreate the world.
- is able to transform your body and the body of all believers.

> "But the day of the Lord will come as a thief in the night; in the which the heavens shall pass away with a great noise, and the elements shall melt with fervent heat, the earth also and the works that are therein shall be burned up. Seeing then that all these things shall be dissolved, what manner of persons ought ye to be in all holy conversation and godliness, looking for and hasting unto the coming of the day of God, wherein the heavens being on fire shall be dissolved, and the elements shall melt with fervent heat? Nevertheless we, according to his promise, look for new heavens and a new earth, wherein dwelleth righteousness" (2 Pt.3:10-13).

4. *You will receive the crown of righteousness.*

> "Henceforth there is laid up for me a crown of righteousness, which the Lord, the righteous

judge, shall give me at that day: and not to me only, but unto all them also that love his appearing" (2 Tim.4:8).

Thought
This is an unbelievable reward—a crown of righteousness. Imagine! There is a crown of righteousness—a crown that you can receive, a crown that will make you acceptable to God. Even as a minister, you can never live before God unless you are crowned with righteousness—completely covered with righteousness and made perfect. Why? Because God is perfect and only perfection can live in the presence of God. Therefore, the only way you or anyone else can ever become acceptable to God is by receiving the crown of righteousness from God. You are to receive the crown of righteousness for one reason and for one reason only: because you have given your life . . .

- to be a soldier for Christ and His warfare.
- to be an athlete for Christ and His course (race and life).
- to be a steward (a manager) for Christ and His faith.

Think about it: a crown of righteousness that makes you *perfect* before God—*righteous and perfect* so that you can live before God forever and ever. You will be enabled to worship and serve God in perfection—never falling and never coming up short, never grieving and never hurting Him again. What a day of rejoicing that will be! What a glorious contrast with the weaknesses and failures we face today. What a contrast with the fading and deteriorating crowns and trophies given by this world.

Note this: the crown of righteousness will be given by the Lord Himself, by Him who is the righteous and perfect Judge, the only Judge who knows the truth about all men. He knows the heart of every man, and He has seen every man every day and hour of his life. In fact, the Lord has seen every act and heard every word every person has ever done or spoken. He knows all. The Lord knew all about Paul . . .

- that he had been a good soldier for Christ.
- that he had been a good athlete for Christ.
- that he had been a good steward (manager) for Christ.

The Lord is righteous and just; therefore, you can be assured that the Lord will give you the crown of righteousness in that glorious day of redemption.

5. *You will receive the crown of life.*

> "**Blessed is the man that endureth temptation: for when he is tried, he shall receive the crown of life, which the Lord hath promised to them that love him**" (Jas.1:12).
>
> "**Fear none of those things which thou shalt suffer: behold, the devil shall cast some of you into prison, that ye may be tried; and ye shall have tribulation ten days: be thou faithful unto death, and I will give thee a crown of life**" (Rev.2:10).

Thought

You are to receive a great reward for enduring the temptations and trials of this life. Note in James 1:12 above: if you endure temptations and trials in this life, then two great rewards will be given you.

First, you will be "blessed." This refers to this life, to the here and now. The word *blessed* means inward and spiritual joy and satisfaction; an inner assurance and confidence that carries you through all the trials and temptations of life no matter the pain, sorrow, loss, or grief. Simply stated, you will be secure in this life. You will know that God is looking after and caring for you; that He is going to deliver you from all the corruption and evil of this life including death, giving you life eternal.

Second, you shall receive the crown of life in the next world. What is the crown of life? In the Greek this is what is called "the gentive of apposition"; that is, *life itself* is the crown (A.T.Robertson. *Word Pictures In The New Testament,* Vol.6, p.17). If you endure the temptations of life, you shall be crowned with life itself, eternal life—life that will go on and on, never ending. The eternal life that will be given to you will shine more brightly than all the earthly crowns that have ever been worn by the rulers of this world.

Just imagine the actual moment when Christ will crown you with the crown of life. Being crowned with the crown of life . . .

- will fill you with unbroken joy and rejoicing.
- will bestow upon you honor and dignity.
- will give you a deep and perfect sense of victory and triumph.
- will conform you to the image of eternal royalty.

6. *You will receive the crown of incorruption.*

> "And every man that striveth for the mastery is temperate in all things. Now they do it to obtain a corruptible crown; but we an incorruptible" (1 Cor.9:25).
>
> "Blessed be the God and Father of our Lord Jesus Christ, which according to his abundant mercy hath begotten us again unto a lively [living] hope by the resurrection of Jesus Christ from the dead, to an inheritance incorruptible, and undefiled, and that fadeth not away, reserved in heaven for you" (1 Pt.1:3-4).

Thought
As the minister of Christ, you are running in a race to obtain an *incorruptible crown*. The runners in an athletic contest run to obtain a passing fame and a corruptible crown or trophy. The athletes in Paul's day ran for a crown or wreath of olive or pine leaves. Their fame and crown were the same as with our athletes today: they both passed ever so quickly. However, the crown and fame of the genuine Christian runner will never pass away. His crown and fame are incorruptible. He shall live and be rewarded with an eternal fame and with the most real and valued crowns imaginable.

7. *You will receive the crown of rejoicing or soul-winning.*

> "For what is our hope, or joy, or crown of rejoicing? Are not even ye in the presence of our Lord Jesus Christ at his coming? For ye are our glory and joy" (1 Th.2:19-20).

Thought
Paul clearly says that the Thessalonian believers were his hope and joy and *crown of rejoicing*. When? In the day when the

Lord Jesus Christ returns. In that day Paul and believers will all stand in His presence.

- What a hope! The return of the Lord Jesus Christ.
- What a joy! Joining the Lord Jesus Christ with all the believers whom we have known, reached, and grown in Christ down here on earth.
- What a crown! To offer to Christ all the dear people we have *had a part* in reaching and growing for the Lord.

Note the word "crown" (stephanos). It is the victor's crown, the crown worn by the athlete after he has won the contest. The picture is that you are in a contest, a spiritual struggle, against Satan for the souls of men. Therefore, you must strain and struggle and fight for the souls of men. A crown awaits you, a crown that you will miss unless you have souls to present to Christ.

All of us as ministers of Christ need to apply this to ourselves and be very honest about the matter: How many souls have I as a minister won to Christ? In that day, how many souls will I have to present to Him?

- Ten souls?
- Twenty souls?
- Fifty souls?
- One hundred souls?
- Thousands of souls?

The crown of rejoicing awaits the minister who will be able to present souls to the Lord in that day. Ask God to touch your heart and help you to win souls for Him. He will if you will only ask in sincerity.

> "And he saith unto them, Follow me, and I will make you <u>fishers of men</u>" (Mt.4:19).
>
> "He first findeth <u>his own brother</u> Simon, and saith unto him, We have found the Messias, which is, being interpreted, the Christ" (Jn.1:41).
>
> "Philip findeth Nathanael, and saith unto him, We have found him, of whom Moses in the law, and the prophets, did write, Jesus of Nazareth, the son of Joseph" (Jn.1:45).

> "Let him know, that he which converteth the sinner from the error of his way shall save a soul from death, and shall hide a multitude of sins" (Jas.5:20).

8. *You will receive the crown of glory.*

    > "And when the chief Shepherd shall appear, ye shall receive a crown of glory that fadeth not away" (1 Pt.5:4).

Thought

Your reward will be glorious. It is to be a crown of glory that never fades away. Note two things.

First, Jesus Christ is the Chief Shepherd and He is going to appear, that is, return to earth. The idea is that nothing will stop His return; He is going to appear and reward His ministers.

Second, the reward for ministers is glorious: it is to be a crown of glory. What does this mean? It means that the faithful minister shall share in the glory of heaven and be crowned with a very special portion of glory. By crown is meant rule and reign, the assignment of heavenly service for Christ. (See point 10 below for a list of all rewards.)

> "His lord said unto him, Well done, good and faithful servant; thou hast been faithful over a few things, I will make thee ruler over many things: enter thou into the joy of thy lord" (Mt.25:23).
>
> "For our light affliction, which is but for a moment, worketh for us a far more exceeding and eternal weight of glory" (2 Cor.4:17).
>
> "Behold, I come quickly; hold that fast which thou hast, that no man take thy crown" (Rev.3:11).

9. *You will receive the perfection of all things.*

    > "And I saw a new heaven and a new earth: for the first heaven and the first earth were passed away; and there was no more sea . . . .and God shall wipe away all tears from their eyes; and there shall be no more death, neither sorrow, nor crying, neither shall there be any more pain: for the former things are passed away" (Rev.21:1, 4).

> "But the day of the Lord will come as a thief in the night; in the which the heavens shall pass away with a great noise, and the elements shall melt with fervent heat, the earth also and the works that are therein shall be burned up. Seeing then that all these things shall be dissolved, what manner of persons ought ye to be in all holy conversation [behavior] and godliness, looking for and hasting unto the coming of the day of God, wherein the heavens being on fire shall be dissolved, and the elements shall melt with fervent heat? Nevertheless we, according to his promise, look for new heavens and a new earth, wherein dwelleth righteousness" (2 Pt.3:10-13).

Thought

All things are to be remade and perfected: both the universe and believers—all the believers who have ever lived in the universe. There is to be a new creation, a remaking of the heavens and the earth. The heavens (heavenly bodies in outer space) and the earth that you know are going to pass away. God clearly says in His Holy Word that He is going to recreate all things anew, recreate a new heaven and a new earth. Note three significant facts in the above Scripture.

a) All the heavens above—the sun, moon, stars, and planets—are going to be destroyed and remade. God is going to make a new heaven. Think what this will mean.

- There will be no more stars or solar systems that are burned out.

- All of the planets and worlds above and beyond will be remade, created anew and made alive. Think how glorious and beautiful the heavens look now when you look up on a starry night. But imagine what they will be like when God recreates them in all the glory and magnificence of a perfect universe. All things within the universe will be alive and reflect the glory and splendor of God Himself. The universe will be perfect, a place where nothing burns out or wears down or wastes away or dies. Think about the light and brilliance and splendor and glory of all the heavenly bodies when God recreates the heavens. Think what it will mean to have a universe full of *living planets and stars and solar systems*. We cannot imagine the glory and beauty. It is beyond our finite minds. But note the significant point: the Scripture declares emphatically that the heavens are to be remade and recreated into a new heavens.

b) The earth is going to pass away. There is going to be a new earth. The present earth is defective; it is cursed. The earth suffers under all kinds of natural disasters such as earthquakes, volcanic eruptions, destructive storms, floods, scorching heat, deserts, famines, diseases, and death. But the day is coming when God is going to remake the earth. God is going to create a new earth. Think what this will mean.

- No more disasters or destruction
- No more thorns or thistles or unfertile and unproductive soil
- No more hunger or thirst
- No more disease, decay, erosion, or death.

The new earth will flourish and be fruitful, bearing all the good that can be imagined. Think how beautiful, green, lush, productive, and fruitful it will be. Think how peaceful, serene, and comfortable it will be. Think of the security and provision, the abundance and overflowing of every good and perfect gift—the fulness of life that will be possible upon the earth. The earth will be new, perfected by God in every conceivable way.

Note the statement, "there was no more sea" (Rev.21:1). This can mean one of two things. The sea will be eliminated, done away with, and the new earth will have no sea. Or it can mean the same thing that is meant with the heavens and the earth. The heavens and the earth and the sea are to pass away and be made anew and recreated. The sea that causes devastation and destruction will be naturally destroyed right along with the earth and the heavens; but when they are recreated, the sea, being part of the earth, will be part of the new earth, part of the new creation. A perfected earth is beyond our comprehension. But it is exactly what Scripture declares is going to happen. God is going to create a new earth as well as a new heaven.

"Heaven and earth shall pass away, but my words shall not pass away" (Mt.24:35).

"Of old hast thou laid the foundation of the earth: and the heavens are the work of thy hands. They shall perish, but thou shalt endure: yea, all of them shall wax old like a garment; as a vesture shalt thou change them, and they shall be changed: but thou art the same, and thy years shall have no end" (Ps.102:25-27).

"And all the host of heaven shall be dissolved, and the heavens shall be rolled together as a scroll: and all their host shall fall down, as the leaf falleth off from the vine, as a falling fig from the fig tree" (Is.34:4).

"Lift up your eyes to the heavens, and look upon the earth beneath: for the heavens shall vanish away like smoke, and the earth shall wax old like a garment, and they that dwell therein shall die in like manner: but my salvation shall be for ever, and my righteousness shall not be abolished" (Is.51:6).

"For, behold, I create new heavens and a new earth: and the former shall not be remembered, nor come into mind" (Is.65:17).

"For as the new heavens and the new earth, which I will make, shall remain before me, saith the LORD, so shall your seed and your name remain" (Is.66:22).

c) Life will be perfected. This means that your body will be perfected; so will the environment and earth. Life will be totally different from what it is now. The very life and utopia for which you have longed will be a living reality. All the sufferings and evil of life and all the bad and negative experiences of your life will be gone. Scripture explains the change in the most beautiful and striking way: it declares that "God shall wipe away all tears from their [believers'] eyes."

10. *You will receive an eternal inheritance, be made an heir of God and a joint-heir with Christ.*

"The Spirit itself beareth witness with our spirit, that we are the children of God: and if children, then heirs; heirs of God, and joint-heirs with Christ; if so be that we suffer with him, that we may be also glorified together" (Ro.8:16-17).

"That being justified by his grace, we should be made heirs according to the hope of eternal life" (Tit.3:7).

"Blessed be the God and Father of our Lord Jesus Christ, which according to his abundant mercy hath begotten us again unto a lively [living] hope by the resurrection of Jesus Christ from the dead, to an inheritance incorruptible, and undefiled, and that fadeth not away, reserved in heaven for you" (1 Pt.1:3-4).

Thought

Jesus Christ makes you an heir of God. Scripture actually says that you are "joint heirs" with Christ. This is an astounding truth and promise. You shall inherit all that Christ is and has. You shall be given the glorious privilege of sharing all things with the Son of God Himself.

However, note this: to be a joint-heir with Christ does not mean that you are an equal heir in the sense that you will receive an equal amount of the inheritance with Christ. Rather, it means that you are a fellow-heir with Christ; that is, you will share in the inheritance of Christ; you will share Christ's inheritance with Him.

Being a fellow-heir with Christ means at least three glorious things: it means that you shall *share* in the *nature*, in the *position*, and in the *responsibility* of Christ. The following chart shows this with a quick glance.

Fellow Heirs by Nature

Christ is the Son of God, the very being and energy of life and perfection. Therefore, we share in the inheritance of His nature. We receive . . .

- the adoption as children of God (Gal.4:4-7; 1 Jn.3:1).
- the sinless nature of being blameless (Ph.2:15).
- eternal life (Jn.1:4; 10:10; 17:2-3; Jn.3:16; 1 Tim.6:19).

- an enduring substance (Heb.10:34).
- a glorious body (Ph.3:21; 1 Cor.15:42-44).
- eternal glory and honor and peace (Ro.2:10).
- eternal rest and peace (Heb.4:9; Rev.14:13).
- an incorruptible body (1 Cor.9:25).
- a righteous being (2 Tim.4:8).

Fellow Heirs by Position

Christ is the exalted Lord, the Sovereign Majesty of the universe, the Lord of lords and King of kings. Therefore, we share in the inheritance of His position. We receive . . .

- the position of exalted beings (Rev.7:9-12).
- a citizenship in the Kingdom of God (Jas.2:5; Mt.25:34).
- enormous treasures in heaven (Mt.19:21; Lk.12:33).
- unsearchable riches (Eph.3:8).
- the right to surround the throne of God (Rev.7:9-13; 20:4).
- the position of a king (Rev.1:5; 5:10).
- the position of a priest (Rev.1:5; 5:10; 20:6).
- the position of glory (1 Pt.5:4).

Fellow Heirs by Responsibility

Christ is the Sovereign Majesty of the Universe, the One who is ordained to rule and oversee all. Therefore, we share in the inheritance of His responsibility. We receive . . .

- the rulership over many things (Mt.25:23).
- the right to rule and hold authority (Lk.12:42-44; 22:28-29).
- eternal responsibility and joy (Mt.25:21, 23).
- rule and authority over cities (Lk.19:17, 19).
- thrones and the privilege of reigning forever (Rev.20:4; 22:5).

The above Scriptures will give some idea of what Scripture teaches when it speaks of the believer being a *fellow-heir* with Christ. There are an innumerable number of Scriptures that could be added to these. As Paul declares:

> "Eye hath not seen, nor ear heard, neither have entered into the heart of man, the things which God hath prepared for them that love him" (1 Cor.2:9).
>
> "O the depth of the riches both of the wisdom and knowledge of God! how unsearchable are his judgments, and his ways past finding out! For who hath known the mind of the Lord? or who hath been his counsellor? Or who hath first given to him, and it shall be recompensed unto him again? For of him, and through him, and to him, are all things: to whom be glory for ever. Amen" (Ro.11:33-36).

Note how our inheritance is described in 1 Pt.1:4. It is most descriptive, an astounding picture of the new heavens and earth that are coming and of our life in God's new and eternal world. "To an inheritance incorruptible, and undefiled, and that fadeth not away, reserved in heaven for you" (v.4).

a) Your inheritance is "incorruptible" (aphtharton). The word means that it cannot perish; it does not age, deteriorate, or die; it does not have the seed of corruption within it. Matthew Henry points out that everything on earth changes from better to worse, but not our inheritance. It is perfect and incorruptible. It never changes, and it shall never cease to be the most perfect inheritance and gift imaginable (*Matthew Henry's Commentary*, Vol.6, p.1005).

b) Your inheritance is "undefiled" (amianton). The word means that it cannot be polluted or defiled, dirtied or infected. It means that your inheritance will be without any flaw or defect; it will be perfectly free from sickness, disease, infection, accident, pollution, dirt—from any defilement whatsoever. There will never be any pain, suffering, or tears over what happens to you or over the damage or loss of some possession.

c) Your inheritance *does not fade away* (amaranton). It will last forever and ever. The splendor and beauty of it all—of life and of all the positions and possessions which God shall give you—shall never fade or diminish whatsoever. Nothing, not even your energy and body, shall wear out or waste away.

d) Your inheritance is in heaven; it is reserved there for you. It is actually being held there by God for you. God is simply waiting for you to finish your task here on earth and to come to Him. Then He will give you your inheritance. As a minister of God, you have . . .

- received the mercy of God
- been born again
- trusted the resurrection of Jesus Christ to cover your resurrection (1 Pt.1:3).

Therefore, you are to receive the eternal inheritance of God. God has willed the treasures of heaven to you. God counts you as a joint-heir with His very own Son, the Lord Jesus Christ. What a glorious hope and privilege—all through our Lord Jesus Christ!

> **"Knowing that of the Lord ye shall receive the reward of the inheritance: for <u>ye serve the Lord Christ</u>" (Col.3:24).**

Amen and Amen!

INDEXES

Subject Index (pages 319-350)

The page number listed in the Subject Index is only the first page of a subject. The subject usually covers several pages.

The *Point by Point Table of Contents* (pp.iii-xi) gives a helpful subject index when searching for topics that . . .

- meet a personal need.
- will help prepare you to preach at an ordination or to a body of ministers at a conference or ministerial function.

Scripture Index (pages 351-356)

Subject Index

ABANDON - ABANDONED
Duty.
    Must **a**.—be separated from—the world.   231
    Must be totally **a**. to God.   19, 21

ADMINISTRATION
    Duty. To oversee the **a**. of the church.   81

ADULTERY
    Duty. Must not commit **a**.   116, 118

AIM
    Discussed.   11-23

AMBASSADOR
Fact.
    Are an **a**. for Christ.   33
    Called to be an **a**.   8
    Meaning.   9, 33

AMBITION
    Duty. Must not put **a**. above the truth.   187

APOSTASY
    Duty. Must not turn away from the faith.   147

APPEARING
    Of Christ. Meaning.   95, 98, 307

SUBJECT INDEX

ARMOR OF GOD
  Discussed. — 201
  Duty. Must put on the **a.** daily. — 201

ASHAMED
  Duty. To live above reproach. Not to be **a.**
    of anything. — 16, 205

ASSURANCE
  Of victory.
    God causes you to triumph in Christ. — 45
    God counts you trustworthy. — 5

BABBLING
  Meaning. — 181

BACKSLIDING
  Duty. Must restore the fallen minister. — 264

BEHAVIOR, PERSONAL (See **CONDUCT**)
  Duty.
    Must do what we teach. — 68, 116
    Must live a life of godly **b.** — 179, 229
    Must not allow your mind to become corrupt. — 151, 159
    Must not be a hypocrite. (See **HYPOCRISY**)
    Must not be dishonest. — 114
    Must not be filled with pride. — 157
    Must not be inconsistent. — 17
    Must not break or violate the Word of God. — 119
    Must not commit adultery. — 118
    Must not commit apostasy. — 147
    Must not commit idolatry. — 119
    Must not deceive people. — 140
    Must not dishonor God. — 119
    Must not enter the ministry for gain nor
      as a profession or a livelihood. — 126, 157, 161
    Must not enter the ministry out of
      covetousness. — 126, 157, 161
    Must not fear established, worldly religion. — 32
    Must not glory in self. — 127
    Must not hold to man's empty ideas
      & speculations. — 185
    Must not lie, deny Christ. — 141, 146, 152
    Must not lift up yourself. — 131
    Must not live a hypocritical life. — 120
    Must not live in the past. — 15
    Must not mishandle the Word of God. — 114
    Must not offend in anything. — 17
    Must not pervert the gospel. — 139, 153, 162, 164

Must not preach the thoughts and ideas of men.	137,175
Must not preach with enticing words.	122
Must not put ambition above the truth.	187
Must not seek to please men.	138
Must not seek worldly recognition.	127
Must not steal.	116
Must not stress statistical numbers.	129
Must not twist the Word of God.	154,164
Must not use flattery or flattering words.	124,126
Must not walk deceiving others.	114
Must not walk in craftiness.	114
Must not waste time in empty conversation.	240
Outline of subjects discussed.	223-246
You and your body and mind.	223-229
You and your conduct.	229-242
You and your financial support.	242-246

BELIEVE - BELIEF
Duty.
    Must **b**. Christ and His Word.   93
    Must **b**. God.   13
    Must have the right kind of **b**.   191
    Must test your **b**.   193
    Must test your **b**. and your preaching.   140

BELIEVERS
Duty toward. (See **DUTY - WORK**, Toward others)

BESEECH
Meaning.   9

BIBLE STUDY (See **SCRIPTURES**)

BOAST - BOASTING (See **PRIDE**)
Duty. Must not **b**. in oneself, but in the cross.   127

BODY
Duty.
    Must discipline and subject your **b**.   227
    Must exercise your **b**.   228
    Must glorify Christ in your **b**.   16
    Must present your **b**. as a living sacrifice.   223
    Must struggle to control your mind.   225
Fact.
    Is a temple of the Holy Spirit.   224
    Is perishing, aging, deteriorating daily.   198
    Will receive a new **b**.   304

BOLD - BOLDNESS
Duty. To be a **b**. witness for Christ.   31

CALL - CALLED
Discussed.   6
Fact.

>   Are **c.** because Christ counts you trustworthy. 5
>   Is the minister's great glory. 6
>   The minister's **c.** is the greatest of calls. 7
> Source.
>> God. 3
>> God's grace. 6
>> Holy Spirit. 4
>> Jesus Christ. 4
> To what.
>> To be a servant. 6
>> To be a steward. 7
>> To be a watchman. 77
>> To be an ambassador. 8,33
>> To be under the Holy Spirit's control. 4
>> To the ministry of reconciliation. 8

CASTAWAY
> Meaning. 227

CHARACTER (See CONDUCT; DUTY - WORK)
> Duty. Must live a life of godly **c.** 229
> List of things to flee and to follow after. 233,234

CHARGE
> Meaning. 178

CHILDREN (See FAMILY)

CHOSEN
> Source.
>> God. 3
>> Holy Spirit. 4
>> Jesus Christ. 4

CHRIST
> Meaning. 132

CHURCH
> Basis - foundation.
>> To be centered in the homes. 83
>> Only one foundation: Jesus Christ. 90
> Duty.
>> Must not bring heresy into the **c.** 167,170
>> Must reject heretics in the **c.** 154
> Duty toward.
>> Must manage the organization of the **c.** 81
>> Must pray for the **c.** daily. 210
>> To build the **c.** as a wise masterbuilder. 87
>> To build up the **c.** 69,87
>> To center in the homes. 83
>> To serve & stay with a **c.** for a long time. 133
> Early church. Centered in the homes. 56,84
> Fact. Are false teachers within the **c.** 153,154, 167, 169,170

Staff of. To secure the staff needed. 82
CHURCH DISCIPLINE
  Duty. Discussed. 266
COMFORT
  Meaning. 284
COMMISSION
  Discussed. 55-90
COMMISSION, GREAT (See **MISSION; WITNESSING**)
  Duty.
    To be the Lord's ambassador to the world. 8,33
    To go and make disciples of all nations. 28
    To go to the whole world. 8,27,32,33
COMMIT - COMMITMENT
  Duty. Must c. all you are and have to Christ. 192
COMMUNITY
  Duty. To witness first to your own c. 34
CONDUCT (See **BEHAVIOR, PERSONAL**)
  Must be a man of God. 233
  Must be faithful through trials & temptations. 235
  Must flee youthful lusts. 236
  Must know that perilous times are coming. 240
  Must live a life of godly c. 229
  Must live a life of separation. 231
  Must shun godless & empty talk. 237
CONFESSION
  Duty.
    Must confess that Jesus Christ is the Son of God. 145
    Must confess the incarnation, that Jesus Christ
      has come in the flesh. 140
  Of the false minister. 161,171
  Of the true minister. 142
CONFORM - CONFORMED
  Duty. Must be c. to the image of Christ. 193
CONSISTENT - CONSISTENCY
  Duty.
    Must be a c. witness. 36
    Must be c. in teaching over a long time. 133
    Must be c; must not offend in anything. 17
CONTINUE
  Meaning. 215
CONTROL (See **DISCIPLINE**)

SUBJECT INDEX

CONVERSATION
Duty.
    Must not waste time in empty c.   240
    Must shun empty and godless c.   237

COVET - COVETOUSNESS
Duty. Must not enter the ministry out of c.—as
    a profession or a livelihood.   126

CRAFTINESS
Meaning.   115

CRITICISM
How to handle.   266-280

CROSS, DAILY (See **COMMITMENT; DEDICATION; SELF-DENIAL**)
Duty.
    Must live a crucified life.   195
    Must take up your c. daily.   196

CROWN - CROWNS
Discussed.
    Crown of glory.   311
    Crown of incorruption.   309
    Crown of life.   308
    Crown of rejoicing.   309
    Crown of righteousness.   306
    Crown of soul-winning.   309

CRUCIFIED LIFE
Duty. Must live a c. life in Christ.   195

DAILY WALK (See **WALK, DAILY**)

DEAR
Meaning.   20

DEATH (See **REWARD**)
Discussed.   301-318
    How to face with joy.   19,21

DECEIT - DECEPTION
Meaning.   115

DEDICATE - DEDICATION (See **CROSS, DAILY; SELF-DENIAL**)
Duty.
    Must d. all *you are* and *have* to Christ.   192
    Must not faint in your ministry.   198
    Must sacrifice your body to God.   223
    Must seek God first.   194
Things men d. themselves to.   197

DEFEAT
   Deliverance from.
      By Christ. Always assured.   45
      By God. Always assured.   45

DEMONSTRATION
   Meaning.   123

DENY - DENIAL
   Results of.
      Destroys the hope of salvation.   145
      Makes one a liar.   146
      Means that one denies God Himself.   146
      Means that one denies the New Testament.   146
      Ten results.   144-145
   What it is that some persons deny.
      Jesus Himself.   171
      That Jesus is the Christ, the Son of God.   143
      The Incarnation, that Christ has come in
        the flesh.   144
      The Lord and His death.   167
      The only Lord God and the Lord Jesus Christ.   152

DEPRESSION
   Answer to - Deliverance from. To forget the past
      and press on.   15

DETERMINED
   Meaning.   99

DEVOTIONS, DAILY
   Duty.
      Must pray daily.   208-219
      Must study and obey the Scriptures daily.   202-208
   Outline of subjects discussed.   189-219
   You and Christ.   191-202
   You and prayer.   208-219
   You and Scripture.   202-208

DISCIPLESHIP
   Discussed.   28
   Duty. To go and make disciples of all nations.   28-29
   Meaning.   28

DISCIPLINE
   Duty.
      Must **d**. and control the body.   227
      Must **d**. the mind.   225

DISCOURAGEMENT
   Answer to - Deliverance from. To forget the past
      and press on.   15

SUBJECT INDEX

DISCUSSION
  Duty.
    Must shun empty and godless **d**.   237
    Must shun questionable teaching.   239

DISHONESTY
  Meaning.   115

DISPENSATION
  Meaning.   121

DISTRESS
  Meaning.   42

DOCTRINE
  Duty. Must hold fast sound **d**. and teaching.   93

DOCTRINE, SOUND
  Meaning.   93

DUTY - WORK (See Outline of "Contents, Point by Point" at the beginning of this book. Almost every Point in the *Minister's Handbook* is a duty.)
  Discussed.
    Must go and make disciples of all nations.   28
    Must present every man perfect in Christ.   30
  In edification. (See **EDIFY - EDIFICATION**)
  In evangelism. (See **EVANGELISM; MISSION; WITNESSING**)
  In exhortation. (See **EXHORT - EXHORTATION**)
  In preaching. (See **PREACH - PREACHING**)
  In speech and conversation. To focus upon Christ.   122
  In teaching. (See **TEACH - TEACHING**)
  Toward Christ.
    Must be a steward for Christ.   7
    Must be an under-rower for Christ.   6
    Must be faithful.   19,21,235
    Must complete one's life and ministry
      faithfully.   19,21
    Must exalt Christ whether by life or death.   16
    Must keep the faith.   23
    Must know the power of His resurrection.   14
    Must live a crucified life.   195
    Must live like a faithful soldier.   21
    Must not glory in self, but in the cross.   129
    Must run the race of life like a faithful athlete.   22
    Must *walk* in Christ.   120
  Toward false teaching. (See **TEACHING, FALSE**)
  Toward family. (See **FAMILY**)
    List of duties.   231
  Toward God.
    Must be a steward over the mysteries, the
      truths of God's Word.   7

SUBJECT INDEX

Must be an ambassador for God.	8,32
Must be faithful.	19,21,235
Must be God's watchman.	77
Must not dishonor God.	119
Must put on the armor of God daily.	201
Must seek first the kingdom of God.	194
Toward others.	
Must be a pattern of God's mercy.	27
Must be a wise master builder.	88
Must be consistent and teach over a long period of time.	133
Must edify.	69
Must exhort.	56
Must feed.	72
Must lead others into a pure and faultless religion.	78
Must lead people to worship the Lord.	55
Must live a sacrificial, self-denying life.	195
Must minister and serve even as Christ.	57
Must not enter the ministry for gain, as a profession or a livelihood.	74,126
Must not offend in anything.	17
Must pray for others daily.	217
Must reap the harvest now.	59
Must seek and save the lost.	80
Must serve.	132
Must stay at a church for a long time.	133
Must take the oversight over others willingly.	73
Must teach others in wisdom.	206
Must visit people. A list of who to visit.	79
Must watch over and warn.	76
Must work and labor for God now.	59
Toward yourself.	
List of duties.	230
Must be a new creation in Christ.	192
Must be a person of integrity and honesty.	114
Must be conformed to Christ's image daily.	193
Must be faithful through all trials & temptations.	235
Must be renewed day by day.	197
Must examine yourself constantly.	194
Must fight for the faith.	233,234
Must forget the past and press on.	15
Must guard against becoming a castaway.	227
Must have the right kind of faith.	191
Must hold fast sound doctrine and teaching.	93
Must live a crucified life.	195
Must live what you preach.	116
Must not walk deceitfully.	115
Must not walk in craftiness.	115
Must not walk in dishonesty.	115

Must put on the armor of God daily.	200
Must seek first God's righteousness.	194
Must test yourself, your belief and confession.	140
Things to flee and things to follow.	233,236

DWELL
Meaning. 205

EARTH
Fact. Will be remade and perfected. 312

EDIFY - EDIFICATION (See PREACHING; TEACHING)
Duty.
Must e. or build up believers. 69
Must feed believers. 72

EMPEROR, ROMAN
Preparations made when he visited a city. 98

ENTICING
Meaning. 123

EQUIP - EQUIPPING
Duty. Must equip believers to serve Christ. 70

ETERNAL LIFE
Fact. Will receive eternal life. 301
Meaning. 302

EVALUATE - EVALUATION
Duty. Must e. yourself. 194

EVANGELIZE - EVANGELISM - EVANGELIST (See MISSION; WITNESSING)
Duty.
Must carry the message of reconciliation
  to the whole world. 81
Must do the work of an evangelist. 80
Must go & e. all nations. 28,33
Must seek to present every man perfect in Christ. 30
Fact. Is a gift of the Spirit. 47

EXAMINE - EXAMINATION (See TEST)
Duty. Must e. yourself. 194

EXAMPLE (See TESTIMONY)

EXHORT - EXHORTATION
Duty. Must e. with all longsuffering and doctrine. 66
Meaning. 66

FABLES
Meaning. 178

FAILURE
Duty. Must forget the past and press on for the prize. 15

FAINT
    Duty. Must not faint in your ministry.   197

FAITH
    Duty.
        Must continue in the **f**.   194
        Must have the right kind of **f**.   191
        Must make sure your **f**. is genuine.   194
        Must not turn away from the **f**.   147,150
        Must place your **f**. in Christ.   124
        Must test your **f**.   194
        Must test your **f**. and preaching.   140
    Essential - Importance of. Sustains you, the
        minister, when all else fails.   48
    Saving **f**. Discussed.   191
    Work of. To sustain the minister.   48

FAITHFUL - FAITHFULNESS
    Fact. God counts the minister **f**.   5
    Duty.
        Must be **f**.   17
        Must be **f**. in preaching the gospel.   21
        Must be **f**. in sharing the Word.   17
        Must be **f**. through all experiences of life.   18
        Must be **f**. through all trials and temptations.   17,297
        Must be so **f**. you are totally surrendered to God.   19
        Must complete your life and ministry **f**.   19,22
        Must keep the faith.   23
        Must live like a **f**. soldier.   21
        Must run the race of life like a **f**. athlete.   22
        Toward Christ.   20,21
        Toward God.   19

FALSE TEACHING
    Outline of subjects discussed.   135-188
        You and false teachers or heretics.   137-162
        You and false teaching and doctrine.   175-188
        You and other gospels.   162-175

FAMILY
    Children. What provokes a child. Four things.   257
    Duty.
        Must manage your **f**. well.   256
        Must not provoke your children.   257
        Must witness first to your own **f**.   33
    Minister and wife.
        Must be the husband of one wife.   254
        Must walk in submission and love.   249

FASHION
    Meaning.   305

FEED THE FLOCK OF GOD
Meaning.   72

FINANCES
Duty.
   Must not covet worldly wealth.   243
   Must not seek luxury.   242
   Must receive pay without embarrassment.   242
   Must trust God to meet your needs.   245
   Must work at secular employment if needed.   244

FOUNDATION
Described. As Jesus Christ.   89
Duty. Must build your life upon Christ.   89

GENEALOGY
Duty. Must not teach **g**., godly heritage for salvation.   178

GIFTS, SPIRITUAL
Meaning.   47
Purpose. To equip the minister for his work.   47
Source. God.   47

GLORY (See SELF-GLORY)
Crown of. Discussed.   311

GOD
Duty toward. To know, believe, and understand God.   13
Power of. Does five things.   44
Presence of.
   Does five things.   44
   Is a precious and priceless treasure.   44
Work of. (See **CALL; COMMISSION; MISSION**)
   To call ministers.   3
   To equip the minister.   44
   To give assurance.   44

GODLINESS (See CONDUCT)
Duty.
   Must be a man of God.   233
   Must teach the doctrine of **g**.   156

GOSPEL
Duty.
   Must not pervert the gospel of Christ and preach some other gospel.   162
   Must preach with a sense of urgency.   120
Fact.
   Held accountable for preaching the **g**.   121
   Is a trust, a stewardship, given by God.   121
False. What a false **g**. is.   163

GRACE
Results - work of. Strengthens and empowers you.   41

Source. Christ.	41
Work of. To call ministers.	5

GRAVITY
Meaning.	256

HARVEST
Of souls. Is ripe now.	59

HEAVEN
Duty. Must preach **h**.	110
Fact. Will be carried safely into **h**.	301

HEAVENS, THE
Fact. Will be remade and perfected.	312

HERESY - HERETIC
Duty. Must not bring **h**. into the church.	167
Duty toward. Must reject.	154, 167
Meaning.	168

HERODIANS
Discussed.	183

HOLY - HOLINESS
Meaning.	253

HOLY SPIRIT
Call of. Reasons.	4
Duty toward. (See **FAITHFULNESS**)	
Must be a Spirit-filled witness.	37
Must preach in the power of God's Spirit.	122
Fact. Makes your body His temple.	224
Work of.	
To call ministers.	4
To comfort.	286
To equip ministers.	43

HONEST - HONESTY
Duty. Must be a person of **h**.	116

HOPE
Duty. Must forget the past and press on.	15
Work of. Sustains you in the ministry.	51

HOSPITALITY
Duty. To show **h**.	84

HYPOCRISY - HYPOCRITE (See **TEACHERS, FALSE**)
Duty.	
Must live what you preach and teach.	116, 193
Must make sure you are genuine & not a false teacher.	137
Must not teach different from the Scripture.	148

Error of.
    Brings heresy into the church.   167
    Has a different life-style than God.   153
    Holds a false profession.   141,143,171
    Is disguised as a minister of Christ.   139,171
    Professes, but his heart is far from God.   146,176
    Rejects authority. Is a heretic.   154
  Fact. Is called a liar.   146

IDEAS
  Duty
    Must not preach the **i.**, speculations, of men.   177,178
    Must not put above the truth.   187
  Fact. Are helpful, but belong in the conference rooms of the secular world not in the church.   161

IDOLATRY
  Duty. Must not commit **i.**   118
  Meaning.   119

IMAGE OF CHRIST
  Duty. Must be conformed to the **i.** of Christ.   197

IMMORALITY
  Duty. Must not commit **i.**   118

INCARNATION
  Belief in the **i.** is essential.   141,143
  Confessed and denied.   141

INCORRRUPTION
  Crown of.   309

INFIRMITIES
  Deliverance through.
    By the grace and power of Christ.   41
    By the presence and power of God.   44
  Meaning.   42

INHERITANCE
  Chart of.   315
  Fact. Will receive an eternal **i.**   314

INNER MAN (See **NEW MAN**)

INSTANT
  Meaning.   64

INTEGRITY
  Duty. Must be a person of **i.**   114

INTERCESSION
  Duty. Must take extended times for **i.**   218
  Meaning.   212

JAMBRES
    False religious leader in Egypt.   151

JANNES
    False religious leader in Egypt.   151

JEREMIAH
    Call of.   3

JESUS CHRIST
    Burial. Results. Proves two things.   107
    Death.
        Duty.
            Must glory in the cross.   131
            Must preach Christ and Him crucified.   99
        Results - Effects.
            Crucifies the world to you and you to
                the world.   130
            Twenty-nine results.   100-106
        Was the focus of Paul's preaching.   99
        Why Christ died. Explained.   49,99,130
    Deity. Belief in the deity of Christ is essential.   141,157
    Duty toward. (See **DUTY - WORK**, Toward Christ)
    Incarnation. Belief in the incarnation is essential.   141,158
    Love of. Constrains you to hold fast and endure.   49
    Names - Titles.
        Christ. Meaning.   132
        Jesus. Meaning.   141
        The Foundation. Meaning.   89
    Resurrection.
        Duty.
            Must know the power of His **r**.   14
            Must preach the **r**. of Christ.   106
        Prophecies of.   110
        Results. Proves four things.   107
    Return. Duty. Must prepare for His return.   98
    Work of. (See **CALL; COMMISSION; MISSION**)
        To call ministers.   4
        To commission ministers. (See **COMMISSION**)
        To equip ministers.   41
        To serve man. How?   157

JUDGING OTHERS
    Duty. Must leave **j**. up to God.   261
    Fact. Can never know all the facts.   261

JUDGMENT
    Of whom.
        False teachers.
            Will be accursed.   165
            Will be destroyed swiftly.   170
            Will be judged according to their works.   174
            Will face **j**.   153

Subject Index

    Ministers.   97,121
    What is to be judged.
        Failure to preach.   121
        Labor - works.   259
        Minister's work and preaching.   97,121,125

JUSTIFICATION
    Christ resurrected for our **j**.   108

KINGDOM OF CHRIST
    Surety of. Will be set up.   98

KINGDOM OF GOD
    Duty.
        Must preach the kingdom of God.   110
        Must seek first the kingdom of God.   194
        Meaning.   111-114

KNOW - KNOWLEDGE
    Duty.
        Must **k**. Christ & the power of His resurrection.   14
        Must **k**. God.   13
        Must lead people to know God.   72
        Must not rely on false knowledge.   180

LABOR (See WORK)

LABORERS
    Duty. Must pray daily for more **l**.   213

LEADER - LEADERSHIP
    Duty.
        To oversee the administration of the church.   81
        To oversee the church and its believers.   72

LEAVEN
    Meaning.   183

LIFE (See CONDUCT; PERSONAL LIFE & BEHAVIOR)
    Crown of. Discussed.   308
    Duty.
        Must be conformed to Christ daily.   197
        Must live a crucified **l**.   195
        Must live a **l**. of godly character.   229
        Must live a **l**. of separation.   231
    Fact. Will be perfected.   314
    Meaning.   302

LIVELIHOOD
    Duty. Must not enter the ministry as a **l**. or
        a profession.   74,126

LOST, THE
    Duty. Must seek & save the **l**.   58

LOVE
    Duty. Must l. your wife.   252
    Meaning.   252
    Of Christ. Constrains, motivates you to hold
        fast and endure.   49
    Work of. To compel the minister.   49

LUSTS
    Must flee youthful l.   236

MAN
    State of. Lost and doomed to die.   58

MAN, INNER (See **NEW MAN**)

MAN, NEW (See **NEW MAN**)

MAN, OLD (See **OLD MAN**)

MAN, OUTWARD (See **OLD MAN**)

MANAGEMENT (See **ADMINISTRATION; LEADER - LEADERSHIP**)

MARRIAGE
    Duty.
        Must be the husband of one wife.   230
        Must walk in submission and love.   249

MASTERBUILDER
    Meaning.   87

MEMORIZE
    Duty. Must **m.** Scripture.   205

MERCY
    Duty. To be a pattern of God's mercy.   27
    Meaning.   283

MESSAGE (See **PREACH - PREACHING; TEACH - TEACHING**)
    Duty. Must hold fast and must preach and
    teach sound doctrine.   93
    False. What a false **m.** is.   163
    Outline of subjects discussed.   91-134
        You and your message.   93-115
        You and your preaching and teaching.   116-134

MIND
    Duty. Must control your **m.**—every thought.   225
    What to keep the **m.** upon. Discussed.   226

MINISTER (See Subject Desired. Remember the whole Index applies to the Minister.)
    Discipline of a **m.** by the church. Discussed.   266
    Duty toward other **m.** (See **DUTY - WORK**)
        Must not judge other **m.**   260

Subject Index

Must restore fallen **m**.	264
Must support travelling **m**.	263
Not to ordain **m**. too quickly.	264
To receive and support other **m**.	263
Fact. Is a gift of the Spirit (Pastor).	47
Meaning.	6
Must know you are a co-worker with other **m**.	258
Qualifications and duties. List of.	230-231
Relationship with other **m**.	
Are not rivals, but co-workers.	258
Some plant; some water.	259

MINISTER, FALSE (See **TEACHERS, FALSE**)

MINISTERING (See **DUTY**; Subject Desired)
Duty. Must **m**. & serve even as Christ served.	57

MINISTRY
Duty.
To be faithful to the end.	21
To fight like a faithful soldier.	21
To run like a faithful athlete.	22
To serve even as Christ served.	57
To stay at your **m**. for a long time.	133
Fact. Some enter the **m**. as a profession or for a livelihood.	74,126

MISSION
Discussed.	53-90
Duty.	
Must be the Lord's ambassador to the world.	8,33
Must go and make disciples of all nations.	28
Must go to the whole world.	8,28,32,33
Must pray for laborers. The need is enormous.	213
Must seek and save the lost.	58
Method to use. Discussed.	32
Of Christ. To seek and save the lost.	58
Urgency of. Fields are already ripe for harvest.	59

MYSTERIES OF GOD
Meaning.	19

NAMES - TITLES
Ambassador for Christ.	8
Steward.	7
Under-rower.	6
Watchman.	76

NEEDS - NECESSITIES
Duty. Must trust God to meet **n**.	245
God meets our needs—if we seek Him first.	194
Meaning.	42

NEW CREATION
    Duty. Must be a new creation in Christ.   192

NEW MAN
    Duty.
        Must be a new man in Christ.   193
        Must be conformed to Christ daily.   197
        Must be renewed day by day.   197
    Meaning.   198

OBEDIENT (See **FAITHFUL**)
    Duty. To be an **o**. witness.   35

OFFENDING OTHERS
    Duty. To be consistent; not to offend in anything.   17

OLD MAN
    Duty. Must put off the old man.   193
    Fact. Perishes every day.   198
    Meaning.   198

OPPOSITION (See **PERSECUTION**)
    How to handle. Discussed.   270-273,276
        294,296

ORDAIN - ORDINATION
    Duty. Must be careful who is ordained.   264

ORGANIZATION
    Duty. Must manage the **o**. of the church.   81

ORPHANS
    Duty toward. To visit and minister to.   79

OUGHT
    Meaning.   120

PAST, THE
    Duty. Must forget the **p**. & press on.   15

PEACE (See **RECONCILIATION**)
    Duty.
        To reconcile people to God.   9,33
        To work to bring **p**. between people.   71

PERFECT - PERFECTION
    Fact. All things to be perfected.   311
    Meaning.   30

PERSECUTION
    Attitude toward. Discussed.   268
    Duty.
        Must love those who persecute you.   276
        Must trust God.   269
    Fact. Will face **p**.   270-271
    How to handle **p**.   270-273,276

Meaning 42
Why the world persecutes the minister. 270

PERSONAL LIFE AND BEHAVIOR
Outline of subjects discussed. 221-246
    You and your body and mind. 223-229
    You and your conduct. 229-242
    You and your financial support. 242-246

PHARISEES
Discussed. 183

POSITIVE THINKING
Duty. Must control your mind—every thought. 225
What to think upon. Discussed. 226

POWER
Of the Holy Spirit. Must preach in the Spirit's power. 122
Results and work of. Strengthens through trials and temptations. 42
Source.
    Christ. 42
    God. Does five things. 44
    Holy Spirit. 42

PRAY - PRAYER
Duty.
    Must continue and watch in **p**. 216
    Must **p**. always—moment by moment. 215
    Must **p**. daily. Pray the Lord's prayer. 208
    Must **p**. daily for more laborers. 213
    Must **p**. daily for the church. 210
    Must **p**. daily for the world. 211
    Must take some extended times for **p**. 218
Fact. Is a law of the universe established by God. 218
Kinds of. Discussed. 212
Paul's prayer. For the church. Should be prayed daily. 210

PRAYER, LORD'S
Duty. To be prayed daily. 208

PREACH - PREACHING (See TEACH; TEACHERS, FALSE)
Discussed. 91-134
Duty.
    Must hold fast to sound doctrine. 93
    Must glory in the cross, not self. 131
    Must live what you **p**. 116
    Must not mishandle the Word of God. 114,204
    Must **p**. Reasons why. 61,96
    Must **p**. and teach sound doctrine. 94

Must **p**. and teach the Word of God.	95
Must **p**. Christ and Him alone.	132
Must **p**. Christ and Him crucified.	99
Must **p**. in the power of God's Spirit.	122
Must **p**. over a long period of time.	133
Must **p**. the gospel. Because of sin, death, and judgment to come.	122
Must **p**. the gospel. Three reasons.	120
Must **p**. the gospel with urgency.	120
Must **p**. the incarnation, that Jesus Christ has come in the flesh.	140,145
Must **p**. the kingdom of God and of heaven.	110
Must **p**. the message: "Be reconciled to God."	9
Must **p**. the resurrection of Christ.	106
Must **p**. to please God, not men.	124
Must seek to present every person perfect in Christ.	30
Must turn away from questionable **p**.	239
Must work at secular work if need be in order to **p**.	244
How not to **p**.	
Being filled with pride.	157
Deceiving people.	115,140
Dishonoring God—not living what one **p**.	116,119
Fearing established, worldly religion.	128
Glorying in yourself.	127
Lifting yourself up.	131
Lying, denying Christ.	140,145
Mishandling the Word of God.	114
Perverting the gospel of Christ.	164
P. while one is committing idolatry.	118
P. while one is living in adultery.	118
P. while one is violating the Word of God.	119
Seeking financial gain or a livelihood.	126,157 161,196
Seeking some gain out of greed, covetousness.	126,157 160,196
Seeking the support and approval of men.	125
Seeking to impress people.	126,127
Seeking to please men.	124
Seeking worldly recognition.	127
Stressing statistical numbers.	129
Twisting the Word.	155
Using flattering words.	124
With a corrupt mind.	151,159
With enticing words.	122
With hypocrisy. (See **HYPOCRISY - HYPOCRITE**)	
How to **p**.	
Discussed.	61

Glorying in the cross, not in self.	131
In season, out of season, reprove, rebuke.	64
To please God, not men.	124
With a sense of urgency.	120
Meaning.	61,62
Objective of. To lead people to Christ.	124
Outline of subjects discussed.	91-134
You and your message.	93-116
You and your teaching.	116-134
What not to **p**.	
A different gospel.	163
A different Jesus.	171
Book reviews, politics, economics, etc.	64
Controversial questions.	158
Denial of Jesus Christ.	169
Fables, speculations, ideas of men.	96,175,185
Heresy.	167
List of things.	63
Man-centered and self-help messages.	160
Man's empty ideas and discussions.	185
Persuasive thoughts and ideas of men.	122
Something different from the Word.	149,155
The thoughts & ideas of men.	122,175
Traditions and ideas of men as doctrine.	175,204
Why **p**. - Motivation to **p**.	
God and Christ are watching you.	62,96
Three reasons.	97

PRESS - PRESSING
Duty. Must forget the past & **p**. on.	15

PRIDE - PROUD
Duty. Must not glory in oneself.	127
Meaning.	157

PROFANE
Meaning.	181

PROFESS - PROFESSION
Duty.
Must make sure you are genuine, not a false teacher.	137
Must make sure your profession is true.	191

PROPHECY
Of Christ's resurrection.	109-110

PROVE - PROVING
Duty. Must **p**. you are a true minister of Christ.	17

PURPOSE
Discussed.	25-38

QUIET TIME (See **DEVOTIONS, DAILY**)

REBUKE
Duty. Must **r**. people.   61
Meaning.   66

RECONCILE - RECONCILIATION
Duty.
    To be an ambassador, a minister, of **r**.   9,32
    To **r**., bring people together.   71

REJOICING
Crown of. Discussed.   309

RELATIONSHIPS (See DUTY - WORK)
Outline of subjects discussed.   247-280
    You and other believers.   280
    You and other ministers.   258-267
    You and those who oppose, criticize, and
        persecute you.   268-280
    You and unbelievers.   280
    You and your family.   249-258

RELIGION
Duty toward. To make pure and faultless.   78
Pure **r**. Meaning.   79

RENEW - RENEWED
Duty. Must be renewed day by day.   197

REPROACH
Meaning.   42

REPROVE
Duty. Must **r**. people.   61
Meaning.   65

RESOURCES
Discussed.   39-52

RESURRECTION, THE
Hope of. Motivates the minister.   51

REWARD - REWARDS
Basis - Based upon.
    Faithfulness.   98
    Faithfulness in preaching.   121
Chart of **r**.   315
Outline of subjects discussed.   299-318
    Will be carried into heaven.   301
    Will receive a crown of glory.   311
    Will receive a crown of incorruption.   309
    Will receive a crown of life.   308
    Will receive a crown of rejoicing.   309
    Will receive a crown of righteousness.   306
    Will receive a crown of soul-winning.   309
    Will receive a new body.   304

Will receive an eternal inheritance.	314
Will receive eternal life.	301
Will receive the perfection of all things.	311

RIGHTEOUSNESS
Crown of. Discussed.	306
Duty. Must seek first the **r.** of God.	194

ROMAN EMPEROR
Preparations made when he visited a city.	98

SACRIFICE, SELF (See **CROSS, DAILY; SELF-DENIAL**)
Duty. Must sacrifice your body to God.	223

SACRILEGE
Meaning.	118

SADDUCEES
Discussed.	184

SANCTIFY
Meaning.	252

SATAN
Fact. Has his ministers disguised as ministers of righteousness.	172

SAVE - SAVED - SALVATION
Duty.
Must be a pattern that God saves sinners.	27
Must seek & **s.** the lost.	58
What saving faith is and is not.	191

SCIENCE
False. Must not rely on false **s.** and knowledge.	180
Meaning.	182

SCRIPTURES (See **WORD OF GOD**)
Duty.
Must live as **S.** dictates—be consistent.	207
Must memorize **S.**	205
Must not be hypocritical in teaching the **S.**	148
Must not teach different from the **S.**	148
Must obey and live by the **S.**	202
Must study and obey the **S.** daily.	202
Must study the **S.** daily & consistently.	202,203

SECURITY
Comes by - Source. God's Call. God counts you trustworthy.	5

SEEK - SEEKING
Duty.
Must **s.** & save the lost.	58
Must **s.** first the kingdom of God.	194

SELF-DENIAL
Duty. Must live a life of self-denial.   196

SELF-EXAMINATION
Duty. Must examine yourself.   194

SELF-GLORY
Duty. Must not glory in yourself.   127

SELFISH - SELFISHNESS
Duty. Must turn away from **s.** and ungodly men.   240

SEPARATION
Duty.
    Must live a life of **s.**   231
    Must turn away from selfish and ungodly men.   240

SERVANT - SLAVE
Fact. Are called to be a **s.** for God.   7
Meaning.   58,132

SERVE - SERVICE (See DUTY - WORK)
Duty.
    Must labor for God right now.   59
    Must minister & **s.** even as Christ.   57

SIN - SINS (See BEHAVIOR, PERSONAL - CONDUCT)
List of.
    Adultery.   118
    Boasting.   127
    Covetousness.   126
    Craftiness.   115
    Deceit.   115,138
    Defeatism.   46
    Depression.   15
    Discouragement.   15
    Dishonesty.   115
    Empty talk, godless talk.   237,240
    Enticing.   123
    Failure to pray.   208-219
    Failure to study the Scriptures.   202-208
    Fainting.   213
    False teaching.   135-188
    Heresy.   167
    Hypocrisy. (See **HYPOCRISY**)   119
    Idolatry   118-119
    Immorality.   118
    Inconsistency.   18
    Judging others.   261
    Lust.   236
    Preaching other gospels & false doctrine.   162-188
    Pride.   127,157
    Relying on false science & knowledge.   180,182

Sacrilege. 118
Seeking luxury 242
Self-glory. 127
Sins common to youth. List of. 236
Ungodliness. 237,238
Worldliness. 237

SOUL-WINNING
Crown of. Discussed. 309

SOUND
Meaning. 93

SPIRITUAL GIFTS (See **GIFTS, SPIRITUAL**)

STAFF, CHURCH
Duty. To secure the **s.** needed. 82

STEAL - STEALING
Duty. Must not **s**. 117

STEWARD
Fact. Are called to be a **s.** for God. 7
Meaning. 7

STEWARDSHIP
Duty.
    Must not covet worldly wealth. 243
Must not seek luxury. 242
Must receive pay without embarrassment. 242
Must trust God to meet your needs. 245
Must work at secular employment if needed. 244

SUFFERING
Deliverance from.
    By God. He matches the comfort to equal the **s**. 288
    By the grace and power of Christ. 41
    By the presence and power of God. 43
    Must trust God to deliver you. 283
Discussed.
    Permanent **s.**—your thorn in the flesh. 293
    Why you sometimes suffer. 281-297

SUPPLICATION
Meaning. 212

SURRENDER - SURRENDERED
Duty. To be totally **s.** to God. 19

TALK
Duty.
    Must not waste time in empty **t**. 240
    Must shun empty and godless **t**. 237

TEACH - TEACHERS - TEACHING
   Discussed. 91-134
   Duty.
      Must feed believers. 72
      Must hold fast and teach sound doctrine. 93
      Must instruct, root, and ground people. 67
      Must live what you teach. 68
      Must not turn away from the faith. 149
      Must present every person perfect in Christ. 30
      Must teach faithful believers all you know. 29
      Must teach over a long period of time. 133
      Must teach the Word of God. 68
   Fact. Is a gift of the Spirit. 47
   Gift of. Discussed. 68
   Meaning. 28
   Outline of subjects discussed. 91-134
      You and your message. 93-116
      You and your preaching and teaching. 116-134
   Traits of. Two traits. 68-69
   What makes a teacher true or false. 141-146

TEACHERS, FALSE (See **PREACH - PREACHING**)
   Discussed. 135-188
      Five facts. 171-175
   Duty toward.
      Must guard against those who deny Christ. 152
      Must guard against those who resist the truth. 151
      Must make sure you are not a false teacher. 137
      Must not be a wolf in sheep's clothing. 137
      Must reject heretics, false teachers. 154
      Must teach the words of Christ and godliness. 156
      Must test yourself—your belief in Christ. 140
   Errors of.
      Are carried away with different teachings. 177
      Are heretics. 138
      Bring heresy into the church. 167
      Deny that Jesus is the Christ, the Son of God. 146
      Deny the incarnation, that Jesus Christ
         came in the flesh. 141
      Deny the Lord and His death. 167
      Deny the only Lord God and our Lord
         Jesus Christ. 152
      Depend upon secondary sources, not the Bible. 158
      Do not teach the words of Christ nor godliness. 156
      Fail to do four things. 139-140
      Five errors. 137-140
      Have corrupt minds. 151
      Hold to controversial questions. 158
      Hold to man-centered and self-help messages. 160
      Implant a cancerous growth within the heart. 94
      Must guard against those who resist the truth. 162

SUBJECT INDEX

Pervert the gospel of Christ and teach some other gospel.	154,162
Preach and teach heresy.	138
Put self above love and truth.	185
Rely on false science and knowledge.	180
Resist the truth.	151
Stress the humanity of Jesus.	171
Teach a different gospel.	162
Teach a different Jesus.	171
Teach fables, speculations, ideas of men.	178
Teach hypocritically—different from the Scriptures.	148
Teach man's empty ideas and discussions.	185
Teach tradition and ideas of men as truth.	175
Turn away from Christ and the Word.	154
Turn away from the faith.	149

Names - Titles.
Antichrist - against Christ.	146
Deceitful workers.	171
False ministers.	171
Ministers of Satan.	173,174
Wolves.	138

Outline of subjects discussed.	135-188
You and false doctrine & teaching.	175-188
You and false teachers or heretics.	137-162
You and other gospels.	162-175

Source - Where false teachers are.
In the church.	153,154,167, 169,171

Traits - Characteristics. (See **TEACHERS, FALSE**, Errors of)
Are as wolves.	137
Are deceptive—ministers of Satan.	173
Are disguised as ministers of Christ.	173
Are hypocrites.	116,137,140, 146,148,154, 157,167
Are not attached to Christ.	157
Are proud.	157
Are subverted, twisted.	155
Are ungodly.	154
Have corrupt minds.	151
Rely on false science and knowledge.	180
Trust the fables, ideas, & speculations of men.	141,177,178, 180,185
What makes a teacher true or false.	141,146

TEACHING, FALSE
Description of.	181
Discussed.	135-188

Duty. Must not bring the church.	167
Duty toward.	
Discussed.	137-188
Must fear teaching a different Jesus.	171
Must guard against the false teaching of	
religion and of the state.	183
Must not give attention to false teaching.	148
Must not teach different from the Scriptures.	148
Must turn away from questionable teaching.	239
Outline of subjects discussed.	135-188
You and false doctrine & teaching.	175-188
You and false teachers or heretics.	137-162
You and other gospels.	162-175
Results.	
Accursed.	165
Destroyed swiftly.	170
Judged according to works.	174
Judgment.	153

TEMPTATIONS
Deliverance from.	
By the grace and power of Christ.	41
By the presence and power of God.	43
God's call. God counts you trustworthy.	5
Duty. Must be faithful through all **t**.	17,234

TEST - TESTING
Duty.	
Must prove you are a true minister of Christ.	17
Must **t**. & examine yourself constantly.	194
Must **t**. what you believe and preach.	140

TESTIMONY
Duty. To be a pattern, an example, of God's mercy.	27

THANKSGIVING
Meaning.	213

TRADITIONS
Duty. Must not teach **t**. as doctrine.	175

TRIALS - TRIBULATIONS (See SUFFERING)
Deliverance from.	
By the grace and power of Christ.	41
By the presence and power of God.	43
God's call. God counts you trustworthy.	5
Duty. Must be faithful through all **t**.	17,234
Meaning.	285

TRIUMPH (See VICTORY)

TRUSTWORTHY
Duty. Must be **t**.	5
Fact. God counts the minister **t**.	5

TRUTH
Fact. Some resist the **t**. — 151

UNDERSTAND - UNDERSTANDING (See KNOW - KNOWLEDGE)
Duty. To **u**. God. — 13

UNGODLY - UNGODLINESS
Duty. Must turn away from ungodly people. — 237,238
Traits. List of. — 238

UNITY
Duty. To work to bring **u**. among people. — 71

UNIVERSE
Fact. To be perfected someday in the future. — 112

UNWORTHINESS, SENSE OF
Answer to - Deliverance from. Must forget the past and press on. — 15

URGENT - URGENCY
Duty. Must preach with a sense of **u**. — 120

VAIN
Meaning. — 181

VICTORY
Fact. Is assured. — 44,45
Source.
  Christ. — 41,45
  God. — 43,46

VISIT - VISITATION
Duty. To **v**. orphans and widows. — 79
Who to **v**. List. — 79

WALK, DAILY
Meaning. — 120
Outline of subjects discussed. — 189-219
  You and Christ. — 191-202
  You and prayer. — 208-219
  You and Scripture. — 202-208

WARN - WARNING (See DUTY; TEACHERS, FALSE; TEACHING, FALSE, Results)
Duty. Must **w**. people. — 78

WATCH - WATCHING
Duty.
  Must **w**. in prayer. — 216
  Must **w**. over people. — 76
Meaning. — 216

WATCHMAN, GOD'S
Name - title. Of the minister. Discussed. — 77

WEAK - WEAKNESSES
Deliverance from.
    By the grace and power of Christ.   41
    By the presence and power of God.   43

WIDOWS
Duty toward. Must visit and minister to.   79

WIFE
Duty. Must walk in submission & love.   249

WISDOM
Of man. Cannot save man.   124

WITNESS - WITNESSING (See COMMISSION, GREAT; MISSION)
Discussed. Nine points.   30-38
Duty.
    To be an ambassador for Christ.   8
    To bear **w**. to the death of Christ.   32
    To go and make disciples of all nations.   28
Method. Discussed.   34
Problems confronting **w**. Five problems.   35

WOE
Meaning.   121

WOLVES
Traits of. Describe false teachers.   138

WORD OF GOD (See SCRIPTURES)
Abuse of. (See TEACHERS, FALSE)
    Breaking or violating the **W**.   119
    Depending upon secondary sources instead of the **W**.   158
    Failing to teach the **W**. of Christ.   156
    Handling the **W**. deceitfully.   115
    Mishandling the **W**.   114
    Teaching something different from the **W**.   149
    Turning away from the **W**.   155
Duty.
    Must be a steward over the **W**. of God.   7,18
    Must not mishandle the **W**.   114
    Must not teach different from the **W**.   149
    Must preach and teach the **W**.   61,93
    Must root & ground people in the **W**.   67
Meaning.   63,96

WORD, THE
Meaning.   63

WORK
Discussed.   53-90

WORLD
  Duty.
    Must pray for the **w.** daily.   211
    Must witness to the whole **w.**   33

WORLDLINESS
  Duty. Must be separated from **w.**   231

WORSHIP
  Duty. To lead people to **w.** the Lord.   55
  How to **w.** Discussed.   56

YOUTH
  Lusts of. Listed. Must flee.   236
  Things to follow after.   237

Scripture Index

Genesis	
2:24	255

Exodus	
7:1	151
8:7	151
9:11	151
20:15	117
23:5	278

Leviticus	
19:11	117
19:18	280

Deuteronomy	
5:19	117
11:16	119
17:17	256

Joshua	
1:8	203

1 Chronicles	
16:11	215,216
16:29	55,57

Job	
10:14	274

Psalms	
1:2	203
16:10	110
19:12	274
37:3	246
37:5	246
66:16	38
71:15	36
90:8	274
95:6	55
96:9	55
100:4-5	55
102:25-27	314
103:17	285
108:4	285
119:9,11	205
119:46	31
119:48	203
126:5-6	61

Proverbs	
15:1	279
25:21	278
28:14	151

Ecclesiastes	
10:13	187

Isaiah	
6:8	5,21
7:14	142
9:6	142
26:3	225
29:13	176
34:4	314
40:1	286
40:31	296
41:10	297
42:8	119
43:1-2	297
43:10	3,13
51:6	314
53:5	102
55:11	37
56:10-11	139
62:6	36,76,77
65:17	314
66:22	314

Jeremiah	
1:5-7	3
1:8	291
3:15	72
6:17	76
15:16	205
16:17	274
17:9-10	275
20:9	35
23:1-40	139
23:4	72
29:13	215
30:17	265
50:6	139

Lamentations	
3:22	285

Ezekiel	
2:7	21
3:17	76,77
33:6-9	76,78
34:2-3	139
34:23	72

Hosea	
7:2	274

Amos	
7:14-15	3

Jonah	
1:1-3	19
3:1-3	19

Micah	
3:8	43

Malachi	
3:16	36

Matthew	
1:18-19	286
2:13f	287
2:16f	287
3:2	111
4:10	55
4:17,23	111
4:19	60,310
5:20	174
5:27-28	118
5:31-32	254
5:44	276,277
6:5-8	209
6:9-13	208,210
6:24-34	245
6:25-34	194
6:31-33	246
6:33	113,194
7:1	276
7:7	213
7:15	137
7:15-16	167
7:17	138
7:21-23	116
7:22-23	167,174
7:24	90
8:20	287

Scripture Index

9:36-38	213	5:19	33	22:41-42	218,219
9:37-38	260	6:46-47	218,219	23:34	279
10:7	110,111	7:13	176	24:25-27	109
10:7,27	64	8:15	183		
10:13-15	269	8:36-37	163	**John**	
10:33	145,170	8:38	145,170	1:4	315
11:27	147	10:14	112	1:4-5	304
12:40	109	10:15	112	1:6	3
13:24-25	113	10:28	75	1:14	142
13:43	200	10:43-44	133	1:29	100
13:53-58	287	14:1-2	287	1:41	310
15:6-9	175	14:10-11,18	287	1:45	310
15:9	165,166,187	14:50	287	3:3	112,199
16:1-12	184	16:15	34,64	3:3,5-6	199
16:12	183			3:16	45,96,163,191,285
16:15-18	89,90	**Luke**			301,302,315
16:27	97	1:31	142	3:18	155
18:15-17	156,266	1:37	296	3:36	170,304
18:15-20	155	2:7	286	4:23-24	55,56
19:1-12	254	2:24	286	4:24	56,176
19:4-6	255	2:39	287	4:34	74
19:9	256	3:8	179	4:35	59
19:18	117	3:24-31	110	4:35-36	214,260
19:21	243,316	4:18-19	57	5:24	303,304
19:26	296	4:28-29	287	5:26	302,303,304
20:26-28	57,58	4:43	110	5:28-30	96
21:31	112	6:12	218,219	6:2,26	271
22:16	183	6:46	117	6:27,40	303
22:29	187	7:13	288	6:35	303
23:28	117	8:1	110	6:47	304
23:33	167	8:13	183	6:68	90,163
24:13	289	9:2	110	8:24	163
24:35	314	9:2,4	83	8:31-32	71
24:44	98	9:4	34,85	8:51	90
25:21	316	9:23	15,195,196	9:4	245
25:22-23	260	9:58	287	9:28	180
25:23	200,311,316	9:62	183	10:10	45,303,315
25:31-46	96	10:2	60,213,237	10:12	139
25:34	316	10:2-4	237,240	10:28	303
25:34-36	79	10:3	268	12:32	103
26:28	100	10:4	245	12:44-45	147
26:36-46	294	10:5-6	85	13:14	133
26:40-41	217	10:7	242	13:15	76
26:41	215	11:1-2	209	14:6	89,147
27:30	280	12:1	183		176,302
28:19-20	28,34,67,69	12:2	274	14:9-10	147
		12:33	316	14:15-18	284
Mark		12:42-44	316	14:16-17	224
1:14-15	110	14:33	75	14:18	288
1:35	218,219	18:1	215	15:16	3,61
3:21	287	19:10	58	15:18-25	270
3:22	287	19:17,19	316	15:19	270
3:31-32	287	22:28-29	316	15:20	268,271
4:29	60	22:29-30	99	15:21	271

15:22-24	271	20:24	20,260	12:1	15,284
15:26-27	37	20:25	111	12:1-2	16,223
15:27	38	20:28	4,72,106	12:2	231
16:8-11	124	20:29-30	162,165	12:6-8	47
16:33	288	20:29-31	268	12:13	86
17:2-3	315	20:32	203	12:14	279
17:3	71,302-303	20:33	75,243-244	12:17	280
17:16	271	20:34	244-245	12:20	276,278
17:17	176	20:34-35	244	13:9	117
17:17-20	171	22:15	34	14:4	261,262,275
18:22	280	23:8	183	14:9	106
18:33	287	26:22	96	14:13	276
19:16f	287	26:22-23	109	14:17	111,112
20:9	109	27:25	48	15:1	79
20:21	4,58	28:12	111	15:30-31	293
21:15-17	277	28:27	150	16:3-4	292
21:17	72	28:31	111	16:7	292
				16:5	84
Acts		**Romans**		16:17-18	149,162
1:8	34,37,42,43,124	1:4	107		
2:25	43	1:18	154	**1 Corinthians**	
2:36	132	2:1	276	1:3-4	41
2:38	224	2:6,11	174	1:7	98
4:11-12	90	2:10	316	1:10	71
4:12	90,164	2:17-29	276	1:18	105
4:20	36,123,245	2:21-24	116	1:18,21	62
4:33	124	3:24-25	101	1:23	99
5:20	64	4:20-21	48	1:30-31	99
5:20-21	35	4:25	108	2:1-2	99
5:32	37	5:1	51	2:2	100,164
5:42	67,84	5:1-5	96	2:4-5	122
6:2-4	81,82	5:5	277	2:5	124
7:60	279	5:6	103	2:9	317
8:1-4	84	5:6-11	96	2:12	43
8:5	99	5:8	103,104,285	2:16	225
8:12	111	5:9	101	3:5-9	258
8:35	99	5:10	103	3:8-9	258
9:20	132	6:6	195	3:10-11	87
10:42	97	6:11	195,196	3:11	164
11:26	133,134	8:2	108	3:16-17	224
12:12	84	8:5	225	4:1	6,7
13:35-37	109	8:9	224	4:1-2	18
15:35	95	8:11	108	4:2	5,69
16:40	84	8:16-17	315	4:3-5	273
17:11	203	8:17	289	4:5	274
18:3	244	8:17-18	200	4:9-13	292
18:5	244	8:29	306	4:11-12	245
18:9-10	32	8:32	103	5:7	105
18:11	68,95,133,134	8:34	101	6:11	51
19:23-40	292	9:3	166	6:19-20	4,224
19:23-41	290	10:9	108,132	6:20	104
20:18-19	292	10:9-10	139,191,192	7:1	6
20:18-27	292	10:14-15	214	7:17	81
20:20	84	11:33-36	317	8:11	103

Scripture Index

9:12-15	245	4:17	311	3:13	101
9:14	242	4:17-18	290	3:28	251
9:16	62,73,120,245	5:1	198	4:4-5	102
9:17	121	5:5-8	301	4:4-7	316
9:23-27	23	5:6-8	301	4:13-15	294
9:24-27	20-21	5:10	97	5:16-21	270
9:25	309,316	5:14	49,73	5:22-23	304
9:27	227	5:15	104	5:24	196
10:13	18,44-45,291	5:17	44,140,192,199	6:1	265
10:24	75	5:18-21	8	6:2	57,80,133
11:11-12	250	5:20	32	6:6	242
11:34	81	5:21	104	6:8-9	60
12:28	47	6:1	260	6:9	214
13:11	72	6:3-10	17	6:11	294
14:3	70	6:4-11	292	6:12	127
14:26	70	6:14	232	6:12-13	127
15:1-58	96	6:14-16	232	6:13	129
15:2-4	108	6:14-18	232	6:14	127,129
15:3	100	6:15	233		
15:3-4	106,107	6:16	224,233	**Ephesians**	
15:24	114	6:17-18	80,232,233,271	1:6-7	100
15:32	292	8:1	6	1:20	107
15:42-44	305,316	9:1	6	2:2,4-5	199
15:44	306	9:8	41	2:4-7	96,285
15:50-53	114	10:3-5	197	2:13-14	105
16:19	84	10:5	216,225,226	2:16	105
		10:10	294	2:18	105
2 Corinthians		11:4	171	2:20-21	90
1:3	283,288	11:4, 13-15	171	3:7	7
1:3-7	284,285	11:7-9	245	3:7-8	6,7
1:3-11	283	11:9	244	3:8	316
1:4	285	11:13-15	138,148,153	3:14-19	210
1:5	286	11:16-12:10	294	3:16	296
1:6-7	288	11:23-27	292	3:20	296
1:8-10	290,291-292	11:23-30	235	4:1	6
1:10	291	11:24-27	294	4:11	47,81
1:11	292	12:7	294	4:11-12	67
2:14	45	12:7-10	293	4:11-13	70
2:17	165,205	12:8	294	4:14	178
3:18	198	12:9	295	4:17	6
4:1-2	114	12:9-10	41	4:22	139
4:2	205	12:14	245	4:22-24	193
4:4	140	12:19	70	4:23-24	139
4:5	131	13:1	6	4:24	44,199
4:7	43,44,198	13:5	194	4:28	118,243
4:8-10	17	13:11	71	4:29	70
4:8-12	292			5:2	104,105
4:10	198	**Galatians**		5:11	80
4:10-11	104,195	1:4	102	5:19	6
4:11	198	1:6	163,165	5:20	217
4:13	38,48	1:6-9	153,162	5:22	250
4:14	51	1:6-10	139	5:22-23	249
4:16	198	1:8-9	175	5:25	106,254
4:16-18	198	2:20	104,196	5:25-27	249

6:4	256,257	2:9	245	6:3	159,160
6:10-18	201	2:13	177,181,205	6:3-5	156,188
6:10-20	202	2:19-20	309	6:11-12	233
6:16	48	3:3	268	6:12	22
6:18	210,293	3:6	244	6:14	98
		3:12	276	6:19	316
Philippians		4:1	69	6:20-21	180,237
1:6	262	4:14	108		
1:19	293	4:15	205	**2 Timothy**	
1:20	16	4:16-17	51	1:3	16
1:29	268	5:9-10	102	1:5	207
2:1	284	5:14	286	1:8	30,93
2:1-2	290	5:15	278	1:9	93
2:5-8	197	5:17	215	1:9-10	93
2:8-11	106	5:18	217	1:10	101
2:12	202			1:10-11	68
2:15	316	**2 Thessalonians**		1:13	93
2:27	292	1:7-9	152	2:2	28,29,67,68
3:10	71	3:1	205	2:3-4	232
3:10-11	14,52	3:8	245	2:8	106
3:13-14	15,20			2:12	200
3:20-21	114,305	**1 Timothy**		2:15	202,204
3:21	200,306,316	1:3-4	95,177,178	2:16-18	237,238
4:6	216	1:3	178	2:22-23	236
4:8	225,226	1:5-7	185	3:1-5	241,270
4:11-13	246	1:11-12	19,181	3:1-15	140
4:15	244	1:12	4,5,140	3:5	162
		1:16	27	3:8-9	151
Colossians		2:1-4	211	3:12	268
1:10	71	2:5-6	101	3:13	140
1:14	101	2:7	68	3:14	207
1:20	100	3:1-7	229	3:15	207
1:25	5	3:2	85,230,231,	3:16	63,177,202,203
1:28	30		254,256,263	3:16-17	95,96
2:8	149	3:3	230	4:1-2	61,95,96,97
2:14-15	102	3:4-5	231,256	4:2	64,70
3:1-2	243	3:5	257	4:3-4	177
3:1-4	301	3:7	231	4:4	178
3:4	200	3:8-13	82	4:5	81
3:9-10	193,236	3:16	142	4:6-8	20
3:10	44,140,193,199	4:1-2	147,186	4:7-8	21
3:12	284	4:7	178	4:8	307,316
3:16	205	4:8	228	4:18	291,301,365
3:24	318	4:11	67		
4:2-4	215	4:12	27	**Titus**	
4:4	218	4:15	203	1:3	181
4:15	84	4:16	94	1:5	81,82
		5:10	86	1:6	230,231,
1 Thessalonians		5:17	242		256,257
1:8	205	5:18	242	1:6-9	230
1:10	102	5:19-20	264,266	1:7	7,230,231
2:4	181	5:19-22	264	1:8	180,231
2:4-5	125	5:20	66	1:9	66,70,231
2:6	127	5:22	264	1:10	187
2:8	74	5:24-25	260	1:10-11	148

Scripture Index

1:14	175,179	2:5	316	3:1	316		
1:16	116,149	4:2	212,218	3:2	306		
2:1	93,94	4:12	275	3:5	100		
2:6	254	5:16	293	3:16	105		
2:6-8	27	5:16-18	213	3:18	117		
2:7	76	5:20	61,265,311	3:23	174,177		
2:11-13	31			4:1	145		
2:12-13	51	**1 Peter**		4:1-3	141		
2:14	105	1:3	318	4:7	276		
2:14-15	31,32	1:3-4	108,309,315	5:4-5	49		
2:15	66,70	1:4	317	5:11-12	301		
3:7	315	1:5	262	5:21	119		
3:9	237,239	1:18	101				
3:10-11	154	2:2-3	203	**2 John**			
		2:17	277	7	141		
Philemon		2:24	100,104	10-11	162		
2	84	3:4	199				
		3:7	254	**3 John**			
Hebrews		3:8	71	6-8	263		
1:3	106	3:9	279				
2:9	101,301	3:15	36	**Jude**			
2:14-15	102,143	3:18	103,108	4	152		
2:15	291	4:1	104	24-25	262		
2:16-18	287	4:8	265	**Revelation**			
3:13	67	4:9	83,85,86,263	1:5	316		
4:9	316	4:10	7	2:4	183		
4:15-16	288	4:11	260	2:10	308		
5:9	191	5:2	81	3:11	311		
5:14	72	5:2-3	72,73	5:9	101		
6:1	72	5:4	311,316	5:10	316		
9:12	101			7:9-12	316		
9:14	105	**2 Peter**		7:9-13	316		
9:22	100	1:4	45	12:11	102		
9:26	100	1:16	179	14:13	316		
9:27	122	1:19,21	168	20:4	316		
9:28	100	1:21	169	20:6	316		
10:19-20	104	2:1	156,167	21:1	113,313		
10:24-25	55	2:5	31	21:1,4	311		
10:25	56	2:9	291	21:4-5	114		
10:28	284	2:20-22	151	22:5	316		
10:29	170	3:10-13	113,306,312				
10:32	22						
10:34	316	**1 John**					
11:6	48,191	1:1	144				
12:2	106	1:2	144,304				
12:4	227	1:3	38,145				
13:2	85	1:4	145				
13:3	80	1:7	100				
13:8	111	1:9	145				
13:9	177	2:2	145				
13:17	76,77	2:6	120				
		2:15-16	80,232				
James		2:18-23	145				
1:12	308	2:22	170				
1:27	78	2:22-23	145				

Acknowledgments

Every child of God is precious to the Lord and deeply loved. And every child as a servant of the Lord touches the lives of those who come in contact with him or his ministry. The writing ministry of the following servants have touched this work, and we are grateful that God brought their writings our way. We hereby acknowledge their ministry to us, being fully aware that there are so many others down through the years whose writings have touched our lives and who deserve mention, but the weaknesses of our minds have caused them to fade from memory. May our wonderful Lord continue to bless the ministry of these dear servants, and the ministry of us all as we diligently labor to reach the world for Christ and to meet the desperate needs of those who suffer so much.

Barclay, William. *Daily Study Bible Series*. Philadelphia, PA: Westminster Press, Began in 1953.

Cruden's Complete Concordance of the Old & New Testament. Philadelphia, PA: The John C. Winston Co., 1930.

Greene, Oliver B. *The Epistles of Paul the Apostle to Timothy & Titus*. Greenville, SC: The Gospel Hour, Inc., 1964.

Henry, Matthew. *Commentary on the Whole Bible*. Old Tappan, NJ: Fleming H. Revell Co., n.d.

Hodge, Charles. *Commentary on the Epistle to the Romans*. Grand Rapids, MI: Eerdmans Publishing Co., 1950.

_____. *Commentary on the First Epistle to the Corinthians*. Grand Rapids, MI: Eerdmans Publishing Co., 1950.

_____. *Commentary on the Second Epistle to the Corinthians*. Grand Rapids, MI: Eerdmans Publishing Co., 1950.

Nave's Topical Bible. Nashville, TN: The Southwestern Co., 1921.

Robertson, A.T. *Word Pictures in the New Testament*. Nashville, TN: Broadman Press, 1930.

Strauss, Lehman. *Devotional Studies Galatians & Ephesians.* Neptune, NJ: Loizeaux Brothers, 1957.

Thayer, Joseph Henry. *Greek-English Lexicon of the New Testament.* New York: American Book Co., 1889.

The Amplified New Testament. (Scripture Quotations are from the Amplified New Testament, Copyright 1954, 1958, 1987 by the Lockman Foundation. Used by permission.)

The Expositor's Greek Testament. 5 Volumes. Edited by W. Robertson Nicoll. Grand Rapids, MI: Eerdmans Publishing Co., 1970.

The Four Translation New Testament. (Including The King James; The New American Standard; Williams - New Testament In the Language of the People; Beck - The New Testament In the Language of Today.) Minneapolis, MN: World Wide Publications. Copyright The Iversen Associates, New York, NY, 1966.

The New Thompson Chain Reference Bible. Indianapolis, IN: B.B. Kirkbride Bible Co., 1964,

The Preacher's Outline & Sermon Bible. Chattanooga, TN: Leadership Ministries Worldwide, 1993.

The Pulpit Commentary, 23 Volumes. Edited by H.D.M. Spence & Joseph S. Exell. Grand Rapids, MI: Eerdman's Publishing Co., 1950.

The Tyndale New Testament Commentaries. Grand Rapids, MI: Eerdman's Publishing Co., Began in 1958.

Vincent, Marvin R. *Word Studies in the New Testament.* 4 Volumes. Grand Rapids, MI: Eerdmans Publishing Co., 1969.

Vine, W.E. *Expository Dictionary of New Testament Words.* Old Tappan, NJ: Fleming H. Revell Co., 1940.

Wuest, Kenneth S. *Word Studies in the Greek New Testament.* Grand Rapids, MI: Eerdmans Publishing Co., 1966.

LEADERSHIP MINISTRIES WORLDWIDE

Publishers of Outline Bible Resources

- **THE PREACHER'S OUTLINE & SERMON BIBLE® (POSB)**

NEW TESTAMENT

Matthew I (chapters 1-15)	1 & 2 Corinthians
Matthew II (chapters 16-28)	Galatians, Ephesians, Philippians, Colossians
Mark	1 & 2 Thess., 1 & 2 Timothy, Titus, Philemon
Luke	Hebrews, James
John	1 & 2 Peter, 1, 2, & 3 John, Jude
Acts	Revelation
Romans	Master Outline & Subject Index

OLD TESTAMENT

Genesis I (chapters 1-11)	2 Kings	Isaiah 1 (chapters 1-35)
Genesis II (chapters 12-50)	1 Chronicles	Isaiah 2 (chapters 36-66)
Exodus I (chapters 1-18)	2 Chronicles	Jeremiah 1 (chapters 1-29)
Exodus II (chapters 19-40)	Ezra, Nehemiah, Esther	Jeremiah 2 (chapters 30-52), Lamentations
Leviticus	Job	Ezekiel
Numbers	Psalms 1 (chapters 1-41)	Daniel/Hosea
Deuteronomy	Psalms 2 (chapters 42-106)	Joel, Amos, Obadiah, Jonah, Micah, Nahum
Joshua	Psalms 3 (chapters 107-150)	Habakkuk, Zephaniah, Haggai, Zechariah, Malachi
Judges, Ruth	Proverbs	
1 Samuel	Ecclesiastes, Song of Solomon	
2 Samuel		
1 Kings		

KJV Available in Deluxe 3-Ring Binders or Softbound Edition • NIV Available in Softbound Only

- **The Preacher's Outline & Sermon Bible New Testament** — 3 Vol. Hardcover • KJV – NIV
- *What the Bible Says to the Believer* — **The Believer's Personal Handbook**
  11 Chs. - 500 Subjects, 300 Promises, & 400 Verses Expounded - Italian Imitation Leather or Paperback
- *What the Bible Says to the Minister* — **The Minister's Personal Handbook**
  12 Chs. - 127 Subjects - 400 Verses Expounded - Italian Imitation Leather or Paperback
- **Practical Word Studies In the New Testament** — 2 Vol. Hardcover Set
- **The Teacher's Outline & Study Bible™ - New Testament Books**
  Complete 30 - 45 minute lessons – with illustrations and discussion questions
- **Practical Illustrations — Companion to the POSB**
  Arranged by topic and Scripture reference
- **What the Bible Says Series – Various Subjects**
- **OBR on various digital platforms**
  See current digital providers on our website at www.outlinebible.org
- **Non-English Translations of various books**
  See our website for more information or contact our office

— Contact LMW for quantity orders and information —

LEADERSHIP MINISTRIES WORLDWIDE or Your Local Christian Bookstore
PO Box 21310 • Chattanooga, TN 37424-0310
(423) 855-2181 (9am – 5pm Eastern) • FAX (423) 855-8616
E-mail - info@outlinebible.org • Order online at www.outlinebible.org

LEADERSHIP MINISTRIES WORLDWIDE

PURPOSE STATEMENT

LEADERSHIP MINISTRIES WORLDWIDE
exists to equip ministers, teachers, and laymen in their understanding, preaching and teaching of God's Word by publishing and distributing worldwide *The Preacher's Outline & Sermon Bible®* and related **Outline Bible Resources**, to reach & disciple men, women, boys and girls for Jesus Christ.

MISSION STATEMENT

1. To make the Bible so understandable – its truth so clear and plain – that men and women everywhere, whether teacher or student, preacher or hearer, can grasp its message and receive Jesus Christ as Savior, and...

2. To place the Bible in the hands of all who will preach and teach God's Holy Word, verse by verse, precept by precept, regardless of the individual's ability to purchase it.

Outline Bible Resources have been given to LMW for printing and especially distribution worldwide at/below cost, by those who remain anonymous. One fact, however, is as true today as it was in the time of Christ:

THE GOSPEL IS FREE, BUT THE COST OF TAKING IT IS NOT

LMW depends on the generous gifts of believers with a heart for Him and a love for the lost. They help pay for the printing, translating, and distributing of **Outline Bible Resources** into the hands of God's servants worldwide, who will present the Gospel message with clarity, authority, and understanding beyond their own.

LMW was incorporated in the state of Tennessee in July 1992 and received IRS 501 (c)(3) nonprofit status in March 1994. LMW is an international, nondenominational mission organization. All proceeds from USA sales, along with donations from donor partners, go directly to underwrite our translation and distribution projects of **Outline Bible Resources** to preachers, church and lay leaders, and Bible students around the world.